MAKER
DRAW A COMIC!
COMICS

DRAW A COMIC!

JP Coovert

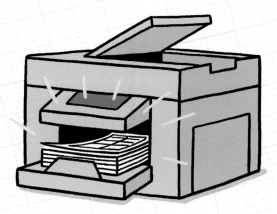

:01
First Second
New York

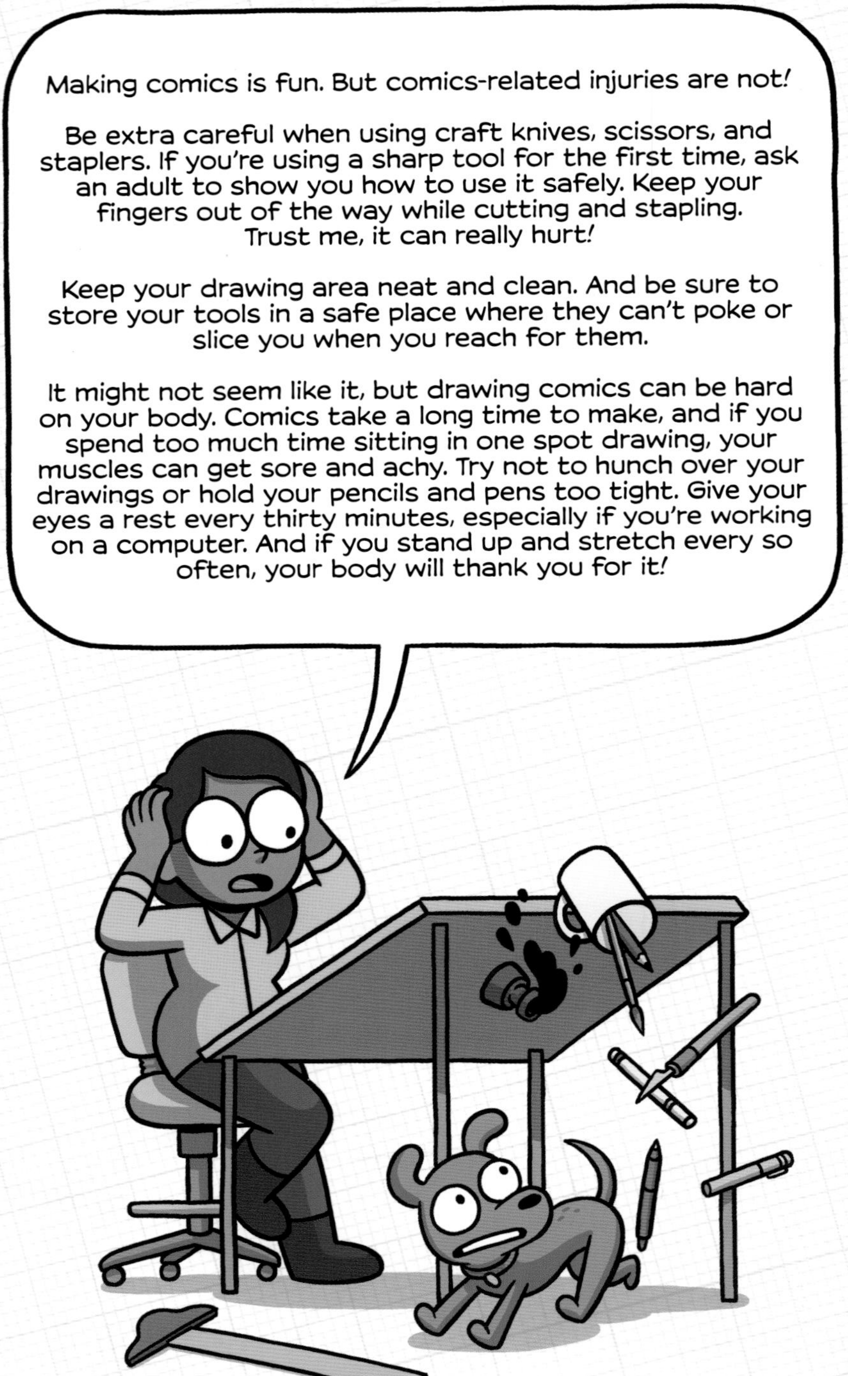
Making comics is fun. But comics-related injuries are not!
Be extra careful when using craft knives, scissors, and staplers. If you're using a sharp tool for the first time, ask an adult to show you how to use it safely. Keep your fingers out of the way while cutting and stapling. Trust me, it can really hurt!
Keep your drawing area neat and clean. And be sure to store your tools in a safe place where they can't poke or slice you when you reach for them.
It might not seem like it, but drawing comics can be hard on your body. Comics take a long time to make, and if you spend too much time sitting in one spot drawing, your muscles can get sore and achy. Try not to hunch over your drawings or hold your pencils and pens too tight. Give your eyes a rest every thirty minutes, especially if you're working on a computer. And if you stand up and stretch every so often, your body will thank you for it!

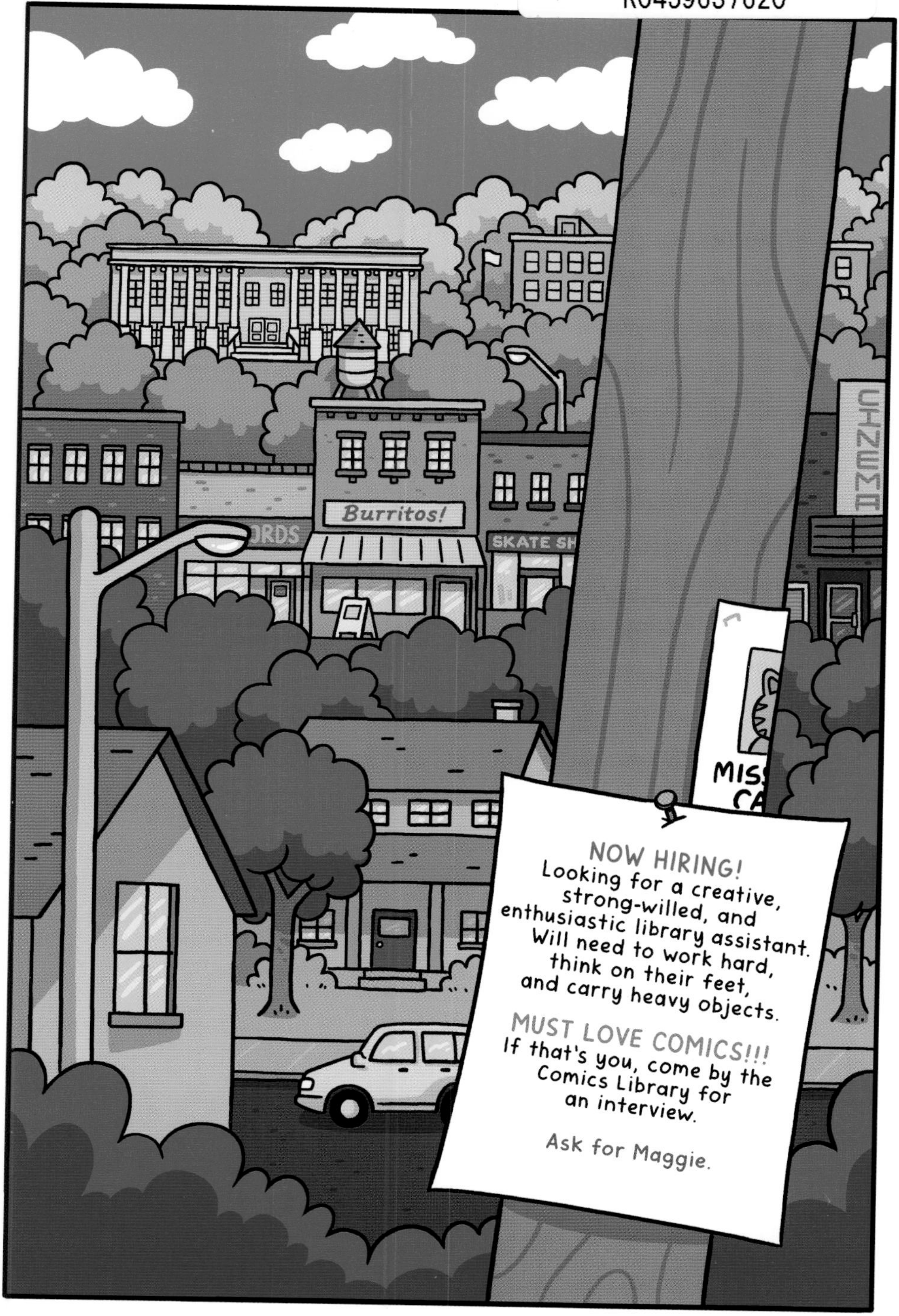

Burritos!
ORDS
SKATE SH
CINEMA
MISS
CA
NOW HIRING!
Looking for a creative, strong-willed, and enthusiastic library assistant. Will need to work hard, think on their feet, and carry heavy objects.
MUST LOVE COMICS!!!
If that's you, come by the Comics Library for an interview.
Ask for Maggie.

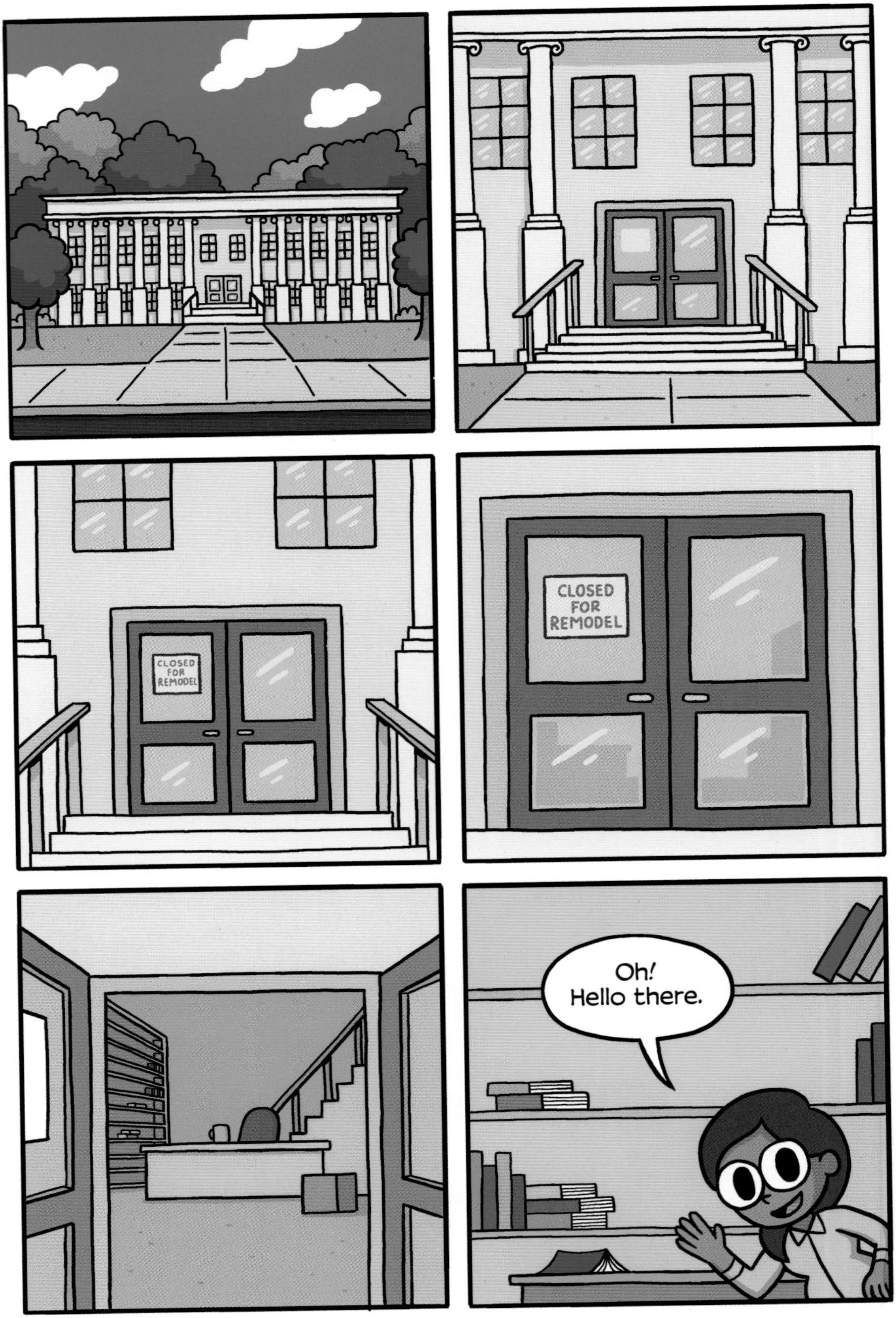
CLOSED FOR REMODEL
CLOSED FOR REMODEL
Oh! Hello there.

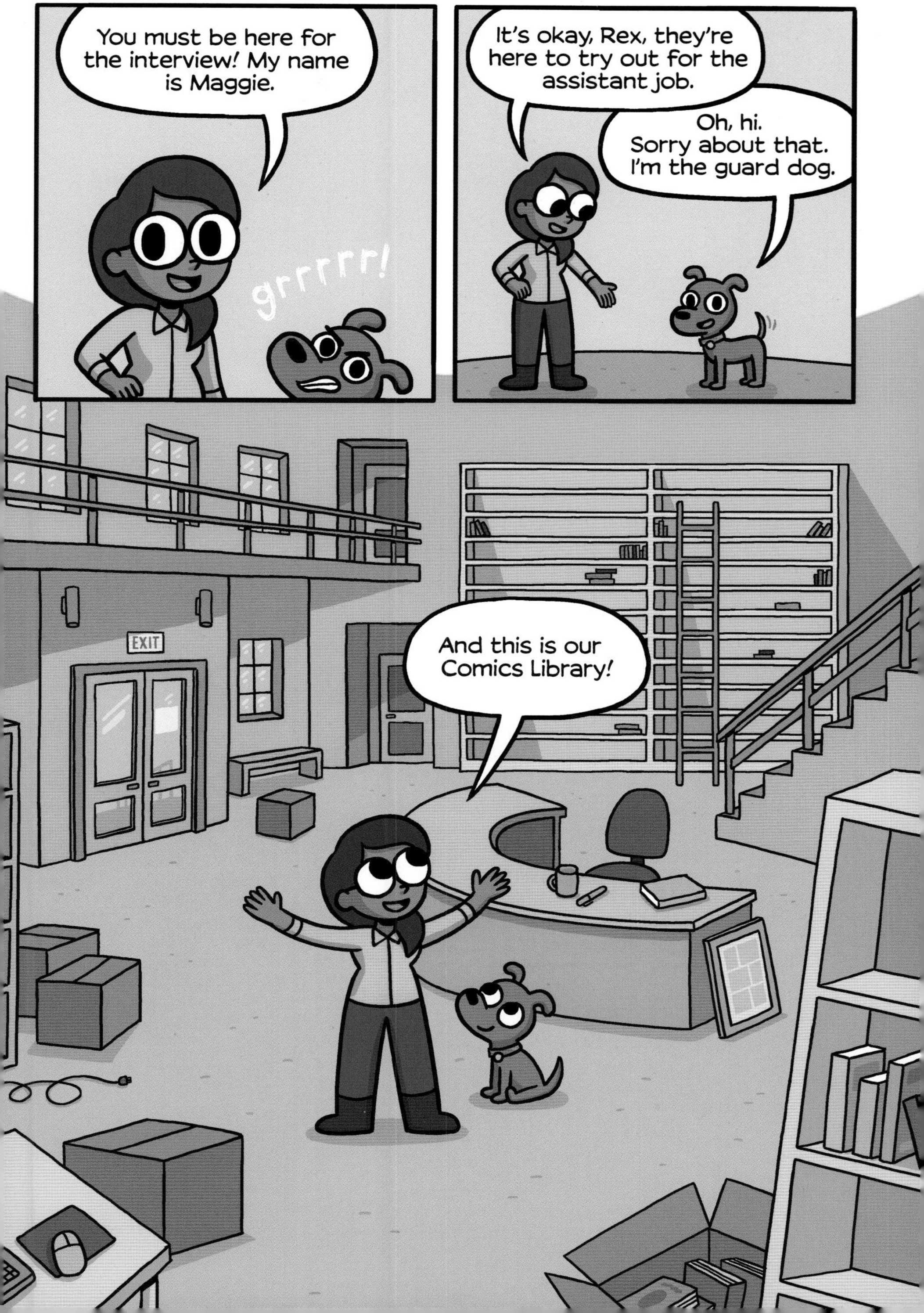
You must be here for the interview! My name is Maggie.
grrrrr!
It's okay, Rex, they're here to try out for the assistant job.
Oh, hi. Sorry about that. I'm the guard dog.
EXIT
And this is our Comics Library!

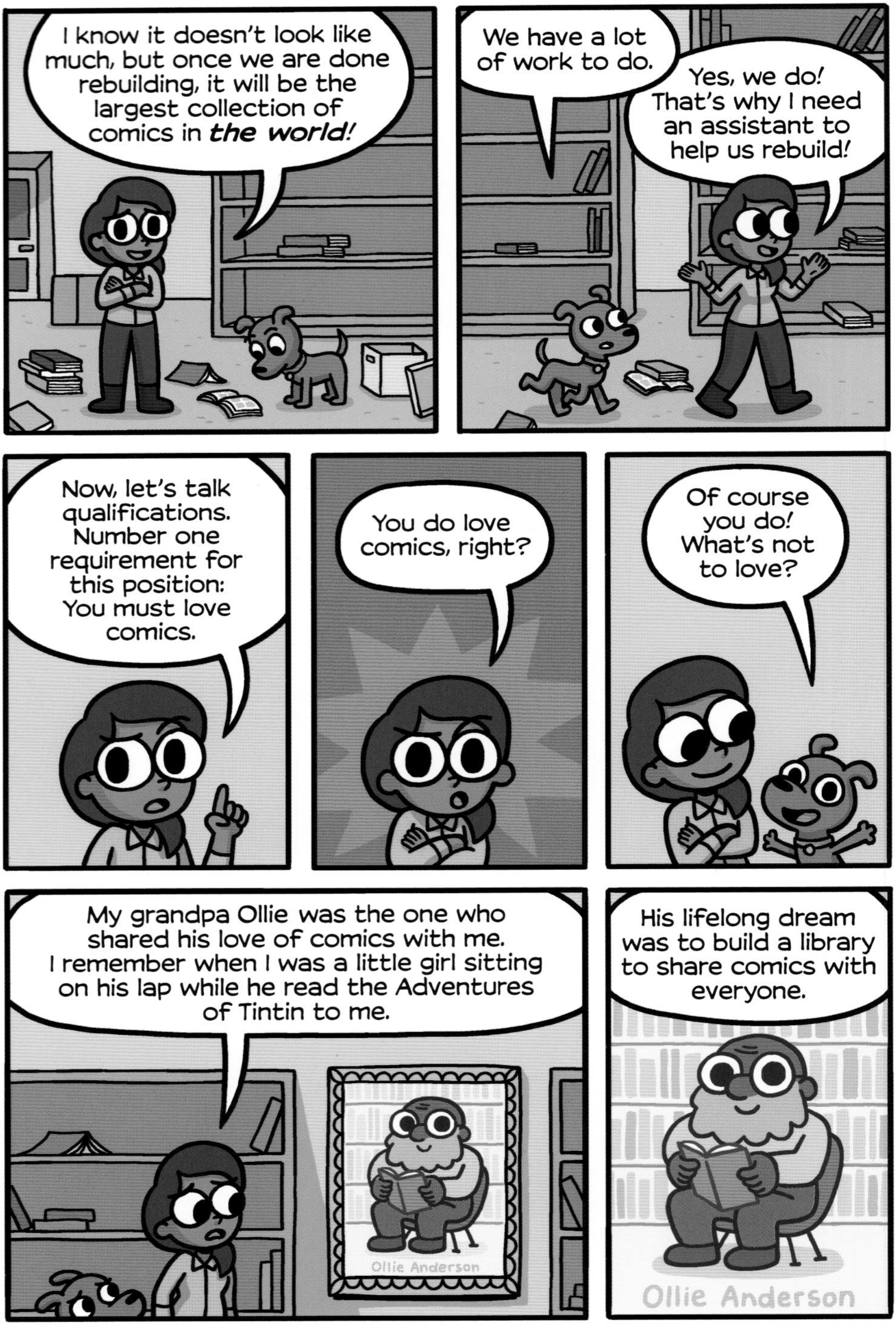
I know it doesn't look like much, but once we are done rebuilding, it will be the largest collection of comics in ***the world!***
We have a lot of work to do.
Yes, we do! That's why I need an assistant to help us rebuild!
Now, let's talk qualifications. Number one requirement for this position: You must love comics.
You do love comics, right?
Of course you do! What's not to love?
My grandpa Ollie was the one who shared his love of comics with me. I remember when I was a little girl sitting on his lap while he read the Adventures of Tintin to me.
Ollie Anderson
His lifelong dream was to build a library to share comics with everyone.
Ollie Anderson

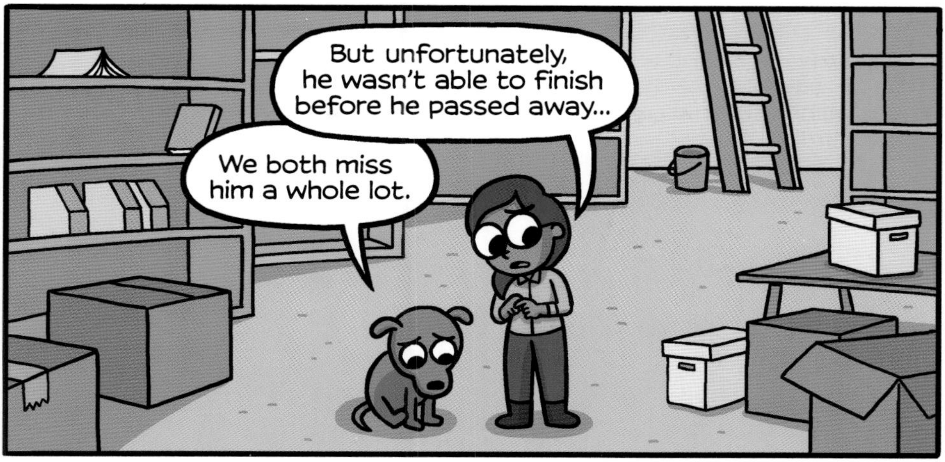
But unfortunately, he wasn't able to finish before he passed away...
We both miss him a whole lot.

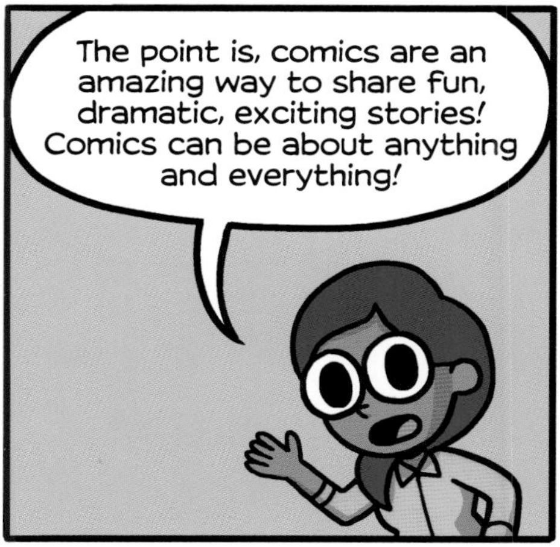
The point is, comics are an amazing way to share fun, dramatic, exciting stories! Comics can be about anything and everything!

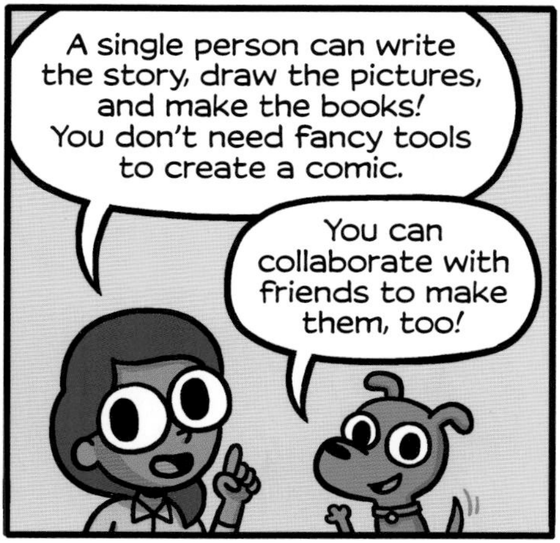
A single person can write the story, draw the pictures, and make the books! You don't need fancy tools to create a comic.
You can collaborate with friends to make them, too!

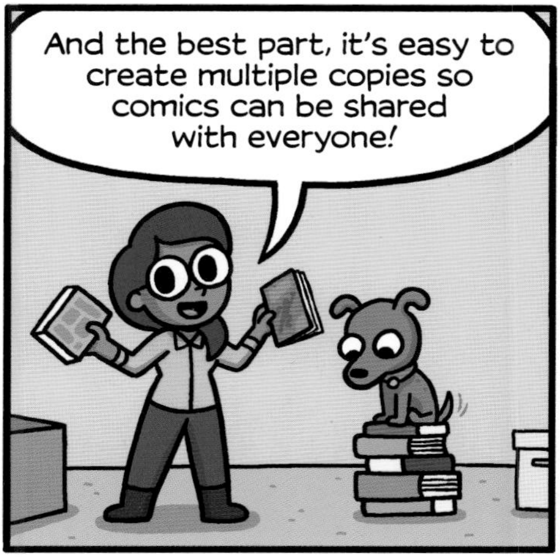
And the best part, it's easy to create multiple copies so comics can be shared with everyone!

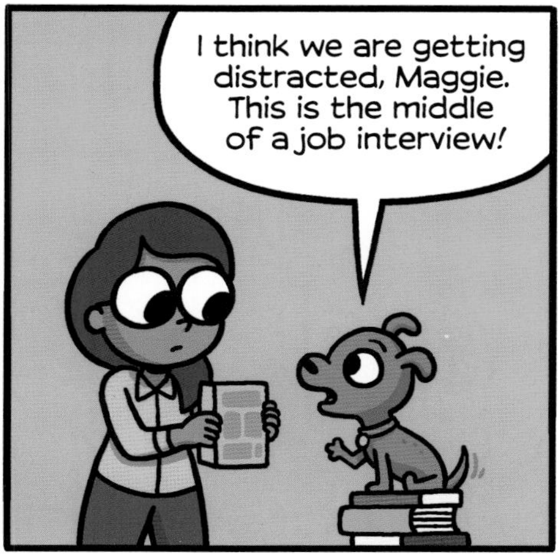
I think we are getting distracted, Maggie. This is the middle of a job interview!

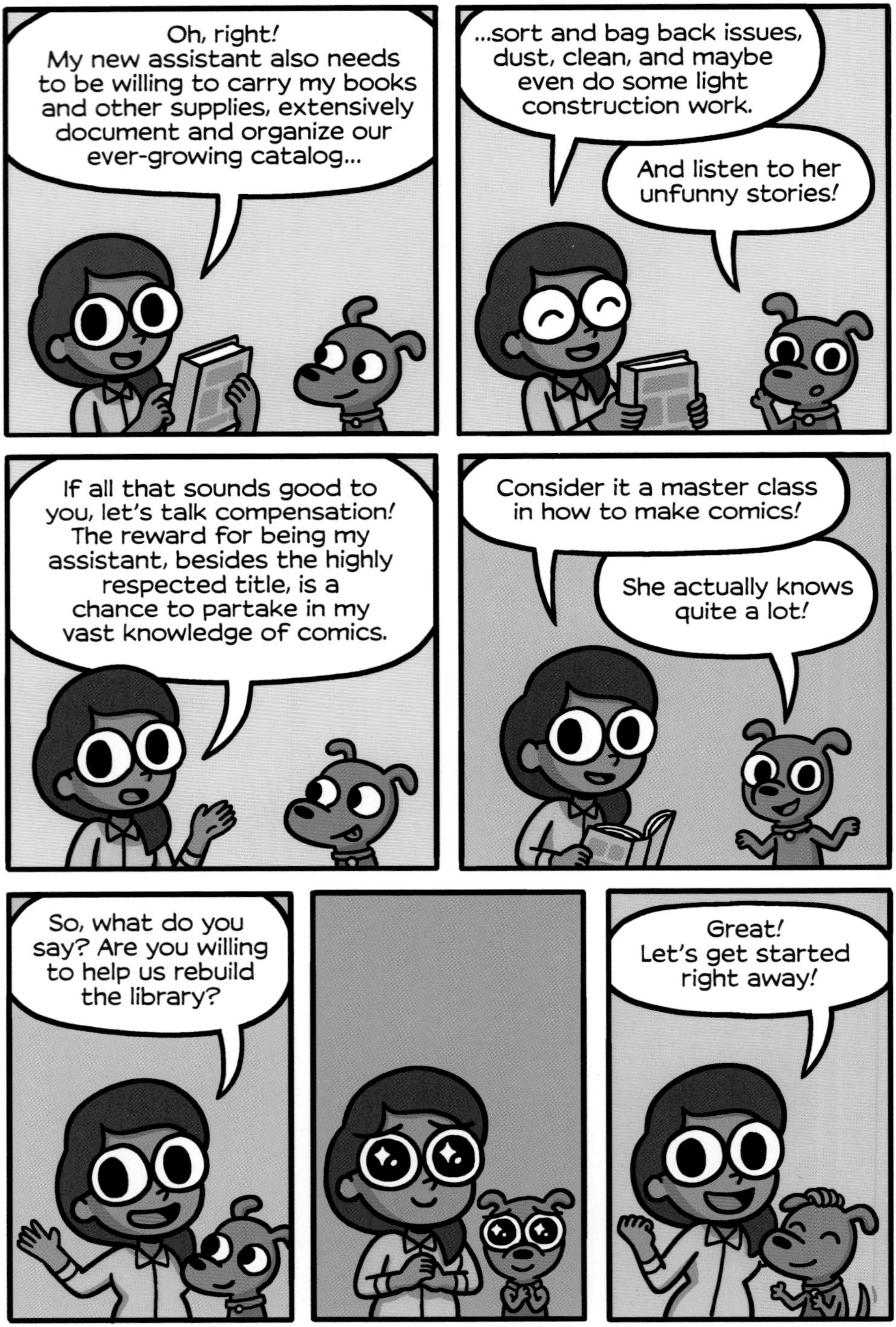
Oh, right! My new assistant also needs to be willing to carry my books and other supplies, extensively document and organize our ever-growing catalog...
...sort and bag back issues, dust, clean, and maybe even do some light construction work.
And listen to her unfunny stories!
If all that sounds good to you, let's talk compensation! The reward for being my assistant, besides the highly respected title, is a chance to partake in my vast knowledge of comics.
Consider it a master class in how to make comics!
She actually knows quite a lot!
So, what do you say? Are you willing to help us rebuild the library?
Great! Let's get started right away!

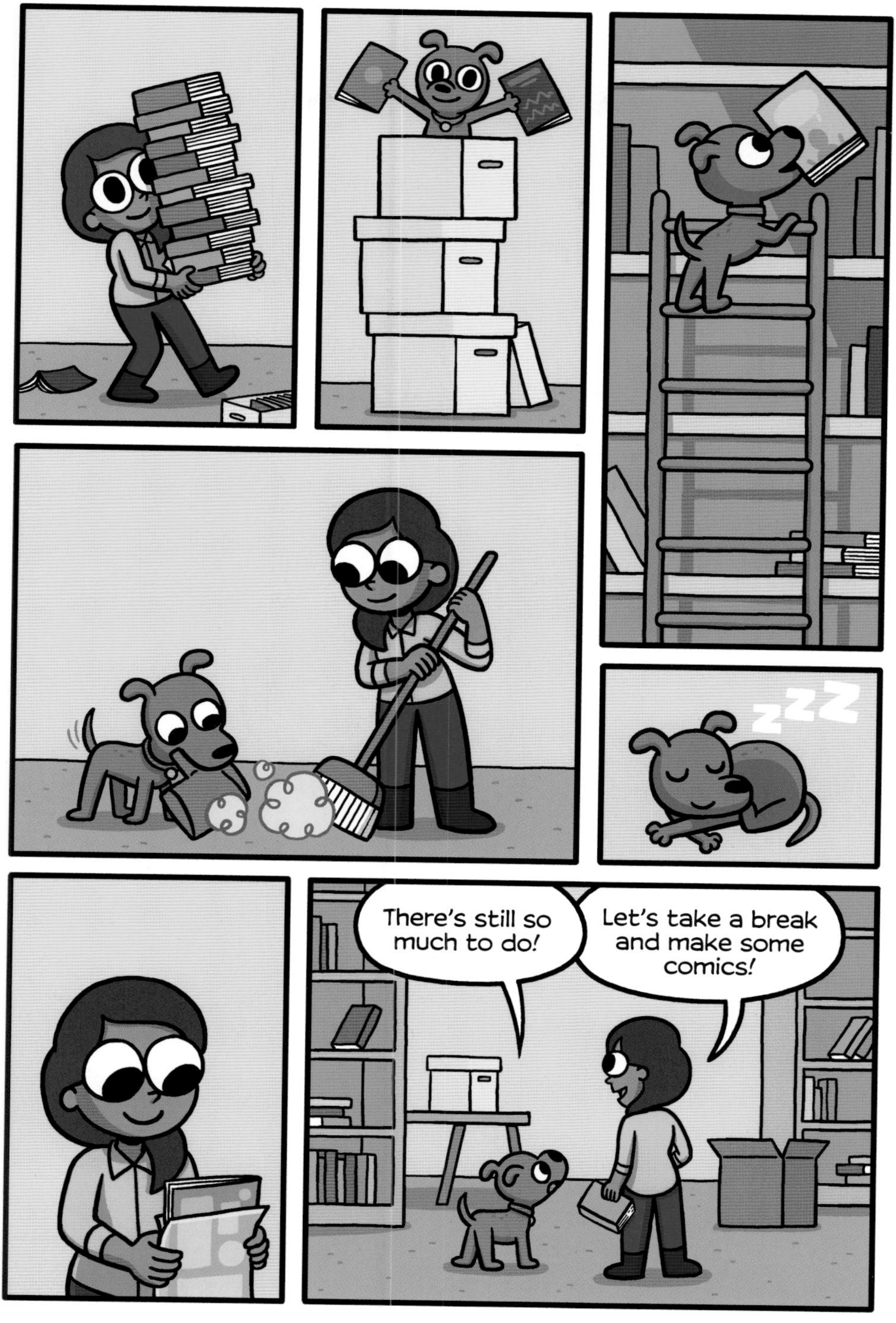
ZZZ
There's still so much to do!
Let's take a break and make some comics!

PROJECT ONE:
LEARNING THE PARTS OF A COMIC!

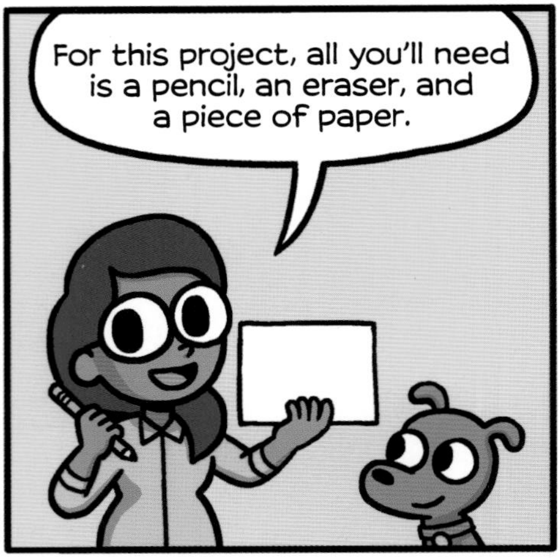
For this project, all you'll need is a pencil, an eraser, and a piece of paper.

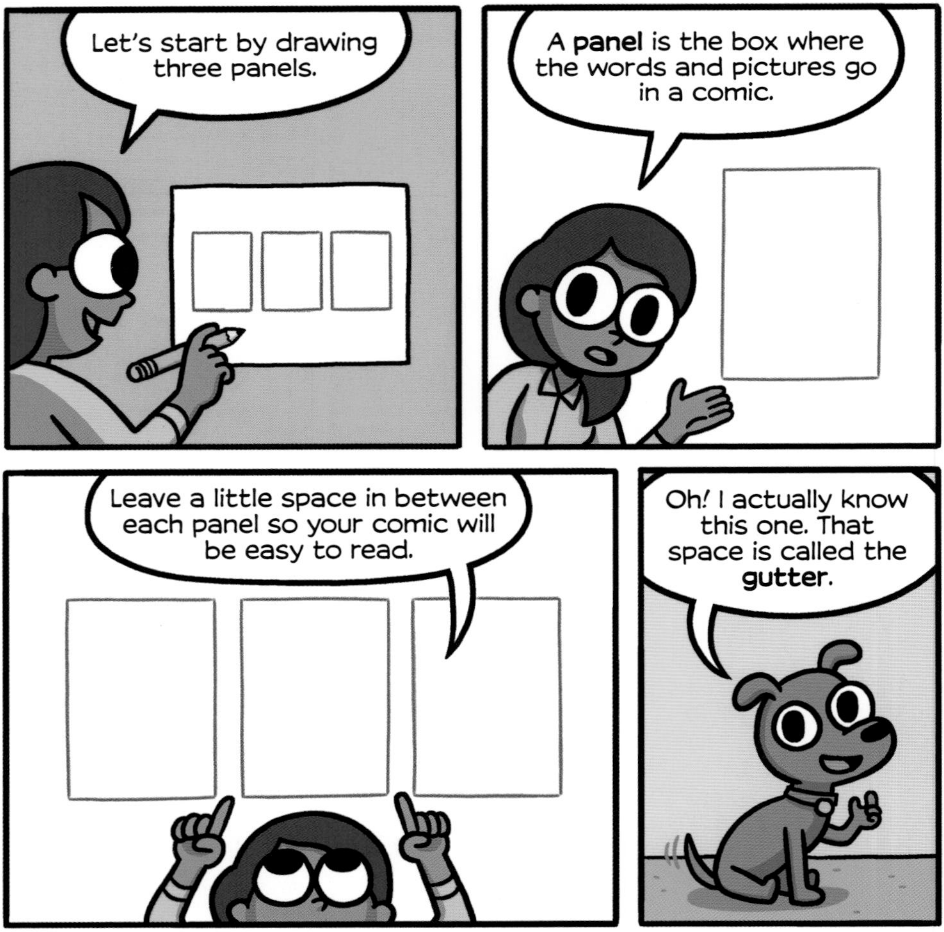
Let's start by drawing three panels.
A **panel** is the box where the words and pictures go in a comic.
Leave a little space in between each panel so your comic will be easy to read.
Oh! I actually know this one. That space is called the **gutter**.

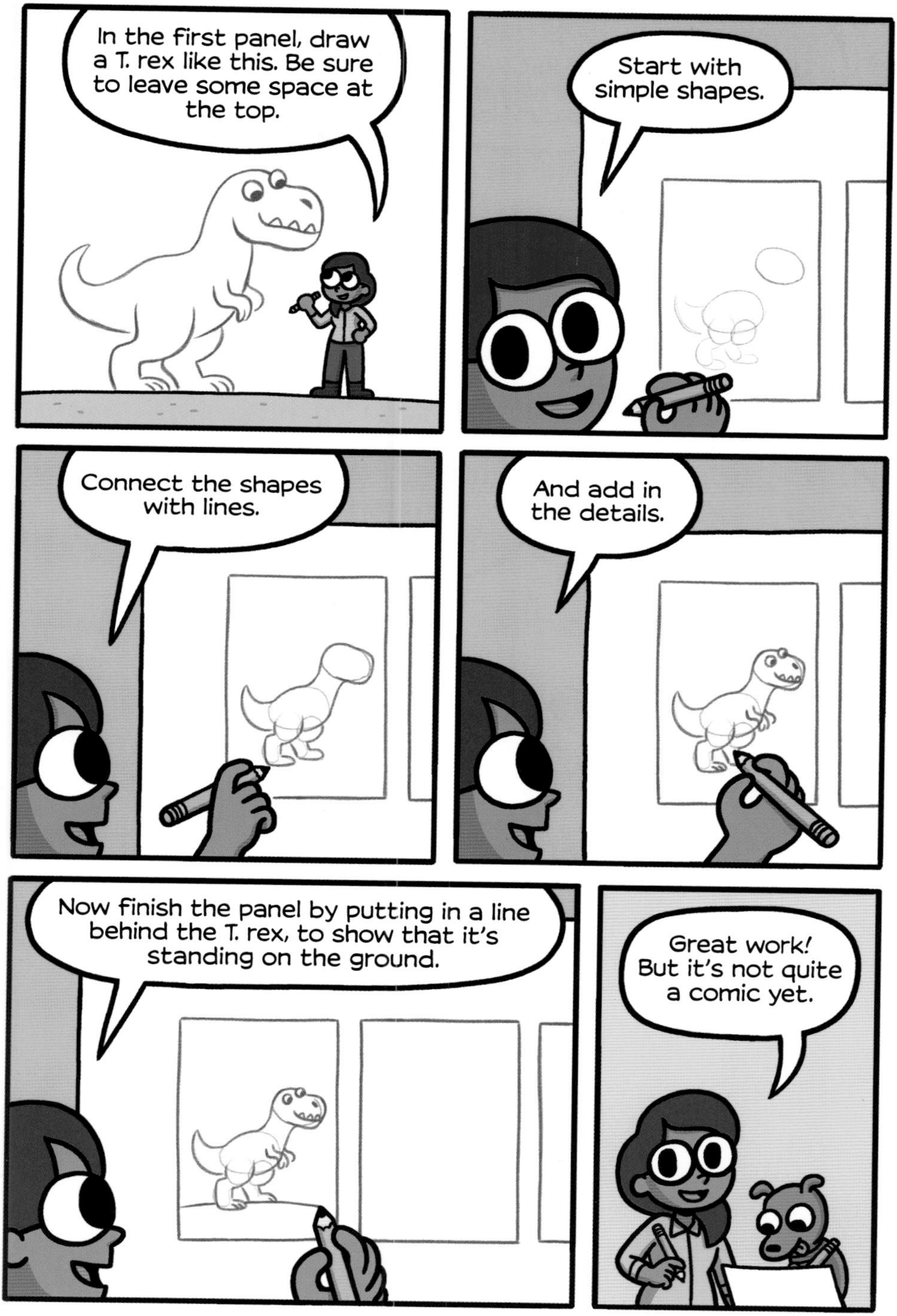
In the first panel, draw a T. rex like this. Be sure to leave some space at the top.
Start with simple shapes.
Connect the shapes with lines.
And add in the details.
Now finish the panel by putting in a line behind the T. rex, to show that it's standing on the ground.
Great work! But it's not quite a comic yet.

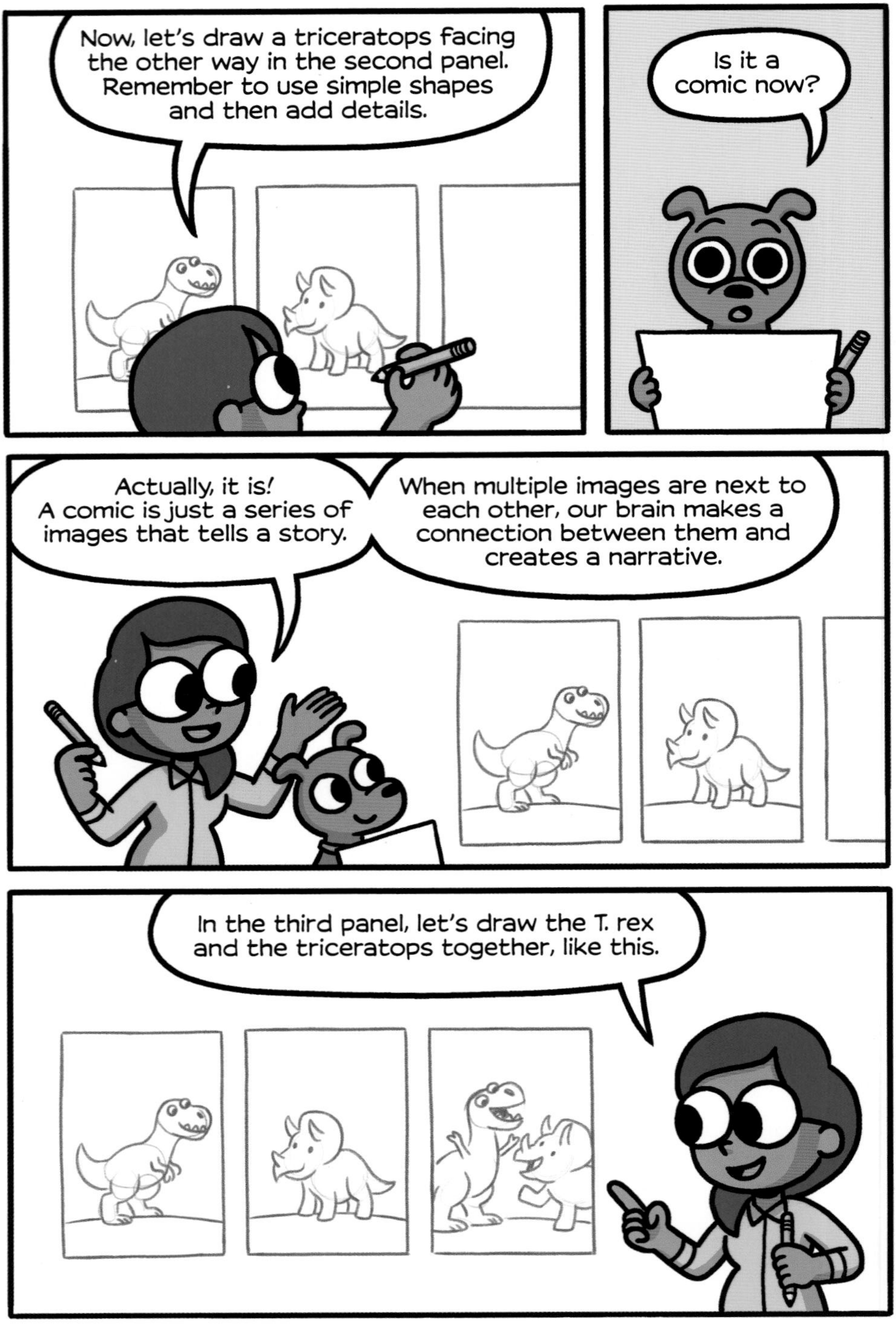

Now, let's draw a triceratops facing the other way in the second panel. Remember to use simple shapes and then add details.
Is it a comic now?
Actually, it is! A comic is just a series of images that tells a story.
When multiple images are next to each other, our brain makes a connection between them and creates a narrative.
In the third panel, let's draw the T. rex and the triceratops together, like this.

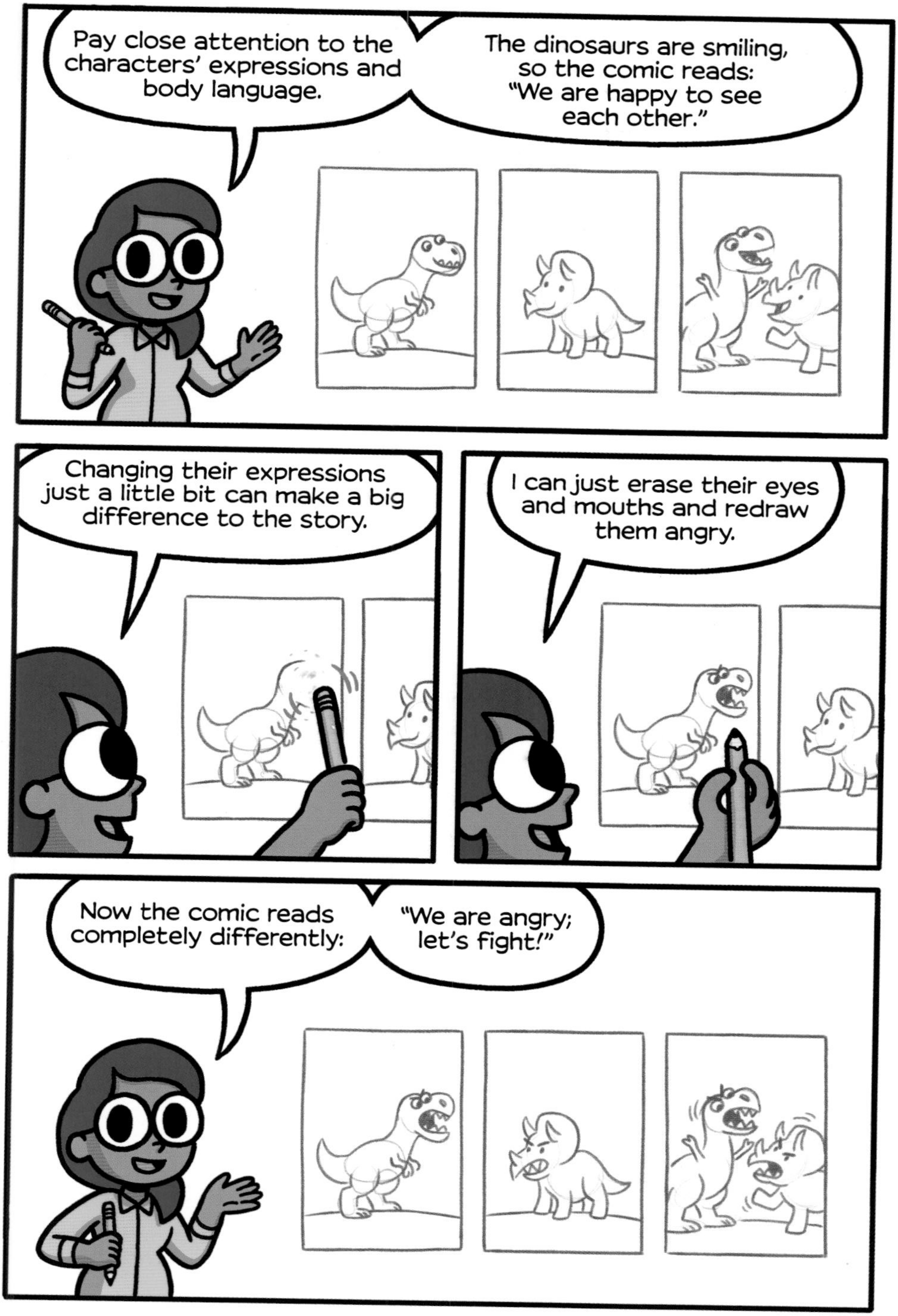

Pay close attention to the characters' expressions and body language.
The dinosaurs are smiling, so the comic reads: "We are happy to see each other."
Changing their expressions just a little bit can make a big difference to the story.
I can just erase their eyes and mouths and redraw them angry.
Now the comic reads completely differently:
"We are angry; let's fight!"

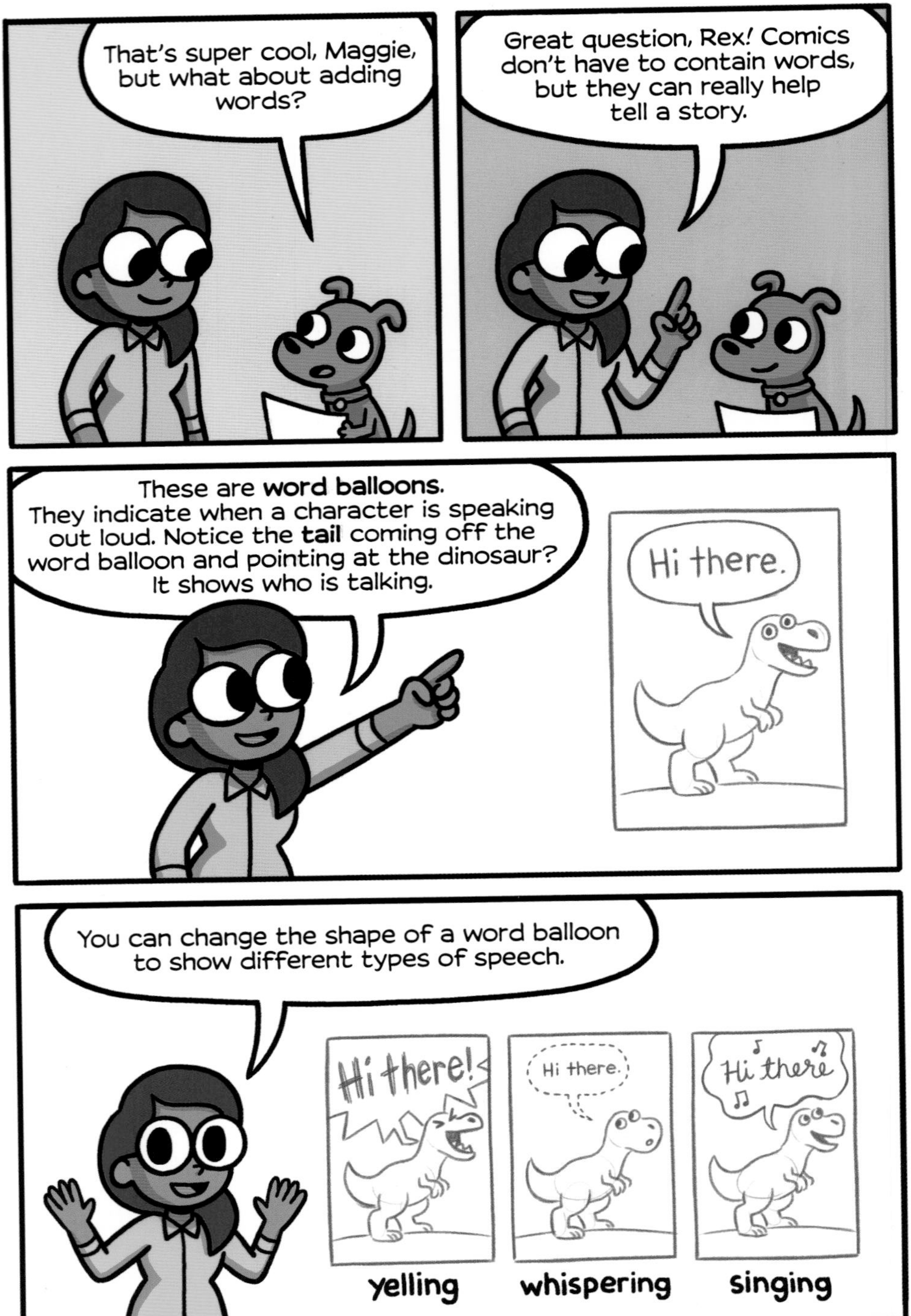

That's super cool, Maggie, but what about adding words?
Great question, Rex! Comics don't have to contain words, but they can really help tell a story.
These are **word balloons**. They indicate when a character is speaking out loud. Notice the **tail** coming off the word balloon and pointing at the dinosaur? It shows who is talking.
Hi there.
You can change the shape of a word balloon to show different types of speech.
Hi there!
Hi there.
Hi there
yelling
whispering
singing

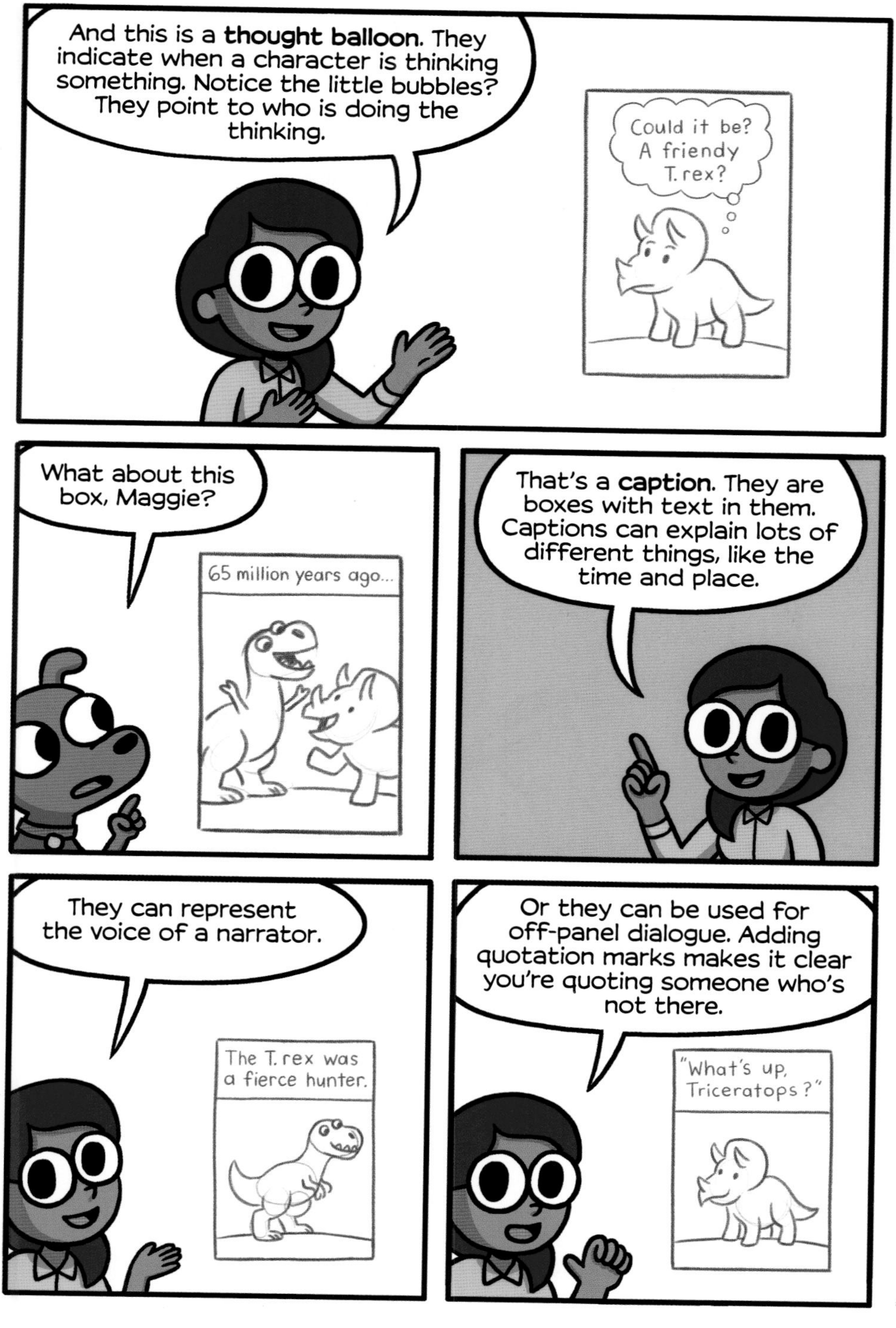
And this is a **thought balloon**. They indicate when a character is thinking something. Notice the little bubbles? They point to who is doing the thinking.
Could it be? A friendy T. rex?
What about this box, Maggie?
65 million years ago...
That's a **caption**. They are boxes with text in them. Captions can explain lots of different things, like the time and place.
They can represent the voice of a narrator.
The T. rex was a fierce hunter.
Or they can be used for off-panel dialogue. Adding quotation marks makes it clear you're quoting someone who's not there.
"What's up, Triceratops?"

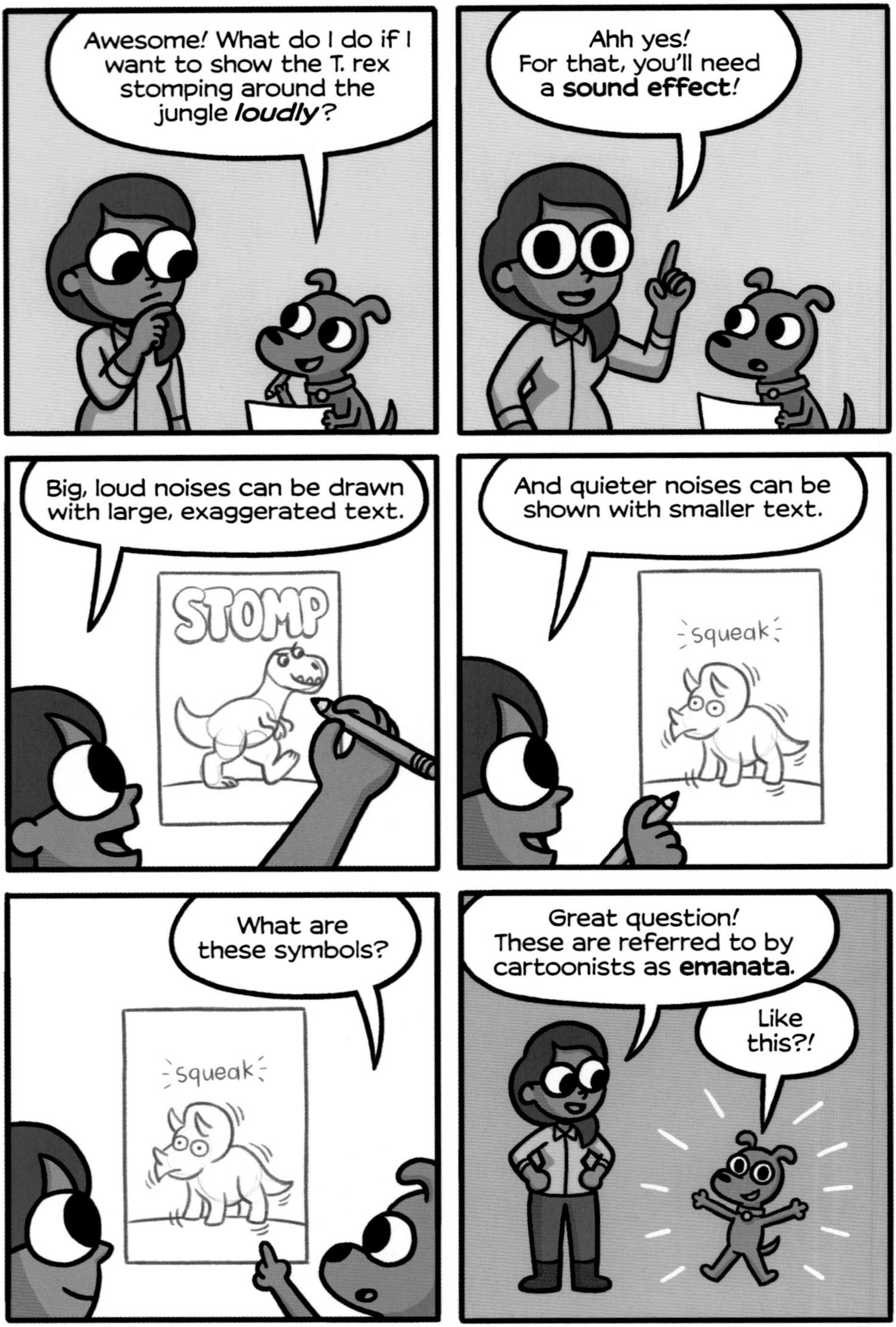
Awesome! What do I do if I want to show the T. rex stomping around the jungle *loudly*?
Ahh yes! For that, you'll need a **sound effect**!
Big, loud noises can be drawn with large, exaggerated text.
STOMP
And quieter noises can be shown with smaller text.
squeak
What are these symbols?
squeak
Great question! These are referred to by cartoonists as **emanata**.
Like this?!

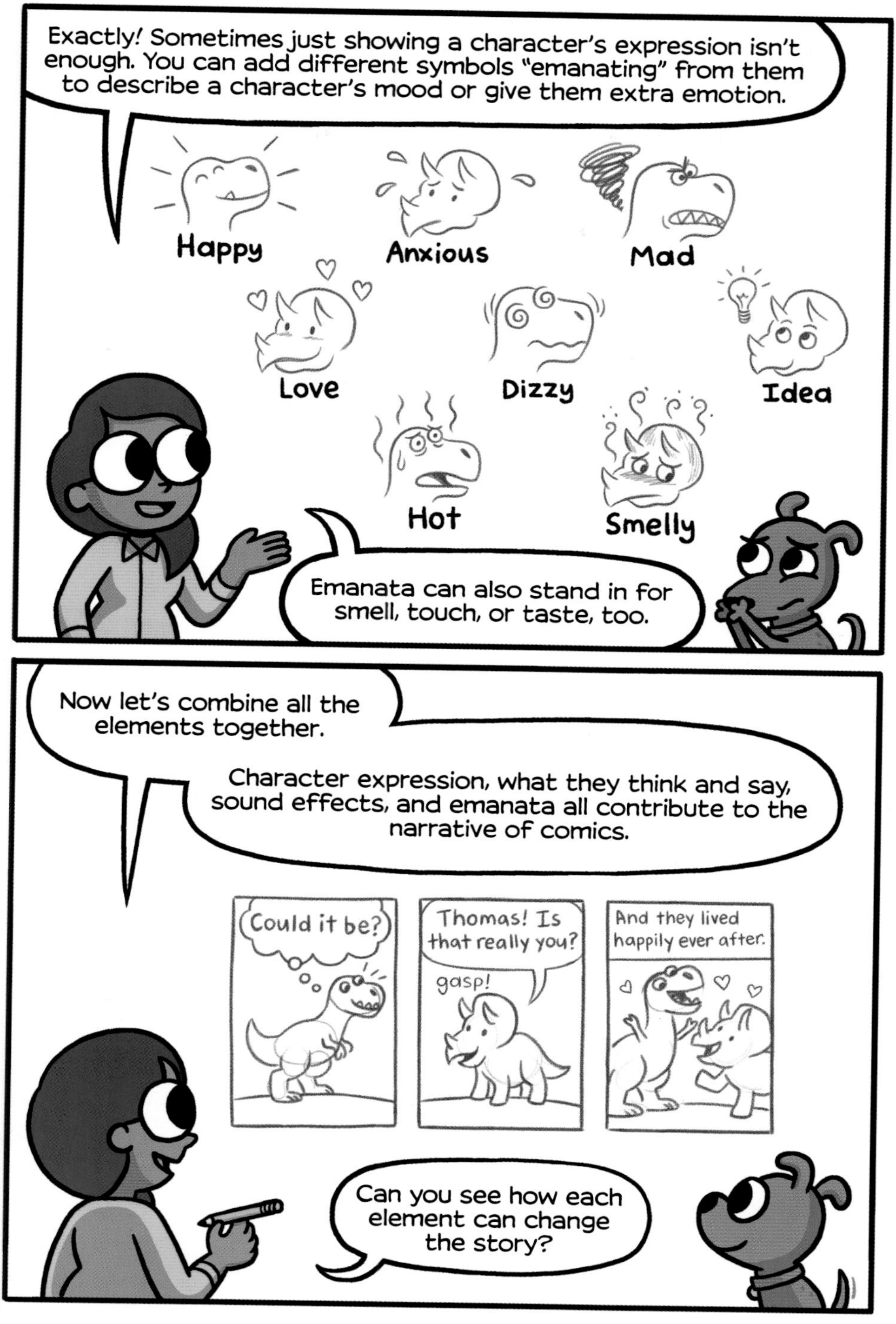
Exactly! Sometimes just showing a character's expression isn't enough. You can add different symbols "emanating" from them to describe a character's mood or give them extra emotion.
Happy
Anxious
Mad
Love
Dizzy
Idea
Hot
Smelly
Emanata can also stand in for smell, touch, or taste, too.
Now let's combine all the elements together.
Character expression, what they think and say, sound effects, and emanata all contribute to the narrative of comics.
Could it be?
Thomas! Is that really you?
gasp!
And they lived happily ever after.
Can you see how each element can change the story?

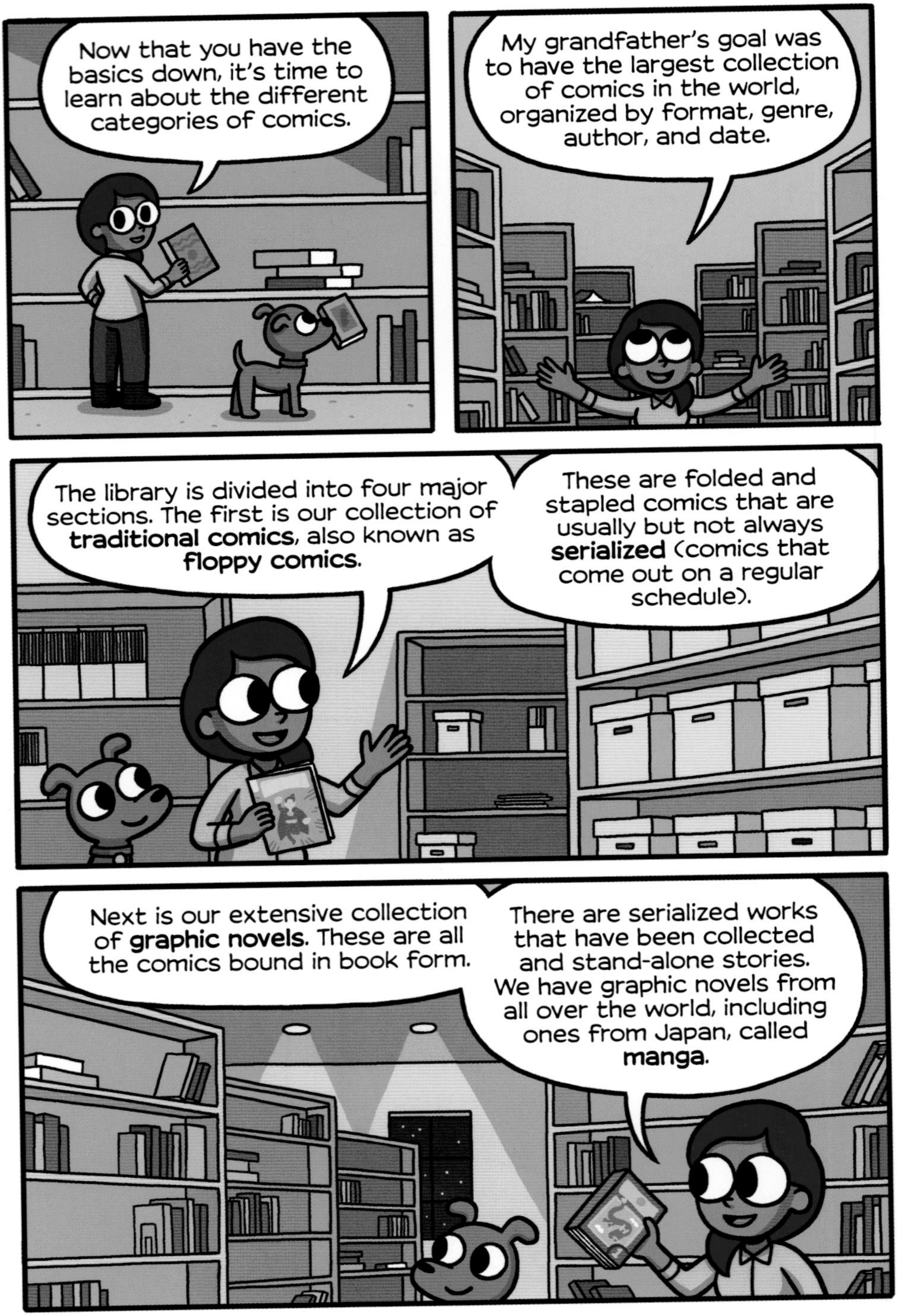
Now that you have the basics down, it's time to learn about the different categories of comics.
My grandfather's goal was to have the largest collection of comics in the world, organized by format, genre, author, and date.
The library is divided into four major sections. The first is our collection of **traditional comics**, also known as **floppy comics**.
These are folded and stapled comics that are usually but not always **serialized** (comics that come out on a regular schedule).
Next is our extensive collection of **graphic novels**. These are all the comics bound in book form.
There are serialized works that have been collected and stand-alone stories. We have graphic novels from all over the world, including ones from Japan, called **manga**.

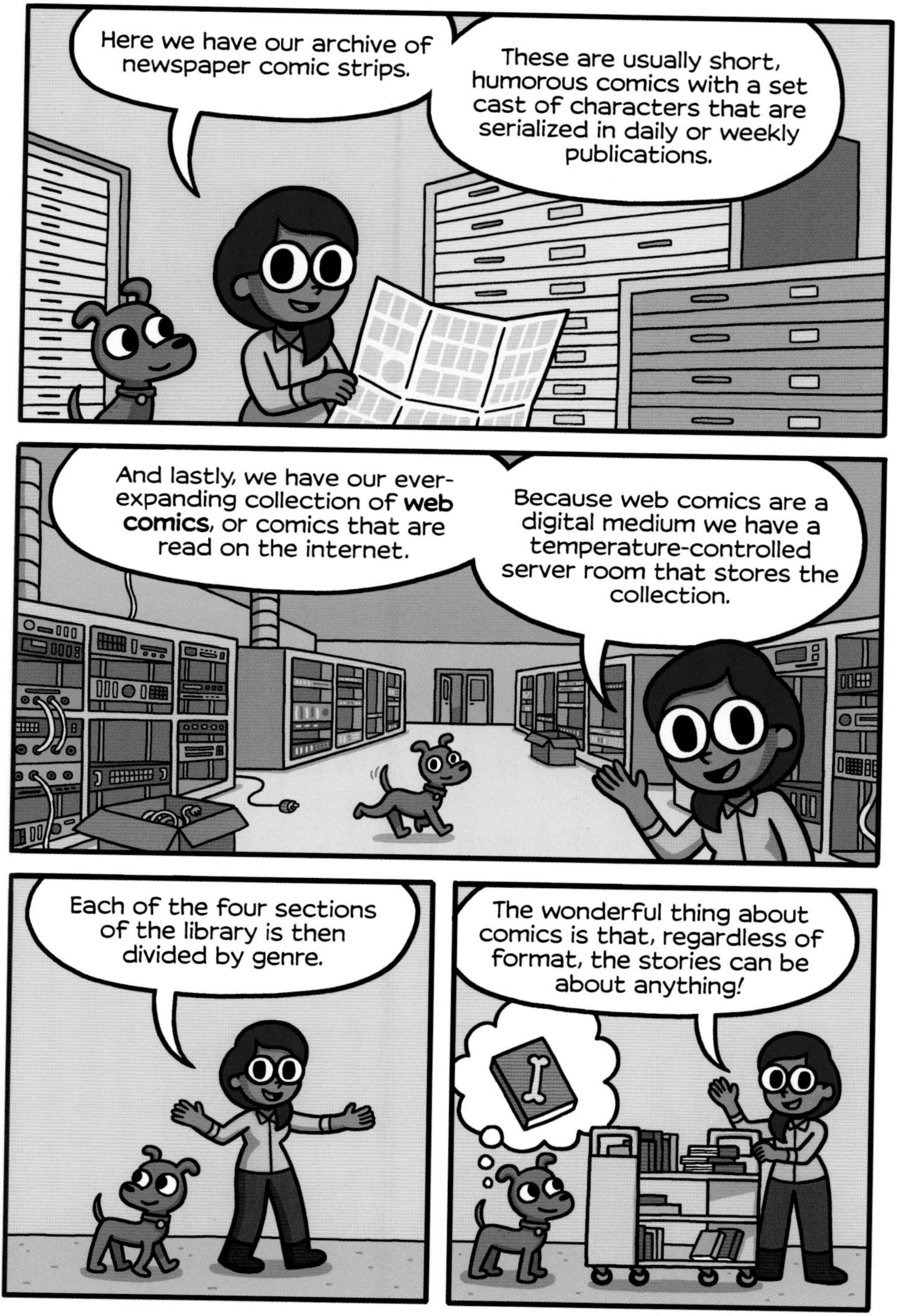
Here we have our archive of newspaper comic strips.
These are usually short, humorous comics with a set cast of characters that are serialized in daily or weekly publications.
And lastly, we have our ever-expanding collection of **web comics**, or comics that are read on the internet.
Because web comics are a digital medium we have a temperature-controlled server room that stores the collection.
Each of the four sections of the library is then divided by genre.
The wonderful thing about comics is that, regardless of format, the stories can be about anything!

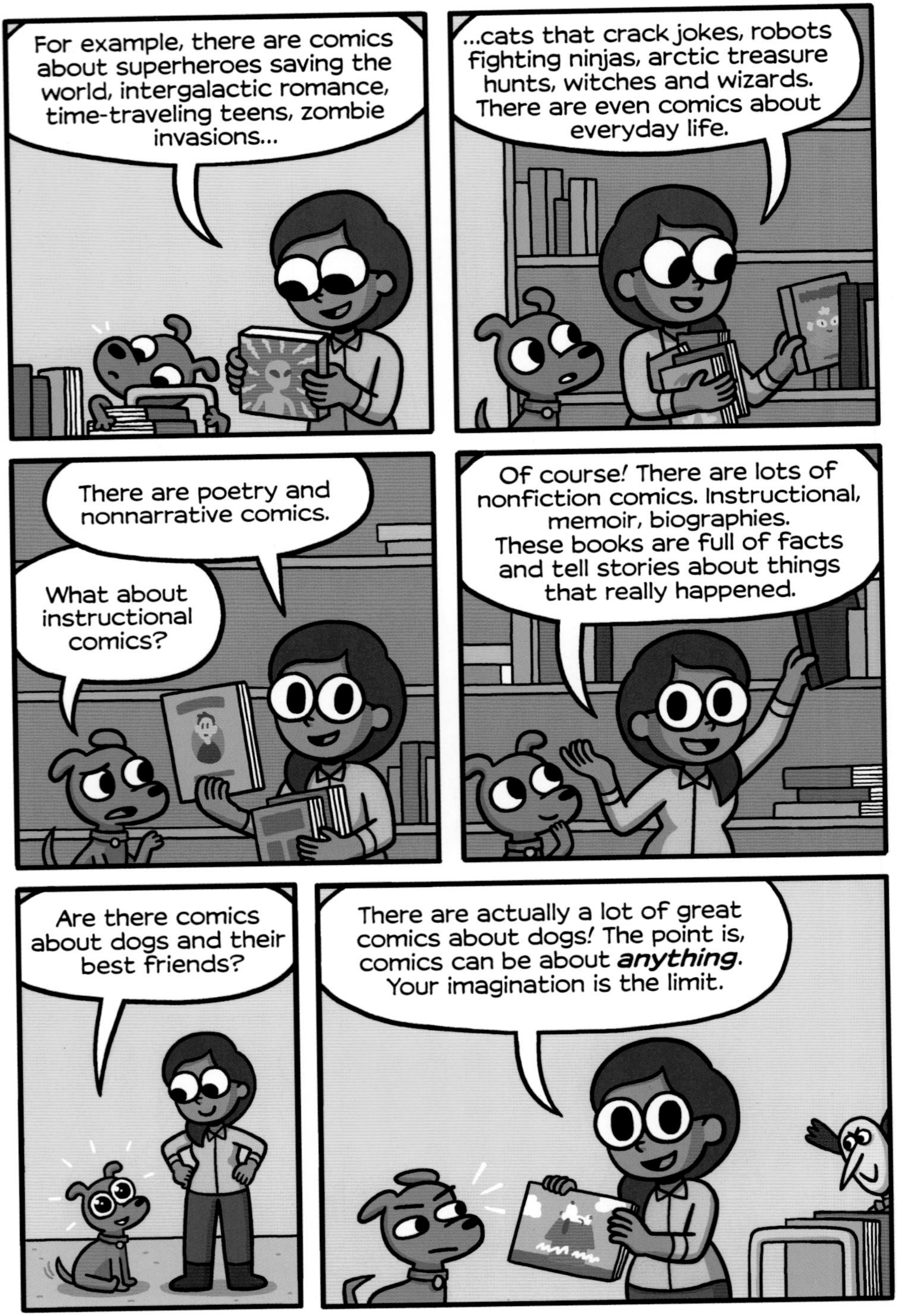
For example, there are comics about superheroes saving the world, intergalactic romance, time-traveling teens, zombie invasions...
...cats that crack jokes, robots fighting ninjas, arctic treasure hunts, witches and wizards. There are even comics about everyday life.
There are poetry and nonnarrative comics.
What about instructional comics?
Of course! There are lots of nonfiction comics. Instructional, memoir, biographies. These books are full of facts and tell stories about things that really happened.
Are there comics about dogs and their best friends?
There are actually a lot of great comics about dogs! The point is, comics can be about ***anything***. Your imagination is the limit.

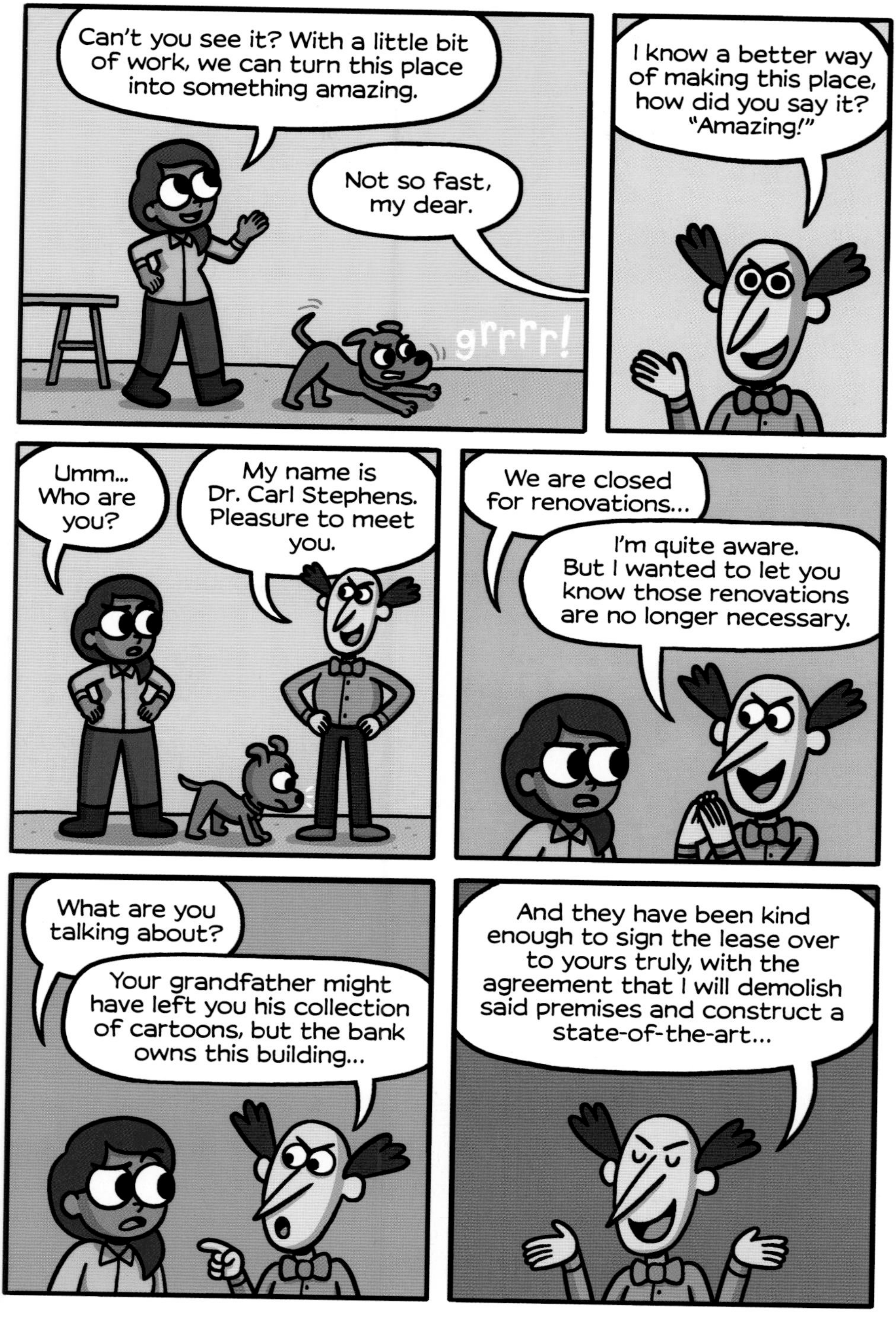
Can't you see it? With a little bit of work, we can turn this place into something amazing.
Not so fast, my dear.
grrrr!
I know a better way of making this place, how did you say it? "Amazing!"
Umm... Who are you?
My name is Dr. Carl Stephens. Pleasure to meet you.
We are closed for renovations...
I'm quite aware. But I wanted to let you know those renovations are no longer necessary.
What are you talking about?
Your grandfather might have left you his collection of cartoons, but the bank owns this building...
And they have been kind enough to sign the lease over to yours truly, with the agreement that I will demolish said premises and construct a state-of-the-art...

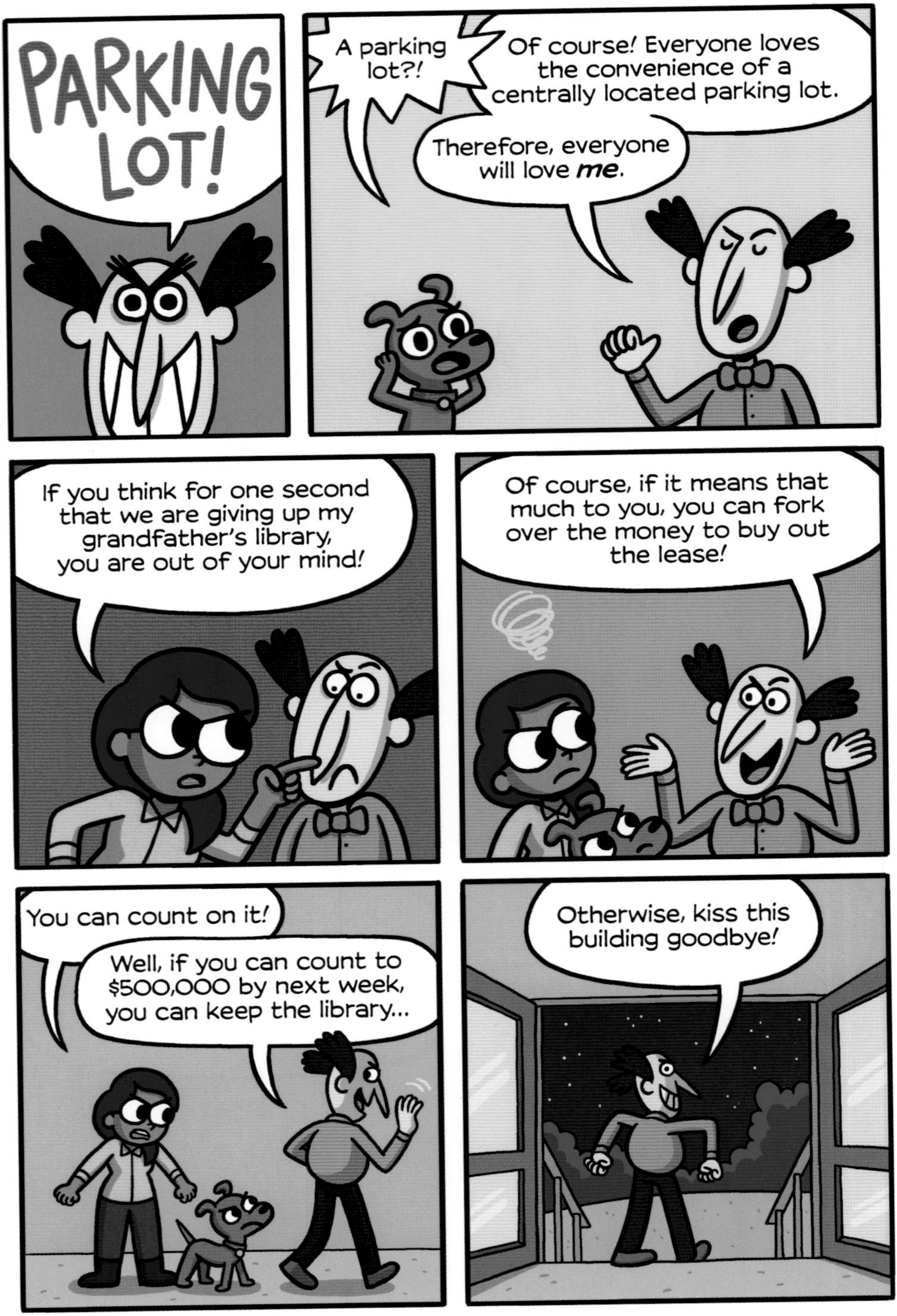

PARKING LOT!
A parking lot?!
Of course! Everyone loves the convenience of a centrally located parking lot.
Therefore, everyone will love *me*.
If you think for one second that we are giving up my grandfather's library, you are out of your mind!
Of course, if it means that much to you, you can fork over the money to buy out the lease!
You can count on it!
Well, if you can count to $500,000 by next week, you can keep the library...
Otherwise, kiss this building goodbye!

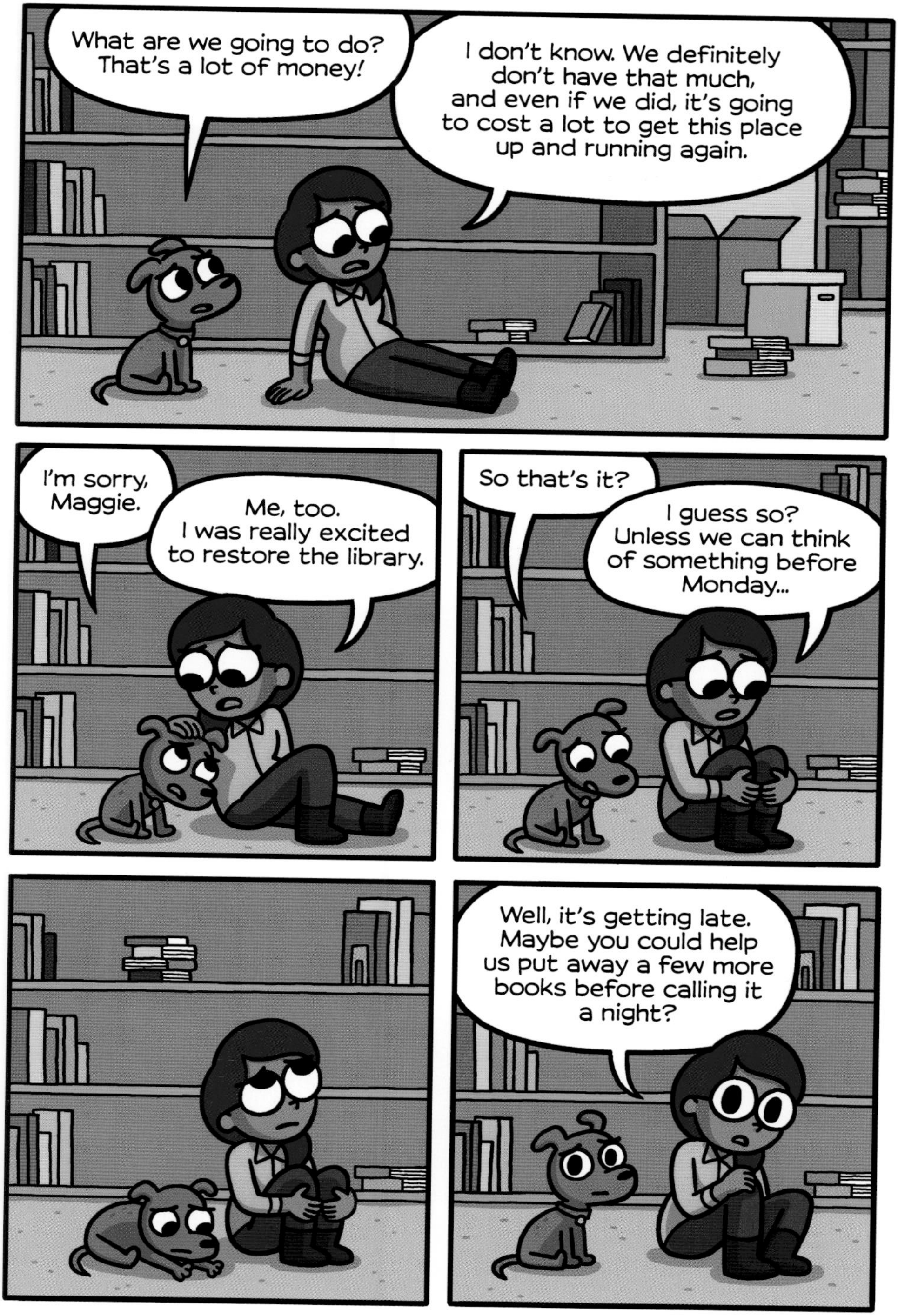
What are we going to do? That's a lot of money!
I don't know. We definitely don't have that much, and even if we did, it's going to cost a lot to get this place up and running again.
I'm sorry, Maggie.
Me, too. I was really excited to restore the library.
So that's it?
I guess so? Unless we can think of something before Monday...
Well, it's getting late. Maybe you could help us put away a few more books before calling it a night?

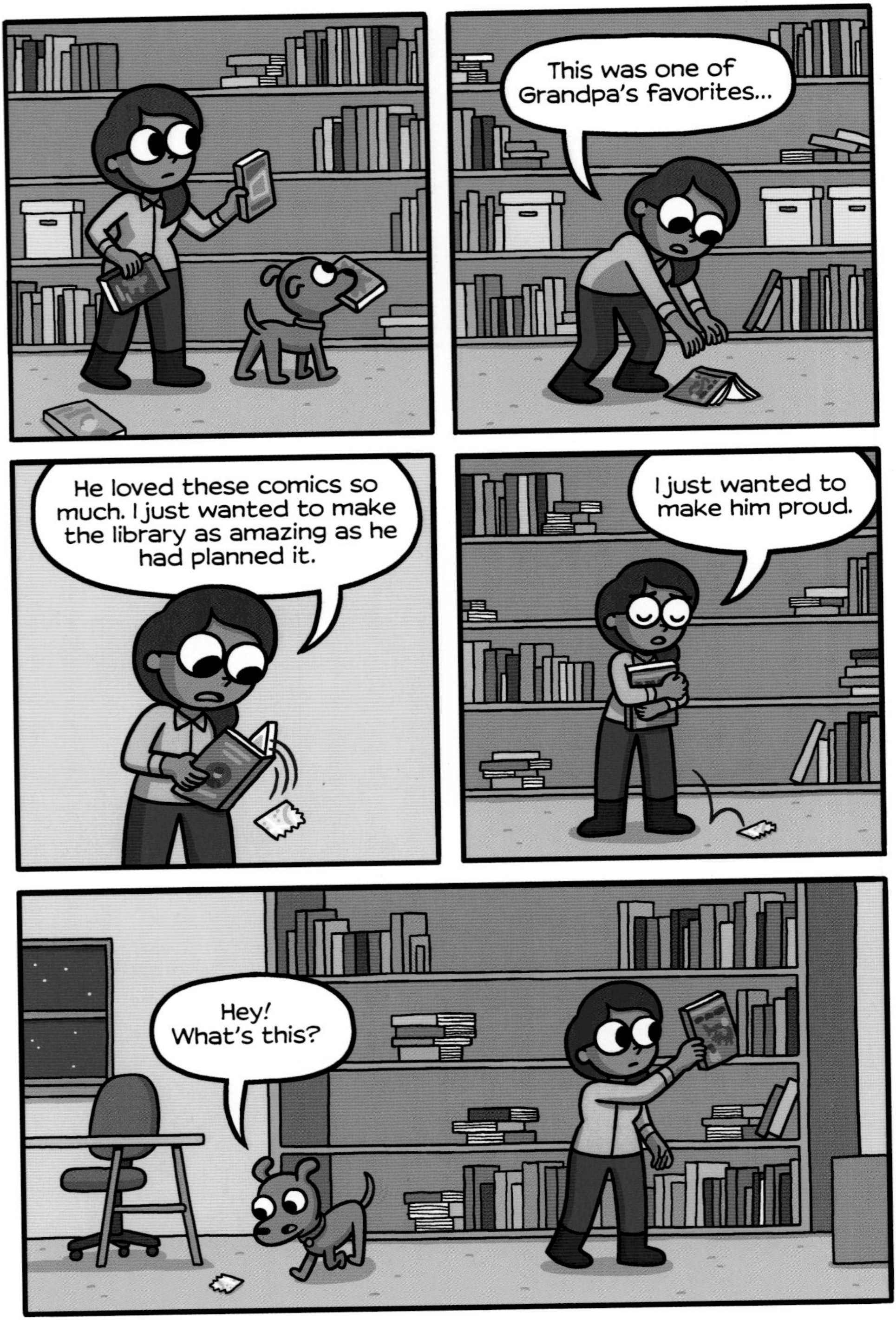
This was one of Grandpa's favorites...
He loved these comics so much. I just wanted to make the library as amazing as he had planned it.
I just wanted to make him proud.
Hey! What's this?

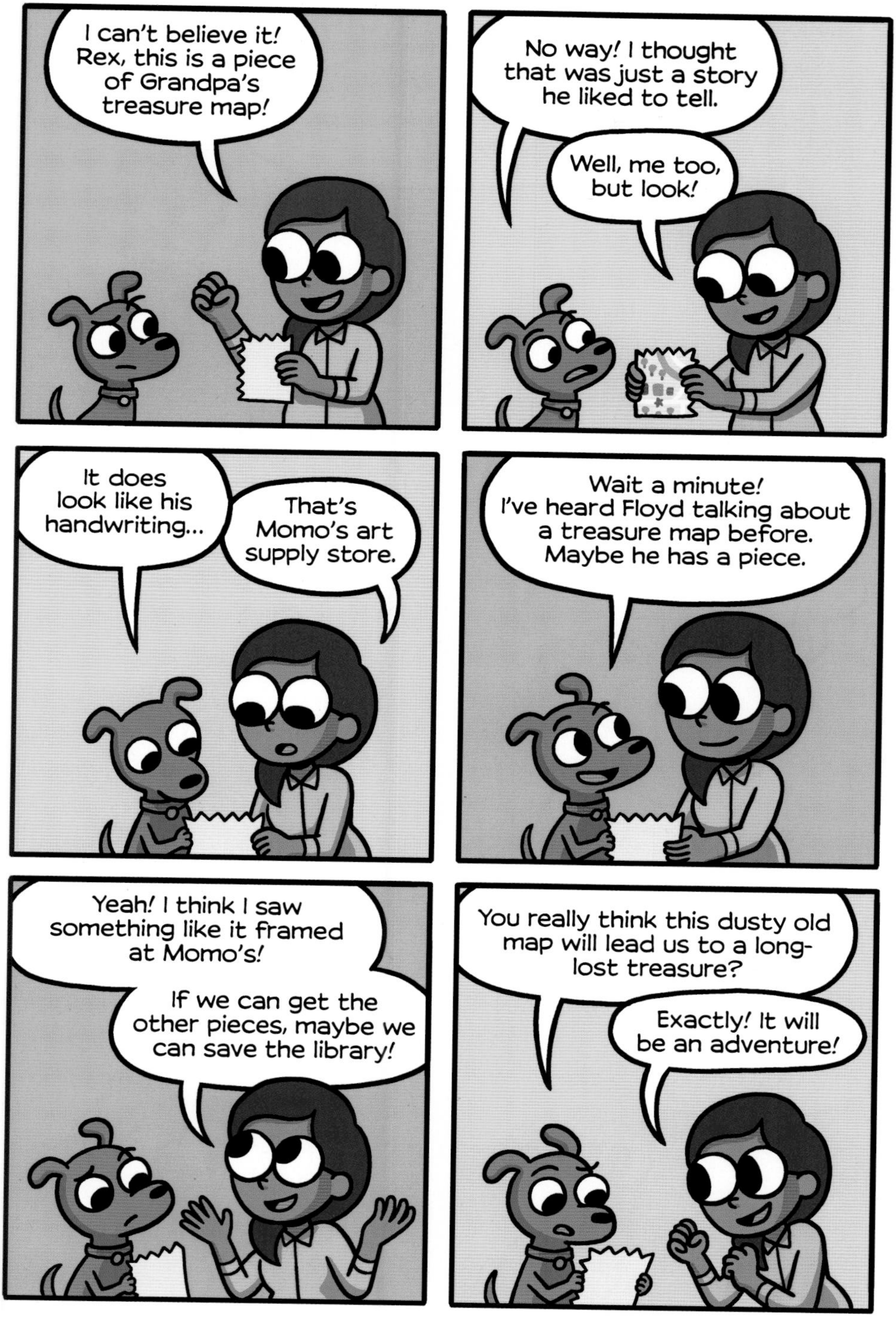
I can't believe it! Rex, this is a piece of Grandpa's treasure map!
No way! I thought that was just a story he liked to tell.
Well, me too, but look!
It does look like his handwriting...
That's Momo's art supply store.
Wait a minute! I've heard Floyd talking about a treasure map before. Maybe he has a piece.
Yeah! I think I saw something like it framed at Momo's!
If we can get the other pieces, maybe we can save the library!
You really think this dusty old map will lead us to a long-lost treasure?
Exactly! It will be an adventure!

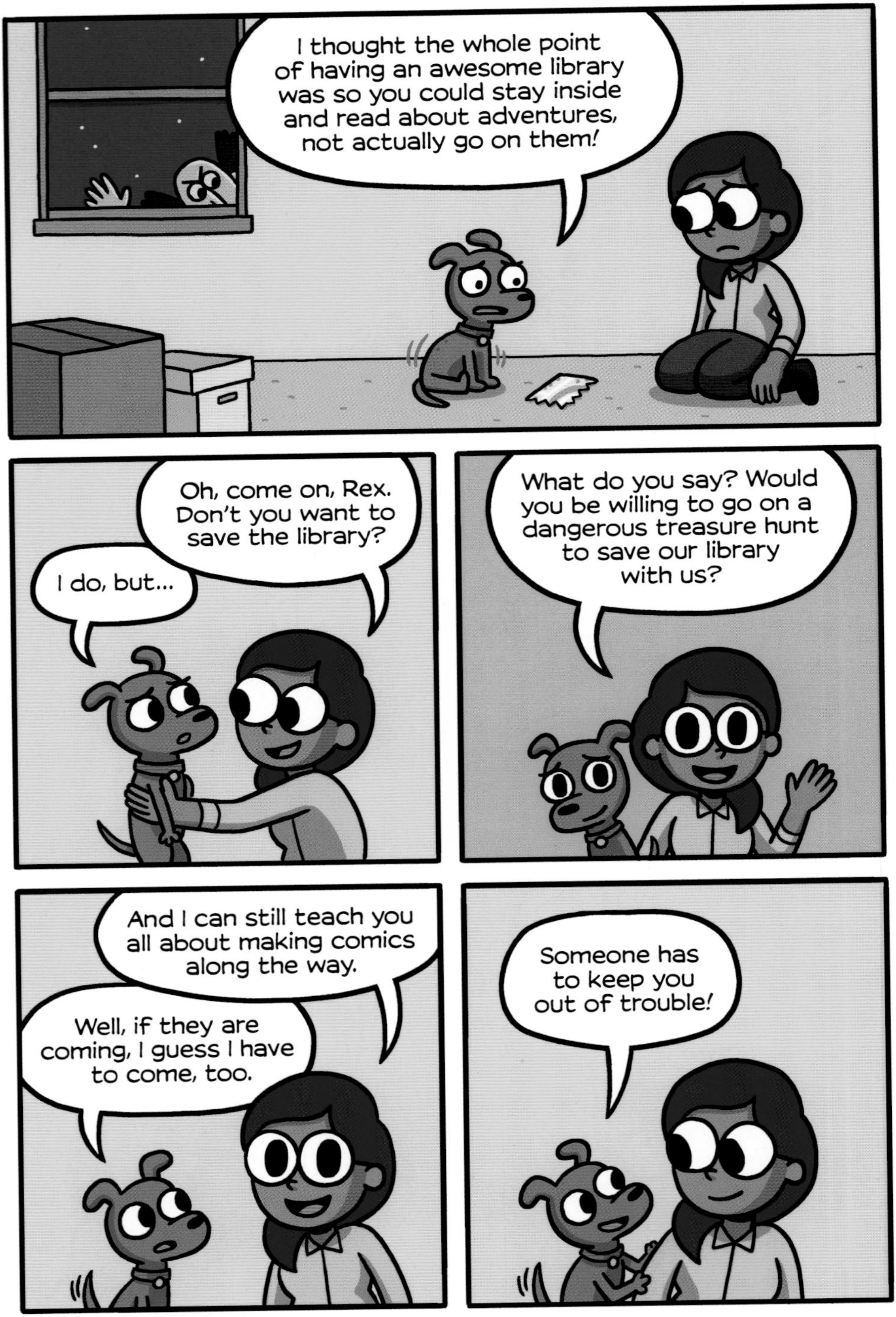
I thought the whole point of having an awesome library was so you could stay inside and read about adventures, not actually go on them!
Oh, come on, Rex. Don't you want to save the library?
I do, but...
What do you say? Would you be willing to go on a dangerous treasure hunt to save our library with us?
And I can still teach you all about making comics along the way.
Well, if they are coming, I guess I have to come, too.
Someone has to keep you out of trouble!

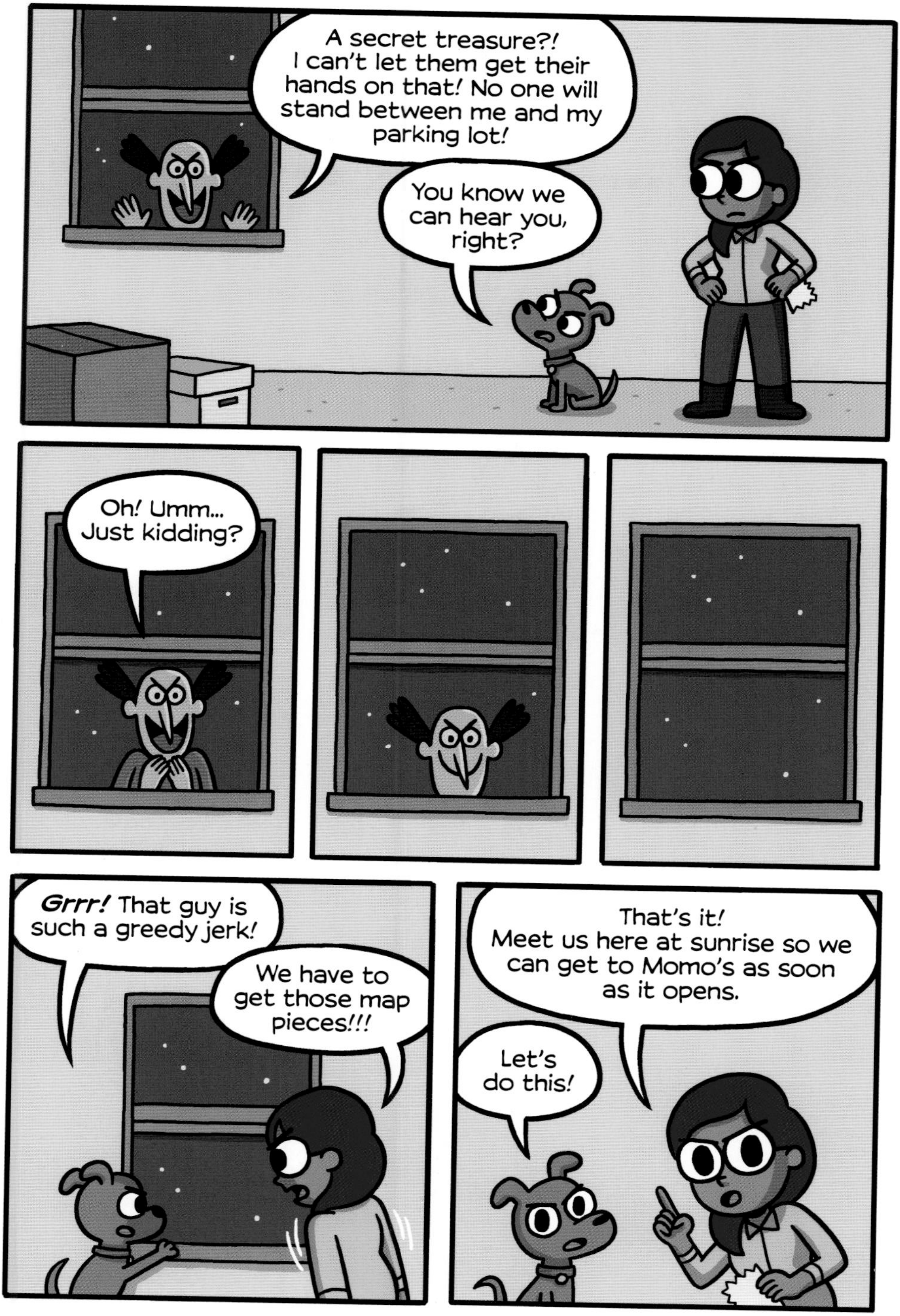
A secret treasure?! I can't let them get their hands on that! No one will stand between me and my parking lot!
You know we can hear you, right?
Oh! Umm... Just kidding?
Grrr! That guy is such a greedy jerk!
We have to get those map pieces!!!
That's it! Meet us here at sunrise so we can get to Momo's as soon as it opens.
Let's do this!

PROJECT TWO: PLANNING A COMIC STRIP

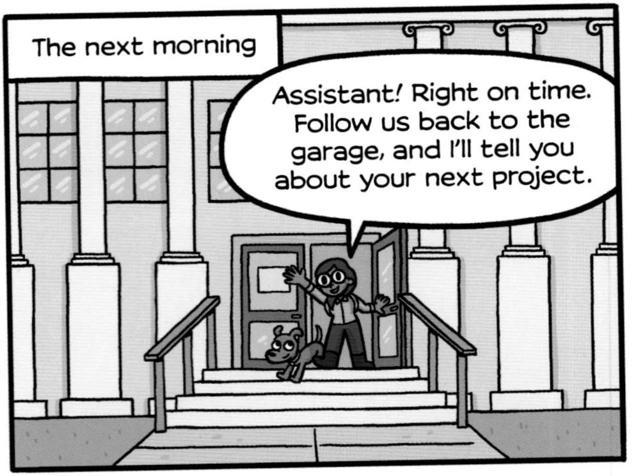

The next morning
Assistant! Right on time. Follow us back to the garage, and I'll tell you about your next project.

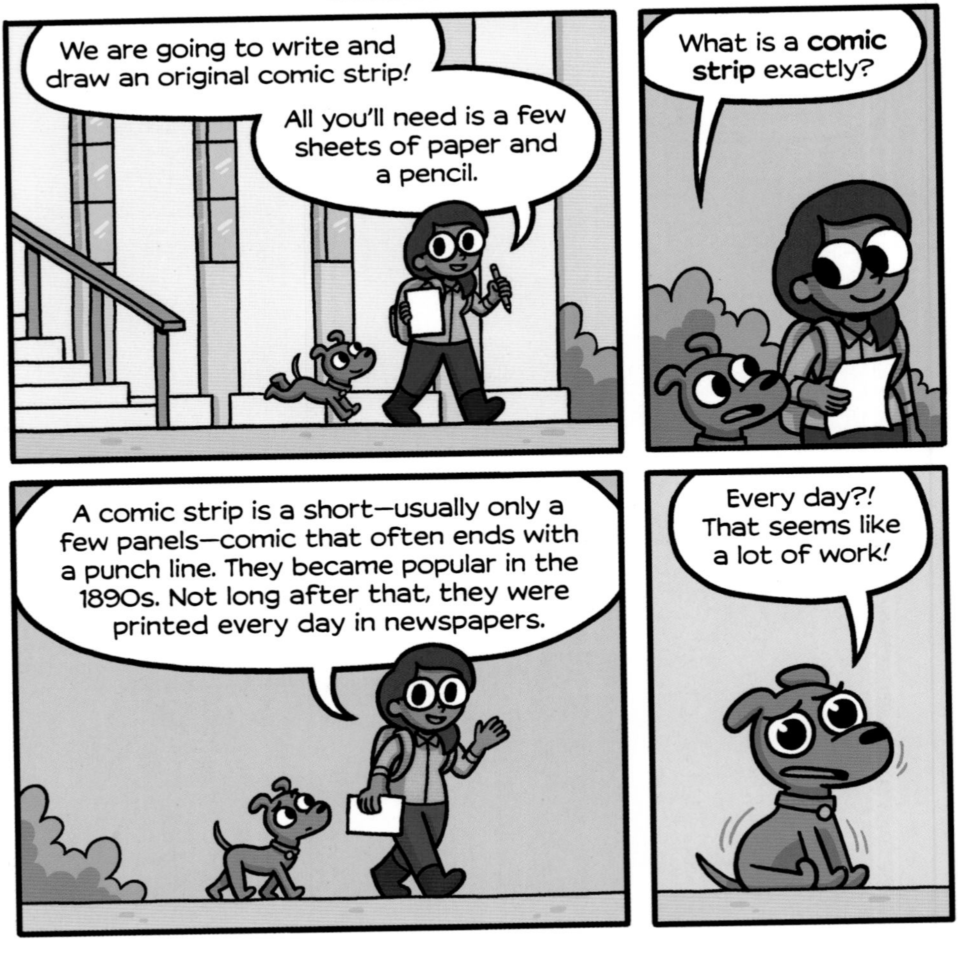

We are going to write and draw an original comic strip!
All you'll need is a few sheets of paper and a pencil.
What is a **comic strip** exactly?
A comic strip is a short—usually only a few panels—comic that often ends with a punch line. They became popular in the 1890s. Not long after that, they were printed every day in newspapers.
Every day?! That seems like a lot of work!

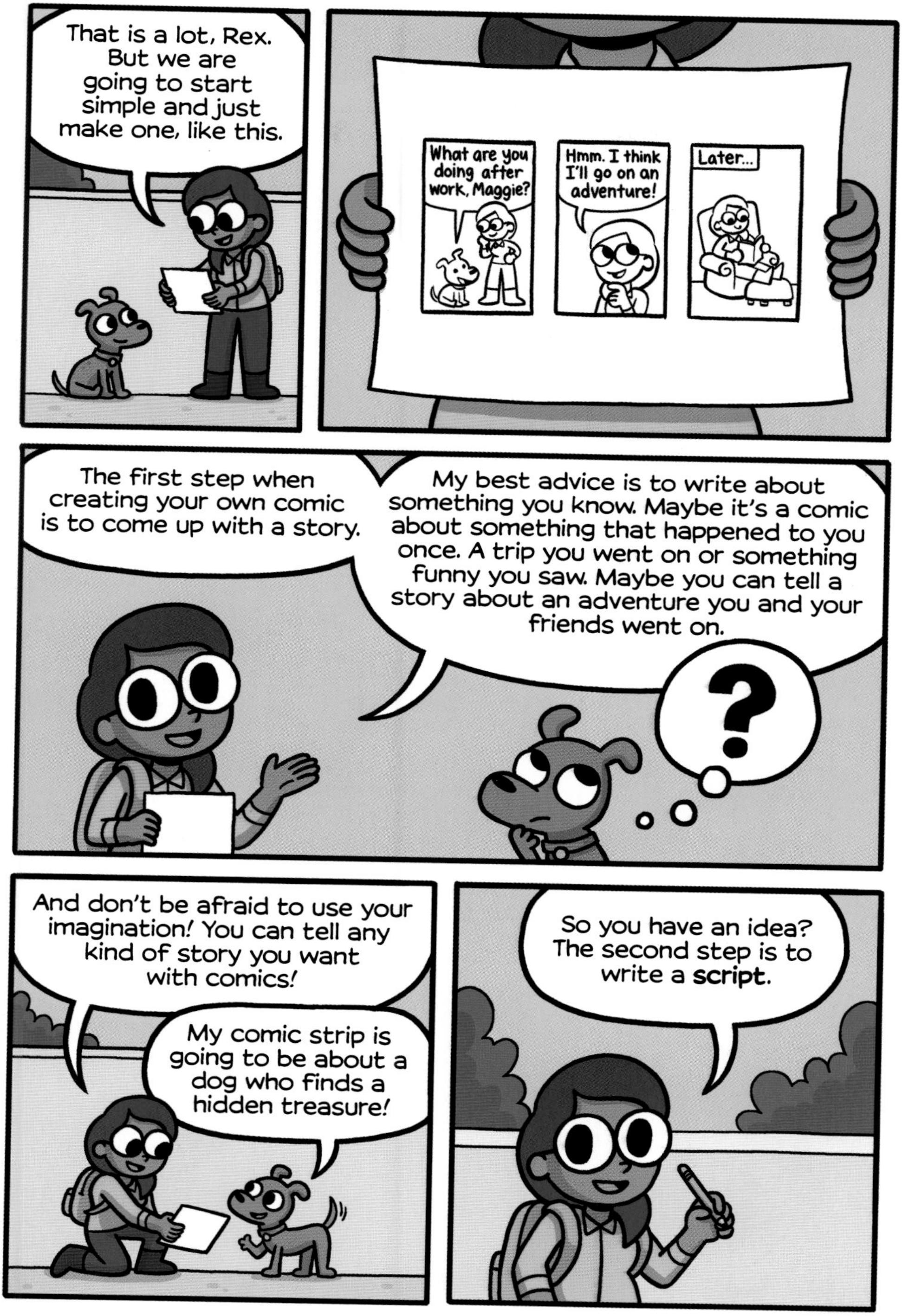
That is a lot, Rex. But we are going to start simple and just make one, like this.
What are you doing after work, Maggie?
Hmm. I think I'll go on an adventure!
Later...
The first step when creating your own comic is to come up with a story.
My best advice is to write about something you know. Maybe it's a comic about something that happened to you once. A trip you went on or something funny you saw. Maybe you can tell a story about an adventure you and your friends went on.
?
And don't be afraid to use your imagination! You can tell any kind of story you want with comics!
My comic strip is going to be about a dog who finds a hidden treasure!
So you have an idea? The second step is to write a **script**.

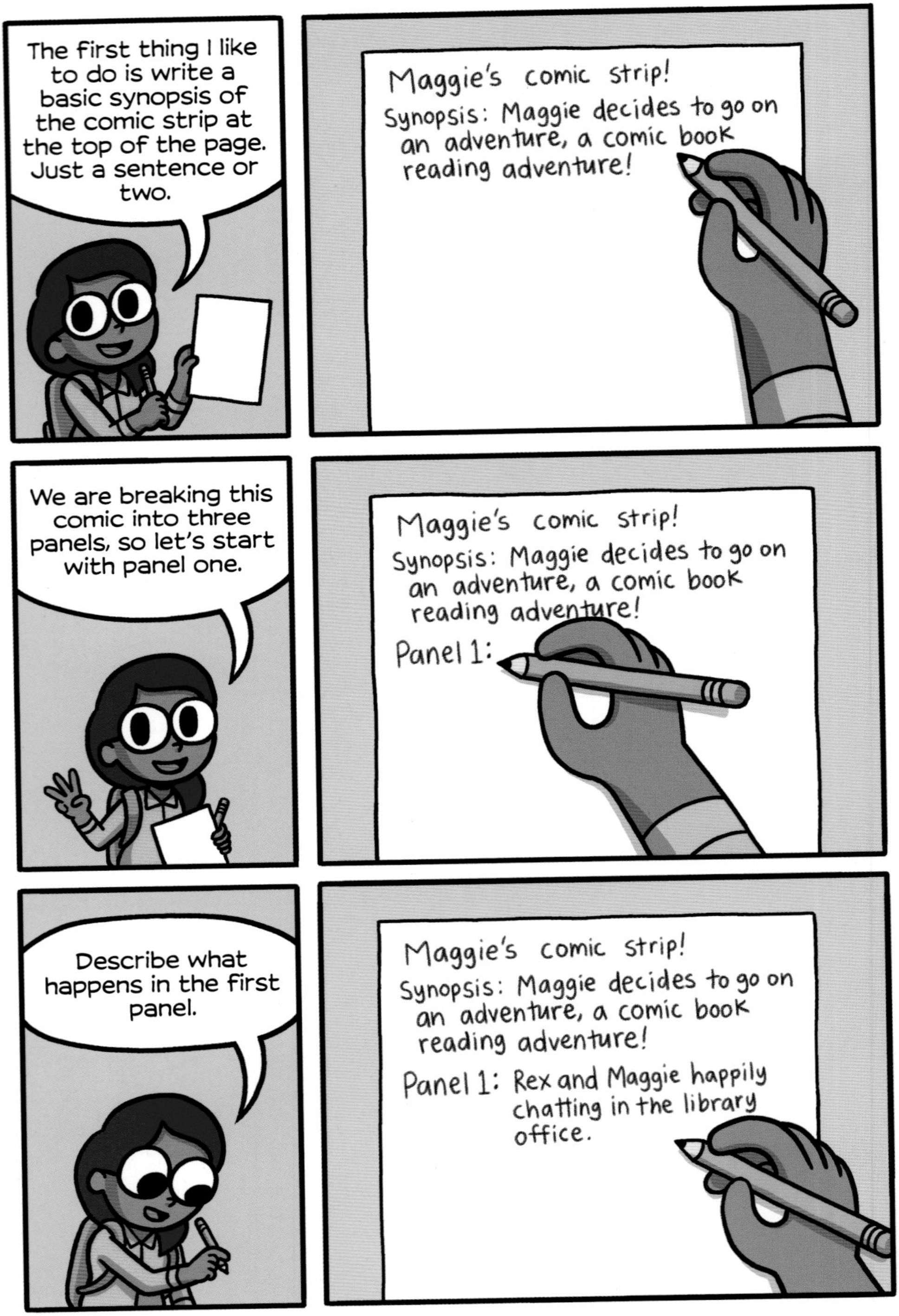
The first thing I like to do is write a basic synopsis of the comic strip at the top of the page. Just a sentence or two.
Maggie's comic strip!
Synopsis: Maggie decides to go on an adventure, a comic book reading adventure!
We are breaking this comic into three panels, so let's start with panel one.
Maggie's comic strip!
Synopsis: Maggie decides to go on an adventure, a comic book reading adventure!
Panel 1:
Describe what happens in the first panel.
Maggie's comic strip!
Synopsis: Maggie decides to go on an adventure, a comic book reading adventure!
Panel 1: Rex and Maggie happily chatting in the library office.

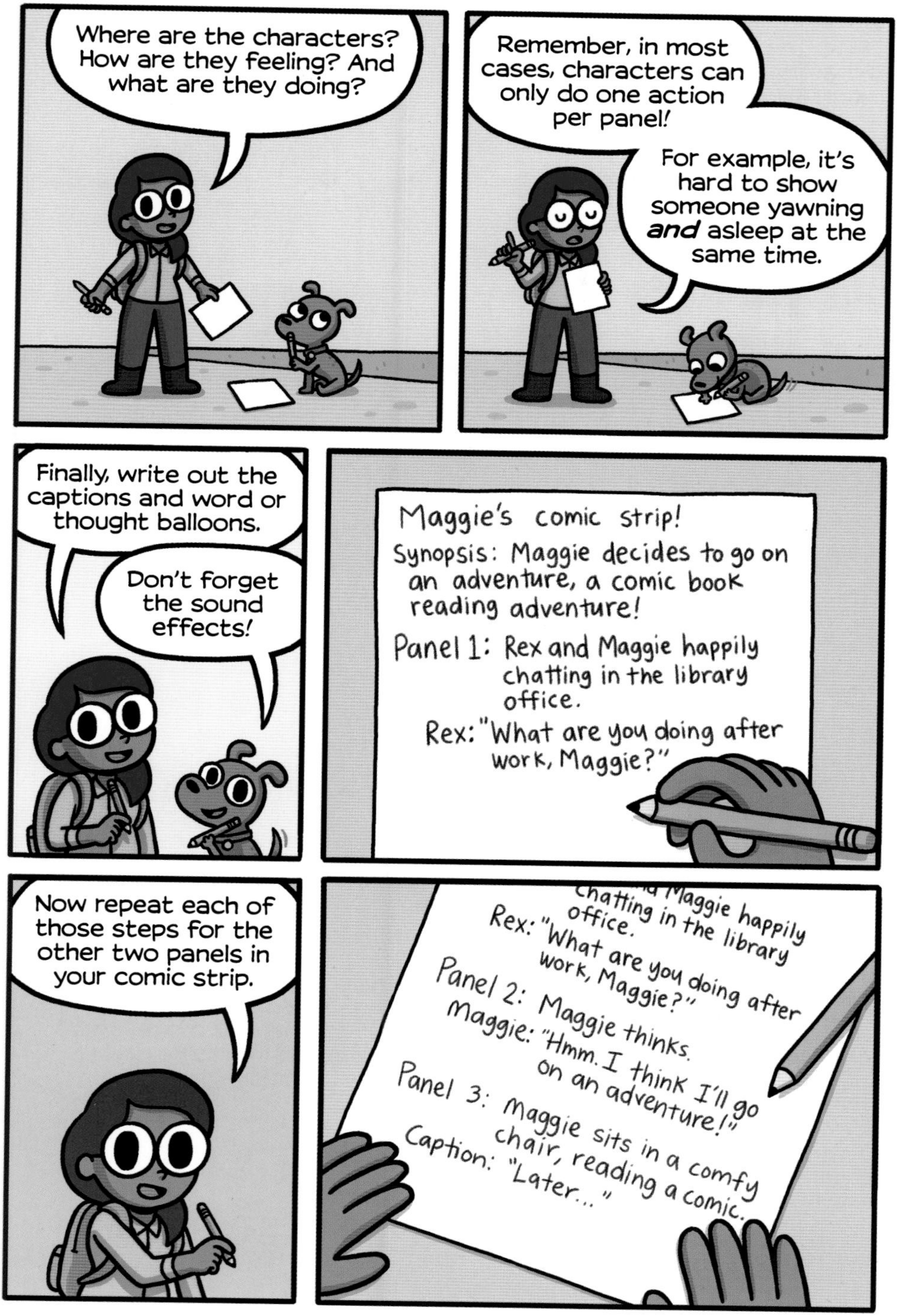
Where are the characters? How are they feeling? And what are they doing?
Remember, in most cases, characters can only do one action per panel!
For example, it's hard to show someone yawning *and* asleep at the same time.
Finally, write out the captions and word or thought balloons.
Don't forget the sound effects!
Maggie's comic strip!
Synopsis: Maggie decides to go on an adventure, a comic book reading adventure!
Panel 1: Rex and Maggie happily chatting in the library office.
Rex: "What are you doing after work, Maggie?"
Now repeat each of those steps for the other two panels in your comic strip.
chatting in the library office.
Rex: "What are you doing after work, Maggie?"
Panel 2: Maggie thinks.
Maggie: "Hmm. I think I'll go on an adventure!"
Panel 3: Maggie sits in a comfy chair, reading a comic.
Caption: "Later..."

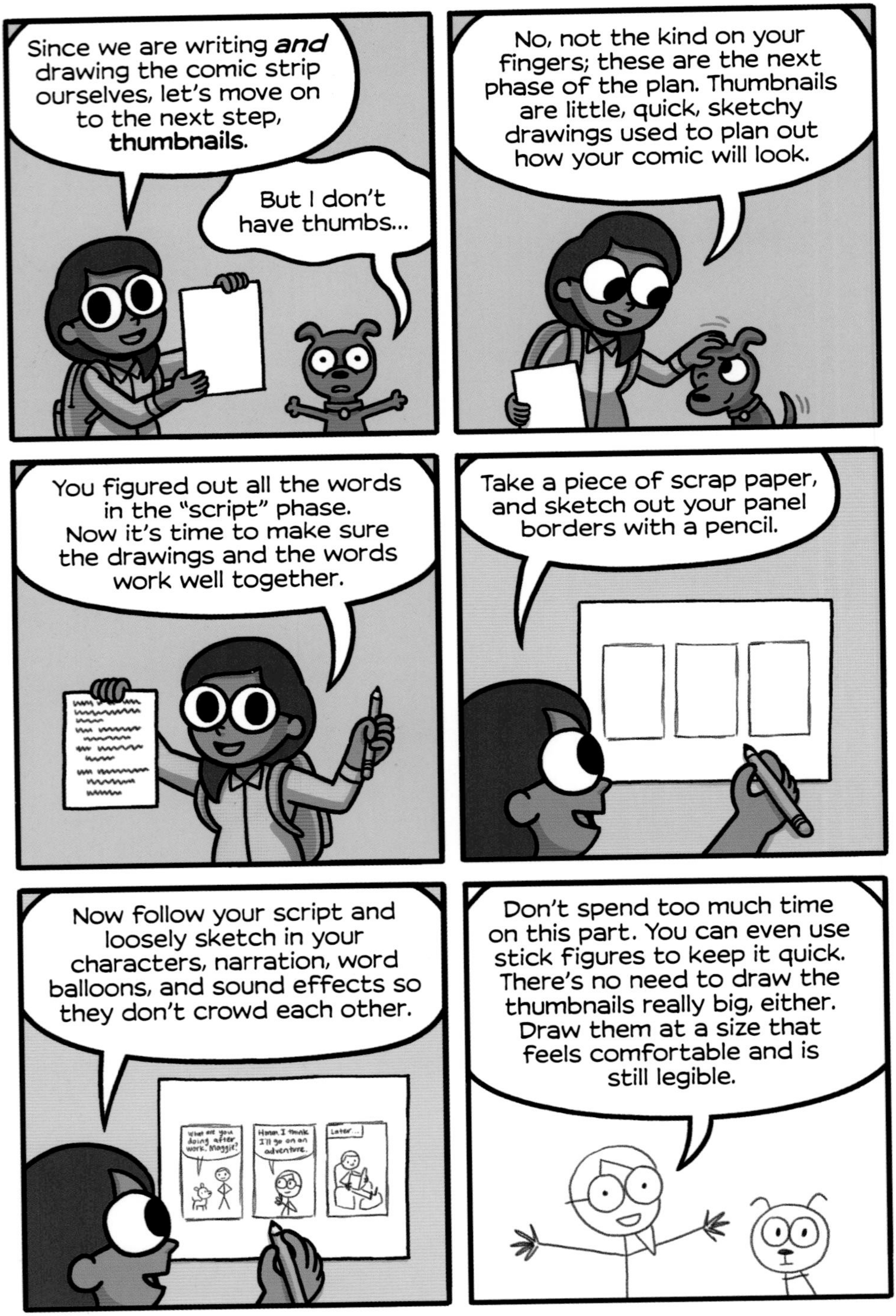
Since we are writing ***and*** drawing the comic strip ourselves, let's move on to the next step, **thumbnails**.
But I don't have thumbs...
No, not the kind on your fingers; these are the next phase of the plan. Thumbnails are little, quick, sketchy drawings used to plan out how your comic will look.
You figured out all the words in the "script" phase. Now it's time to make sure the drawings and the words work well together.
Take a piece of scrap paper, and sketch out your panel borders with a pencil.
Now follow your script and loosely sketch in your characters, narration, word balloons, and sound effects so they don't crowd each other.
What are you doing after work, Maggie?
Hmm, I think I'll go on an adventure.
Later...
Don't spend too much time on this part. You can even use stick figures to keep it quick. There's no need to draw the thumbnails really big, either. Draw them at a size that feels comfortable and is still legible.

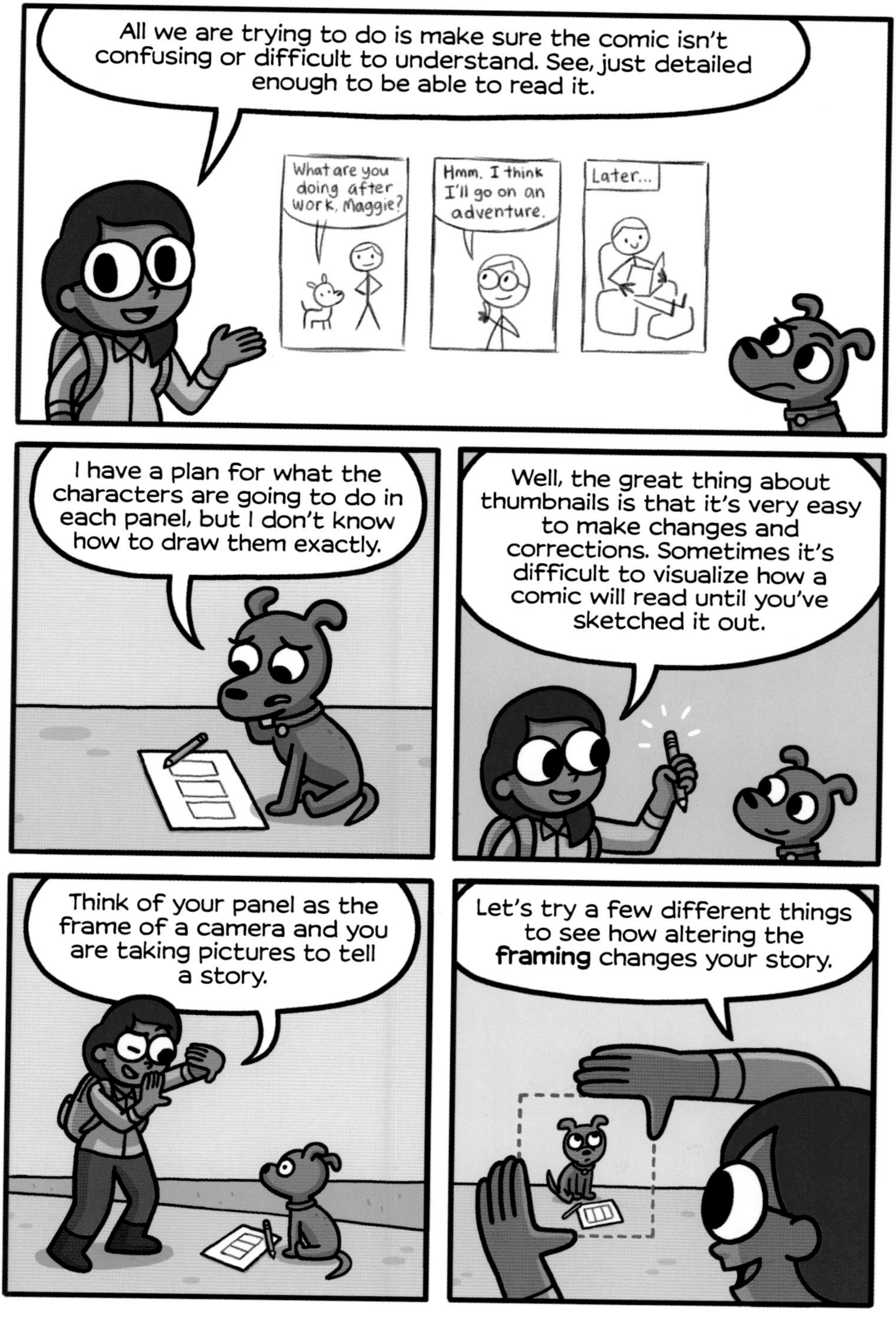
All we are trying to do is make sure the comic isn't confusing or difficult to understand. See, just detailed enough to be able to read it.
What are you doing after work, Maggie?
Hmm. I think I'll go on an adventure.
Later...
I have a plan for what the characters are going to do in each panel, but I don't know how to draw them exactly.
Well, the great thing about thumbnails is that it's very easy to make changes and corrections. Sometimes it's difficult to visualize how a comic will read until you've sketched it out.
Think of your panel as the frame of a camera and you are taking pictures to tell a story.
Let's try a few different things to see how altering the **framing** changes your story.

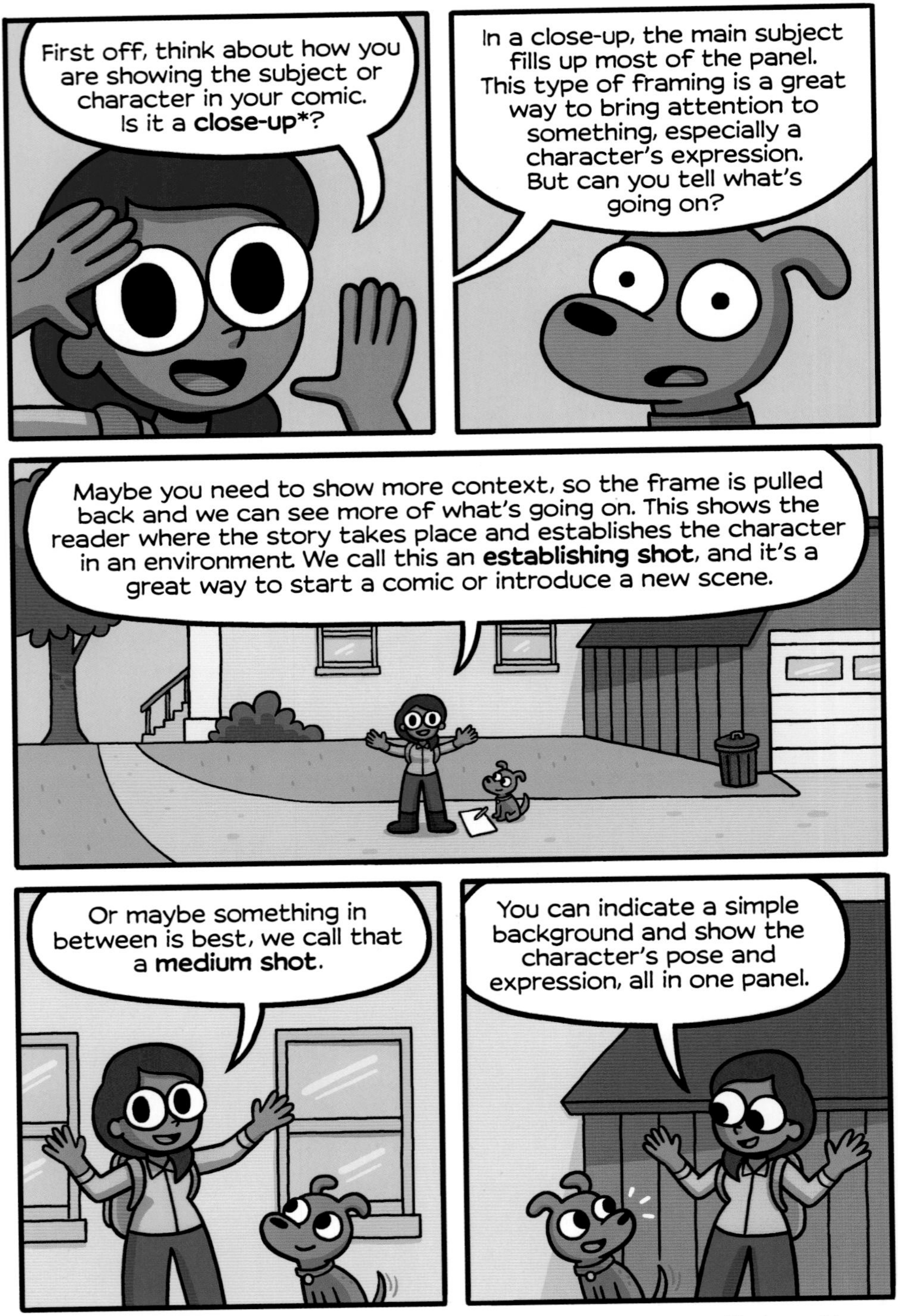
First off, think about how you are showing the subject or character in your comic. Is it a **close-up***?
In a close-up, the main subject fills up most of the panel. This type of framing is a great way to bring attention to something, especially a character's expression. But can you tell what's going on?
Maybe you need to show more context, so the frame is pulled back and we can see more of what's going on. This shows the reader where the story takes place and establishes the character in an environment. We call this an **establishing shot**, and it's a great way to start a comic or introduce a new scene.
Or maybe something in between is best, we call that a **medium shot**.
You can indicate a simple background and show the character's pose and expression, all in one panel.

*Close-up, establishing shot, and medium shot are terms that were first used by filmmakers. Comics and film share some of the same concepts and terminology.

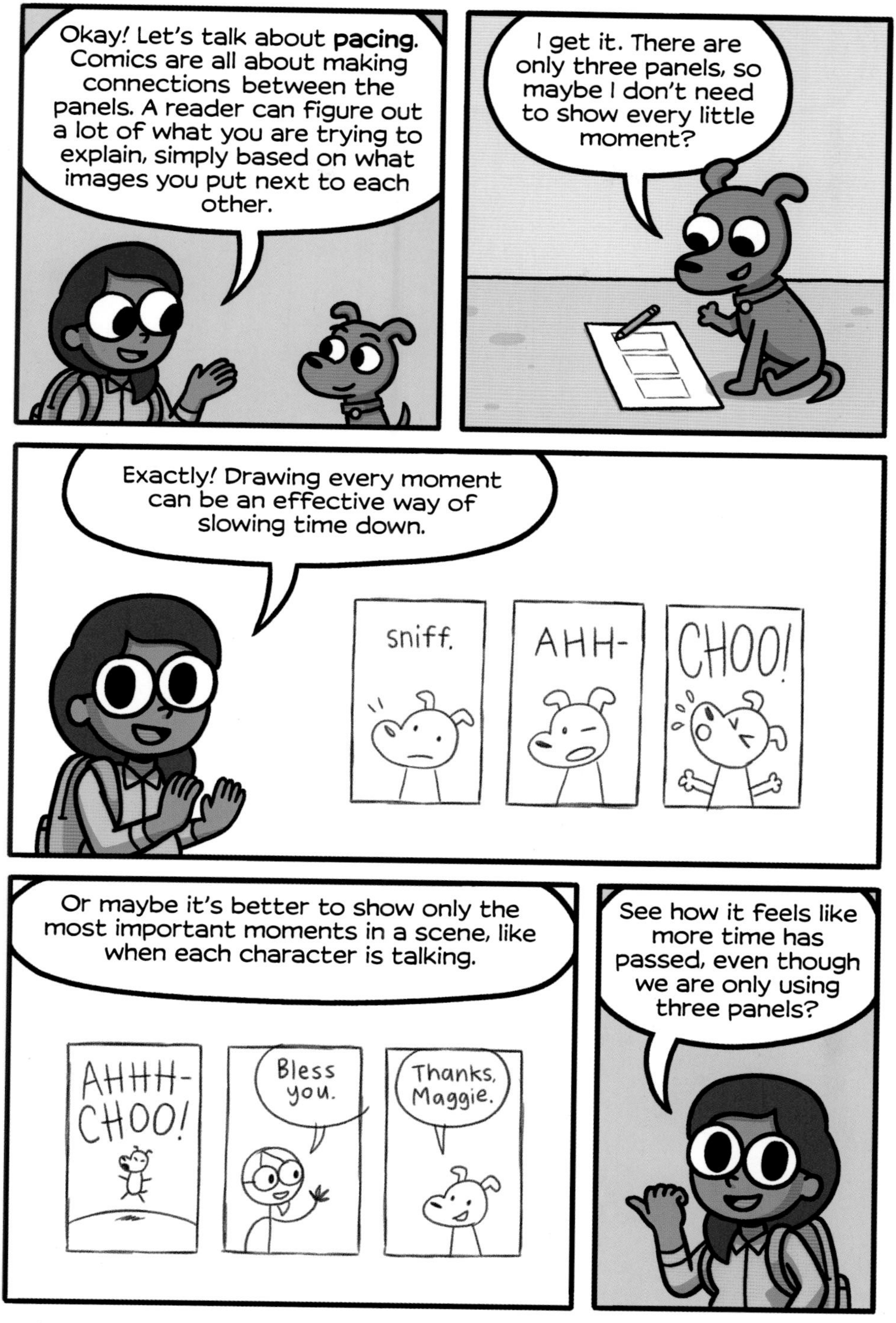
Okay! Let's talk about **pacing**. Comics are all about making connections between the panels. A reader can figure out a lot of what you are trying to explain, simply based on what images you put next to each other.
I get it. There are only three panels, so maybe I don't need to show every little moment?
Exactly! Drawing every moment can be an effective way of slowing time down.
sniff.
AHH-
CHOO!
Or maybe it's better to show only the most important moments in a scene, like when each character is talking.
AHHH-CHOO!
Bless you.
Thanks, Maggie.
See how it feels like more time has passed, even though we are only using three panels?

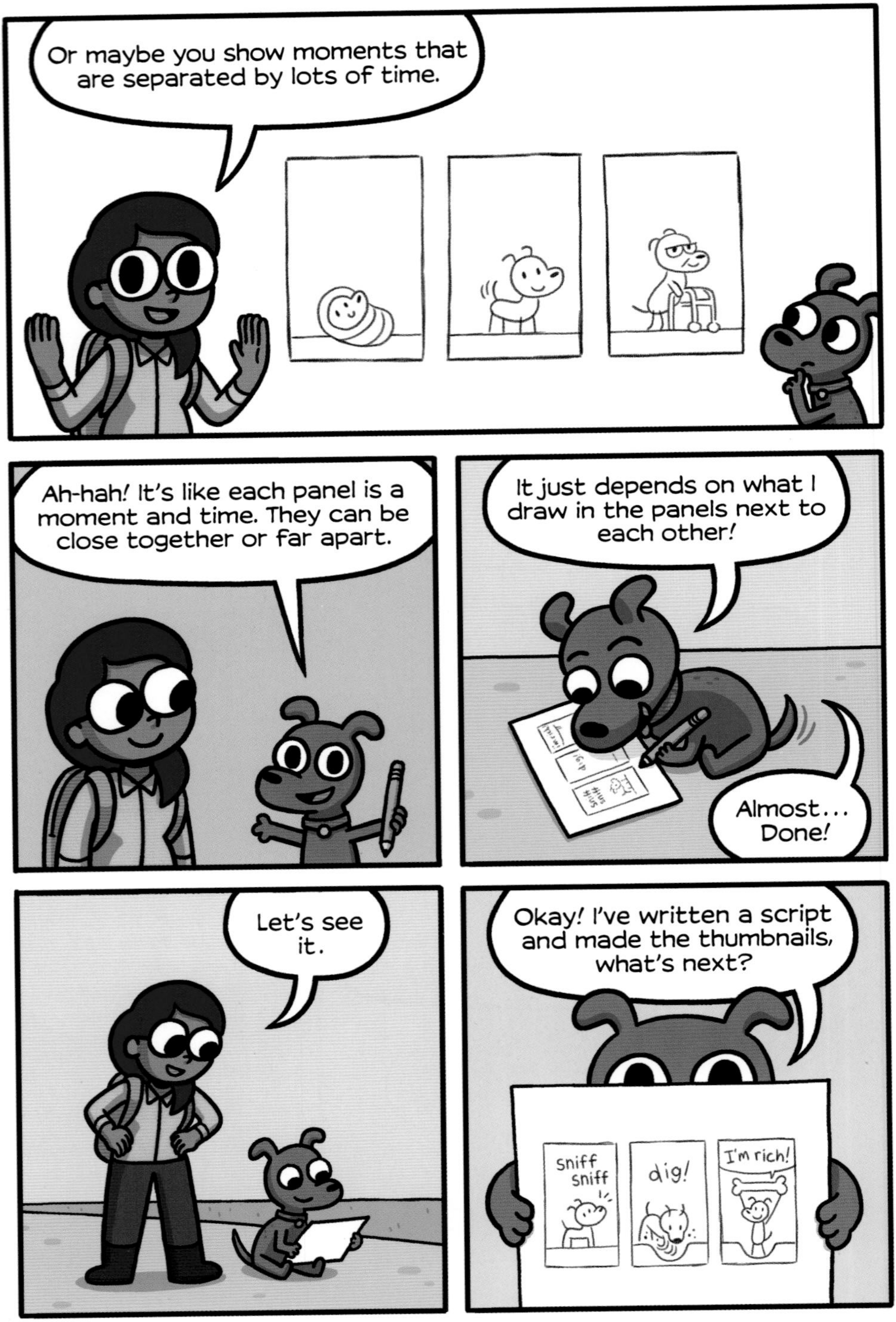
Or maybe you show moments that are separated by lots of time.
Ah-hah! It's like each panel is a moment and time. They can be close together or far apart.
It just depends on what I draw in the panels next to each other!
Almost... Done!
Let's see it.
Okay! I've written a script and made the thumbnails, what's next?
sniff sniff
dig!
I'm rich!

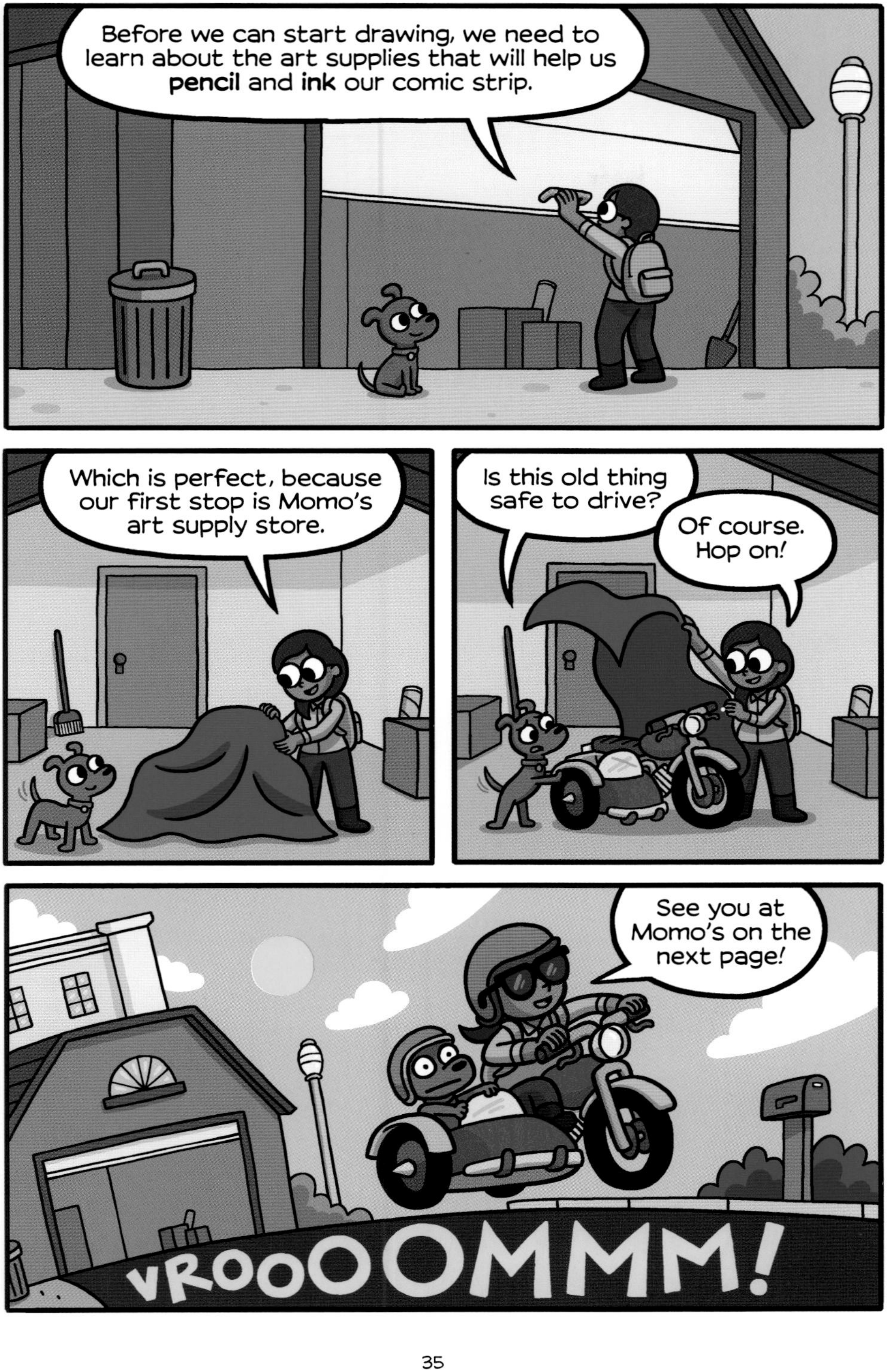
Before we can start drawing, we need to learn about the art supplies that will help us **pencil** and **ink** our comic strip.
Which is perfect, because our first stop is Momo's art supply store.
Is this old thing safe to drive?
Of course. Hop on!
See you at Momo's on the next page!
VROOOOMMM!

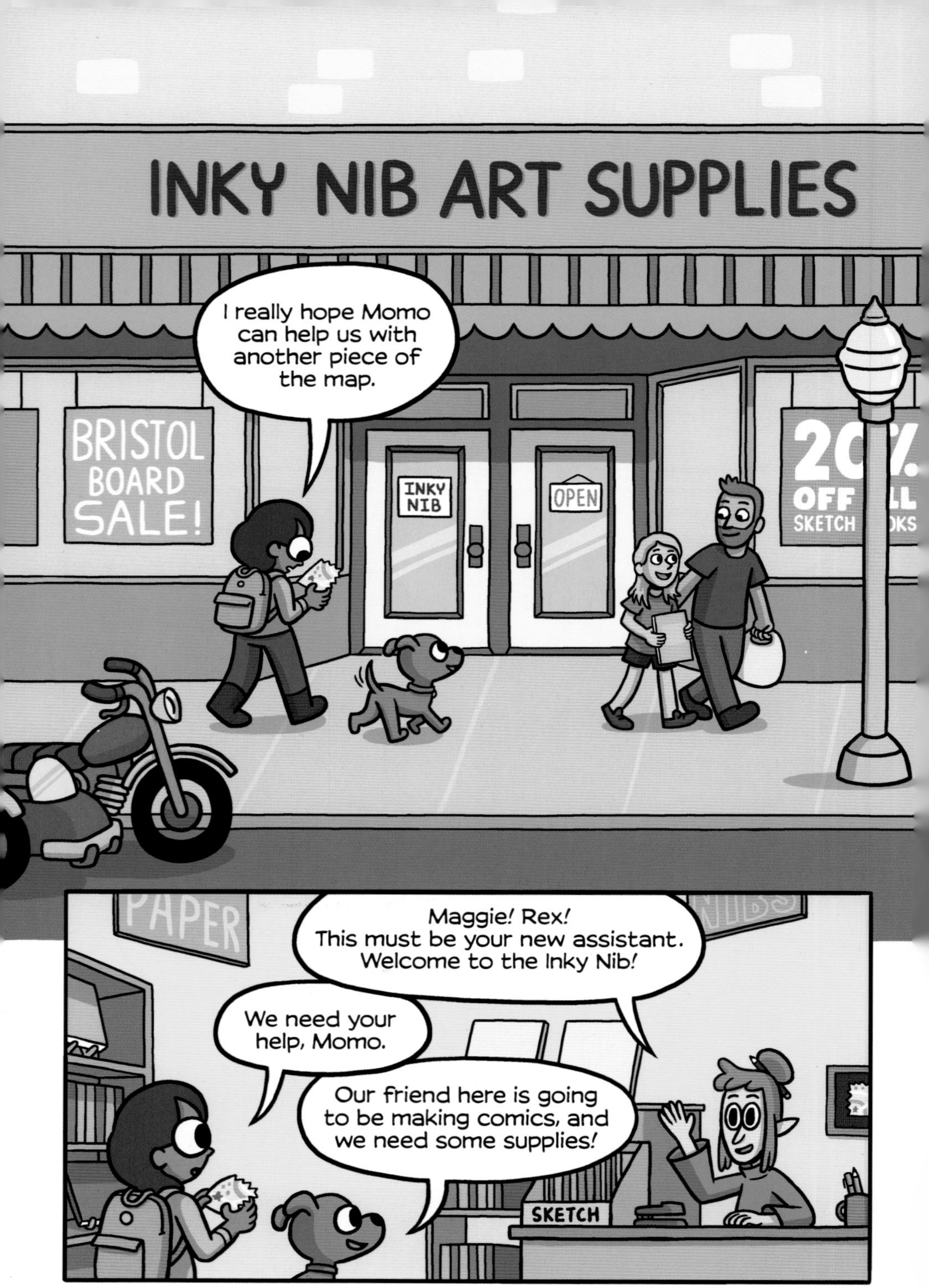
INKY NIB ART SUPPLIES
I really hope Momo can help us with another piece of the map.
BRISTOL BOARD SALE!
INKY NIB
OPEN
20
OFF
SKETCH
PAPER
Maggie! Rex! This must be your new assistant. Welcome to the Inky Nib!
We need your help, Momo.
Our friend here is going to be making comics, and we need some supplies!
SKETCH

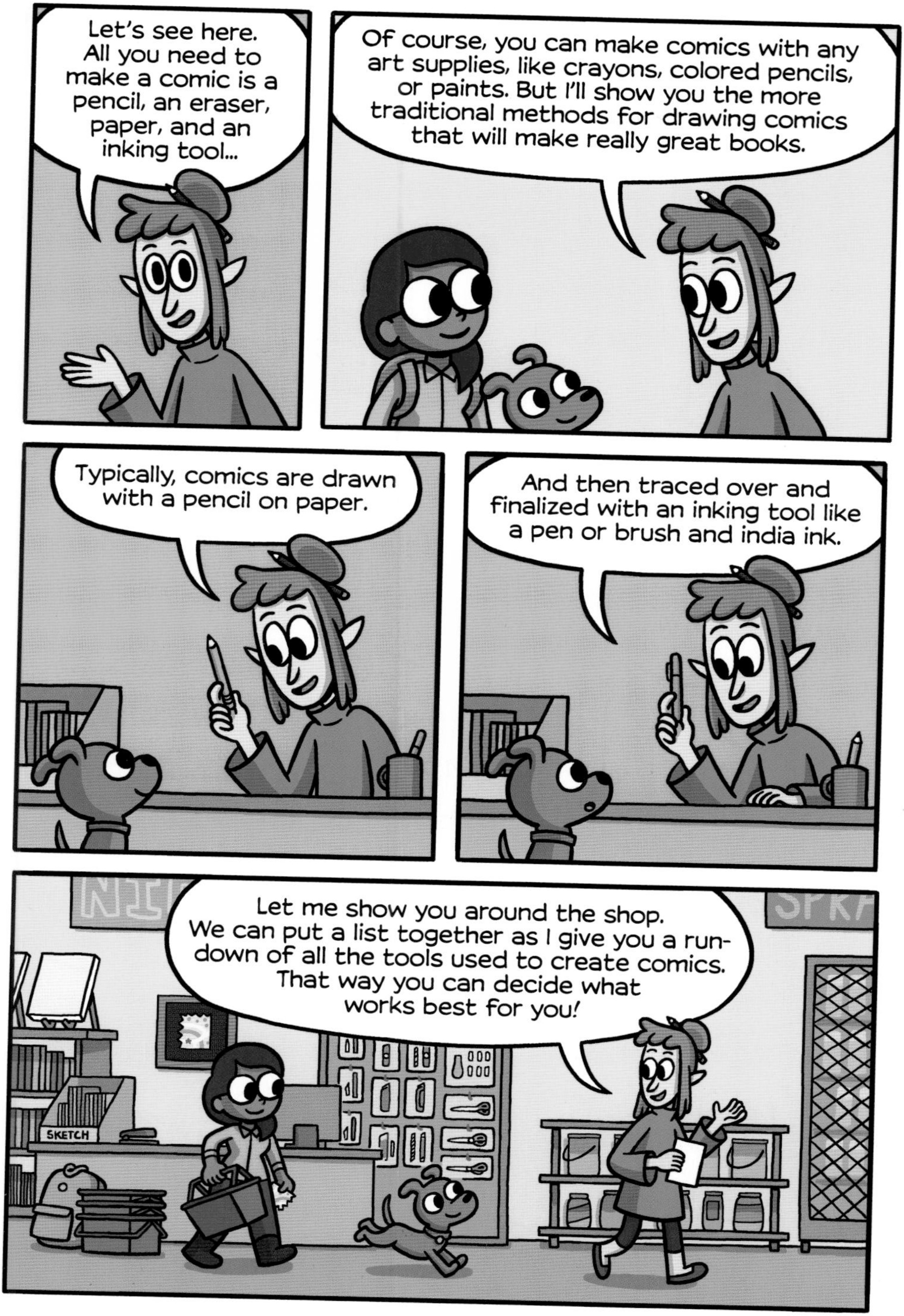
Let's see here. All you need to make a comic is a pencil, an eraser, paper, and an inking tool...
Of course, you can make comics with any art supplies, like crayons, colored pencils, or paints. But I'll show you the more traditional methods for drawing comics that will make really great books.
Typically, comics are drawn with a pencil on paper.
And then traced over and finalized with an inking tool like a pen or brush and india ink.
Let me show you around the shop. We can put a list together as I give you a run-down of all the tools used to create comics. That way you can decide what works best for you!
SKETCH

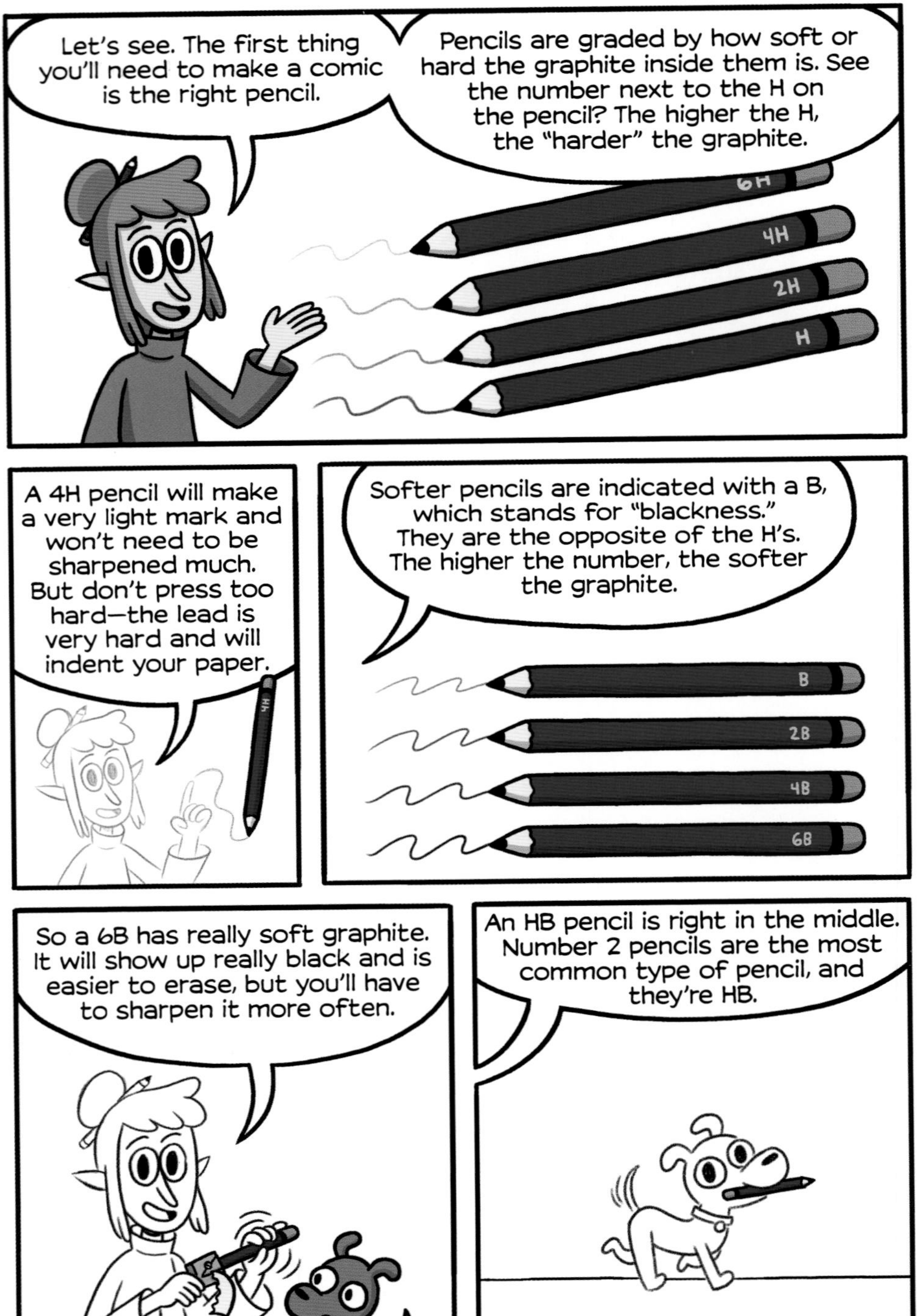
Let's see. The first thing you'll need to make a comic is the right pencil.
Pencils are graded by how soft or hard the graphite inside them is. See the number next to the H on the pencil? The higher the H, the "harder" the graphite.
6H
4H
2H
H
A 4H pencil will make a very light mark and won't need to be sharpened much. But don't press too hard—the lead is very hard and will indent your paper.
4H
Softer pencils are indicated with a B, which stands for "blackness." They are the opposite of the H's. The higher the number, the softer the graphite.
B
2B
4B
6B
So a 6B has really soft graphite. It will show up really black and is easier to erase, but you'll have to sharpen it more often.
An HB pencil is right in the middle. Number 2 pencils are the most common type of pencil, and they're HB.

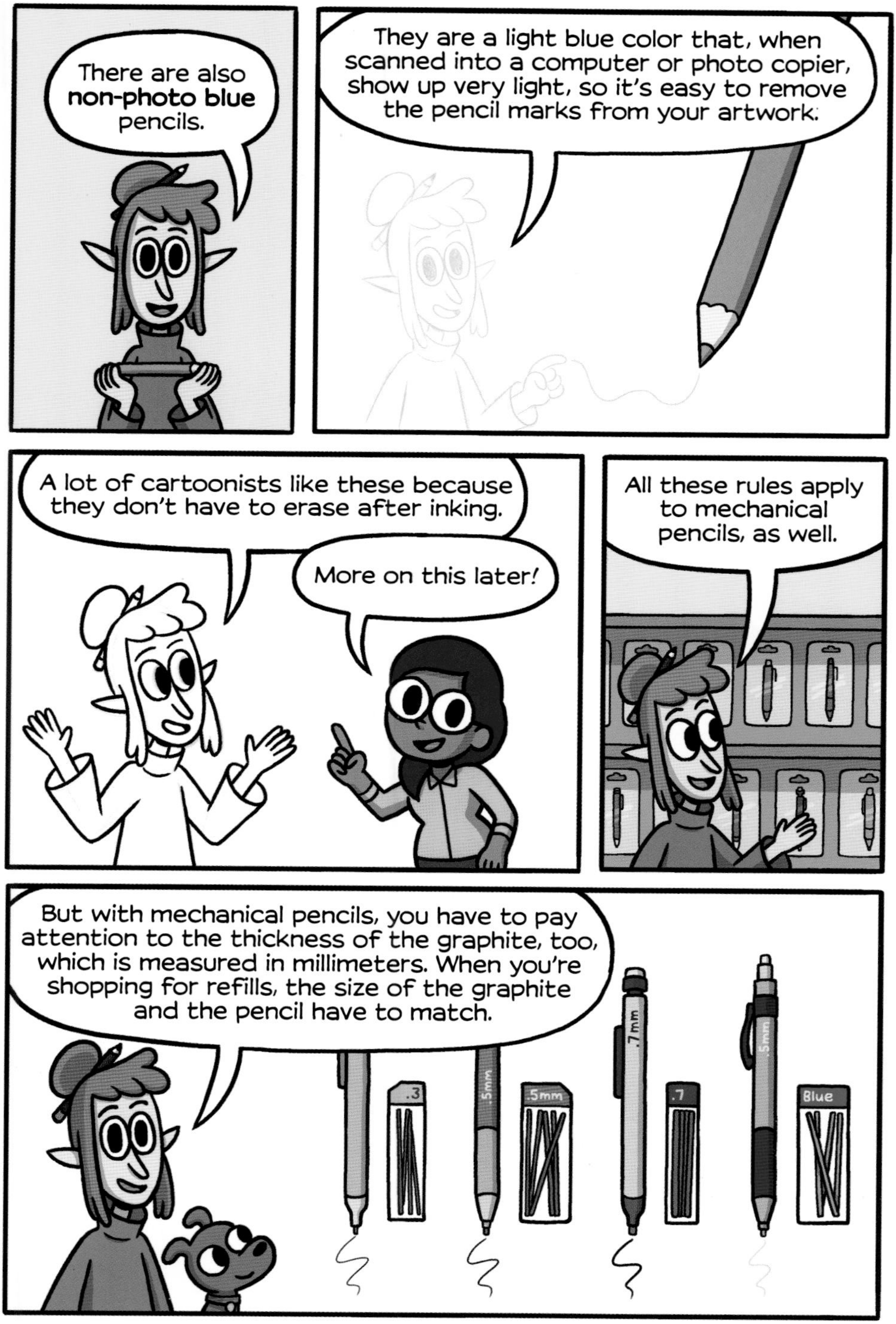
There are also **non-photo blue** pencils.
They are a light blue color that, when scanned into a computer or photo copier, show up very light, so it's easy to remove the pencil marks from your artwork.
A lot of cartoonists like these because they don't have to erase after inking.
More on this later!
All these rules apply to mechanical pencils, as well.
But with mechanical pencils, you have to pay attention to the thickness of the graphite, too, which is measured in millimeters. When you're shopping for refills, the size of the graphite and the pencil have to match.
.3
.5mm
.5mm
.7mm
.7
.5mm
Blue

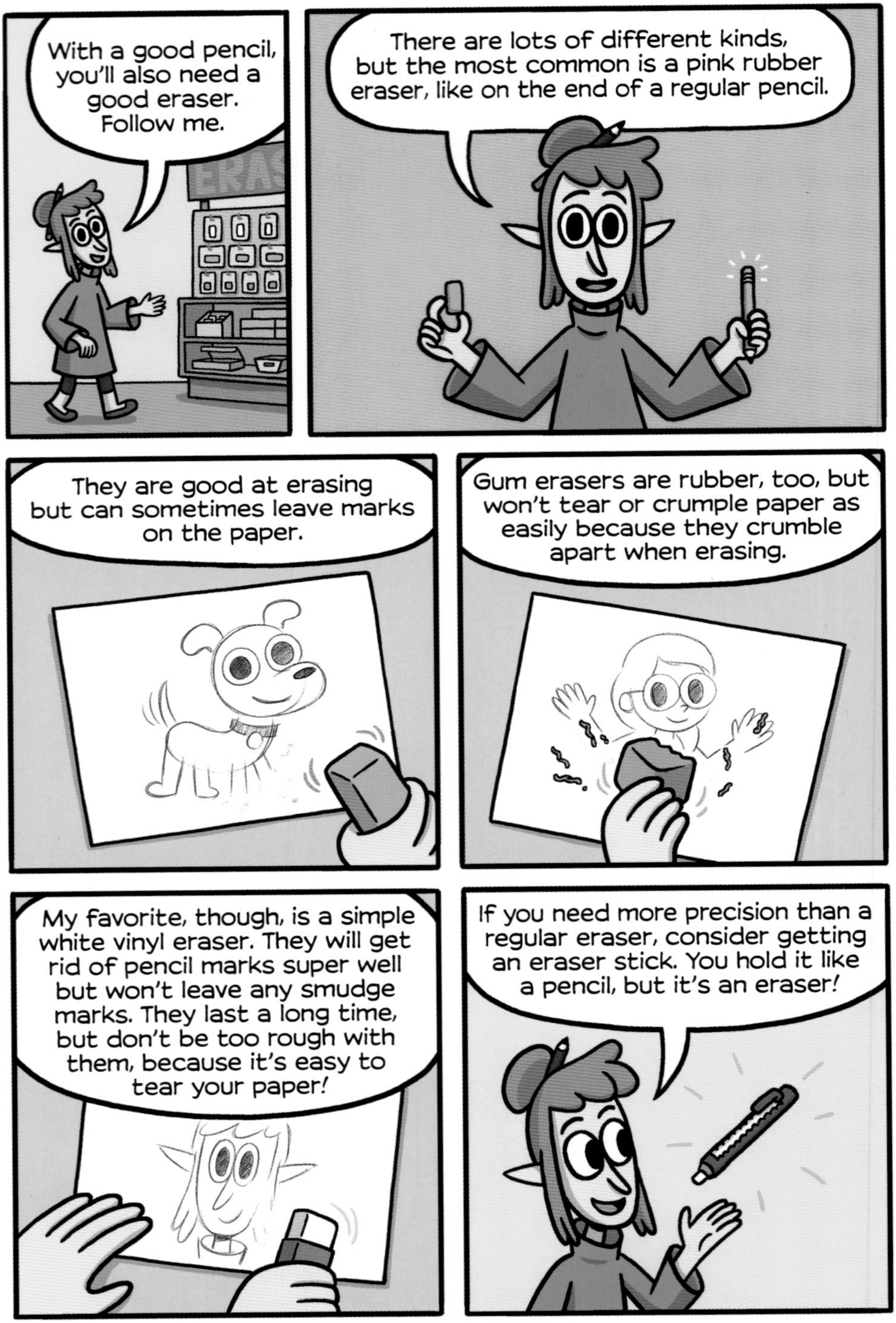
With a good pencil, you'll also need a good eraser. Follow me.
ERAS
There are lots of different kinds, but the most common is a pink rubber eraser, like on the end of a regular pencil.
They are good at erasing but can sometimes leave marks on the paper.
Gum erasers are rubber, too, but won't tear or crumple paper as easily because they crumble apart when erasing.
My favorite, though, is a simple white vinyl eraser. They will get rid of pencil marks super well but won't leave any smudge marks. They last a long time, but don't be too rough with them, because it's easy to tear your paper!
If you need more precision than a regular eraser, consider getting an eraser stick. You hold it like a pencil, but it's an eraser!

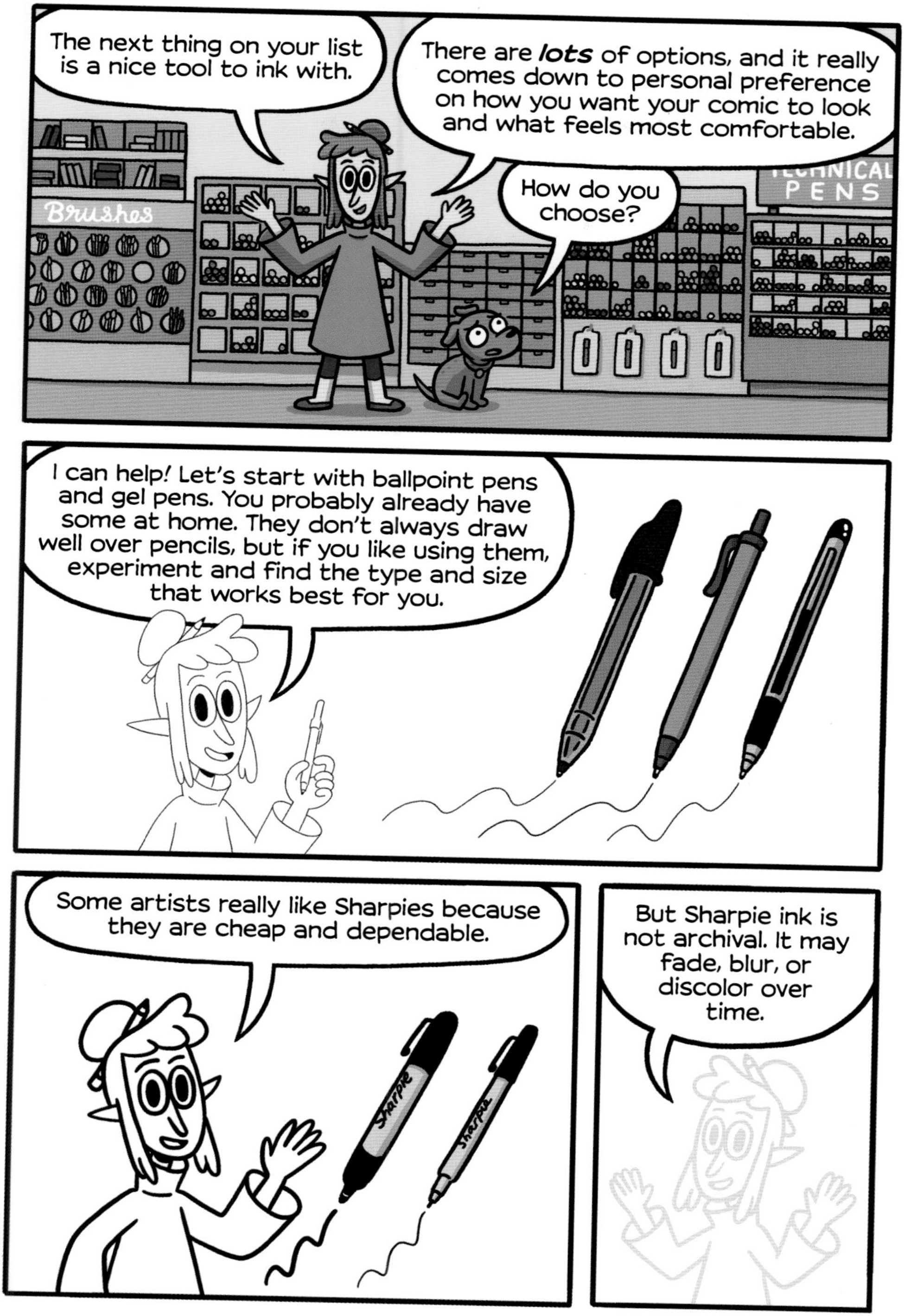

The next thing on your list is a nice tool to ink with.
There are *lots* of options, and it really comes down to personal preference on how you want your comic to look and what feels most comfortable.
How do you choose?
Brushes
TECHNICAL PENS
I can help! Let's start with ballpoint pens and gel pens. You probably already have some at home. They don't always draw well over pencils, but if you like using them, experiment and find the type and size that works best for you.
Some artists really like Sharpies because they are cheap and dependable.
Sharpie
Sharpie
But Sharpie ink is not archival. It may fade, blur, or discolor over time.

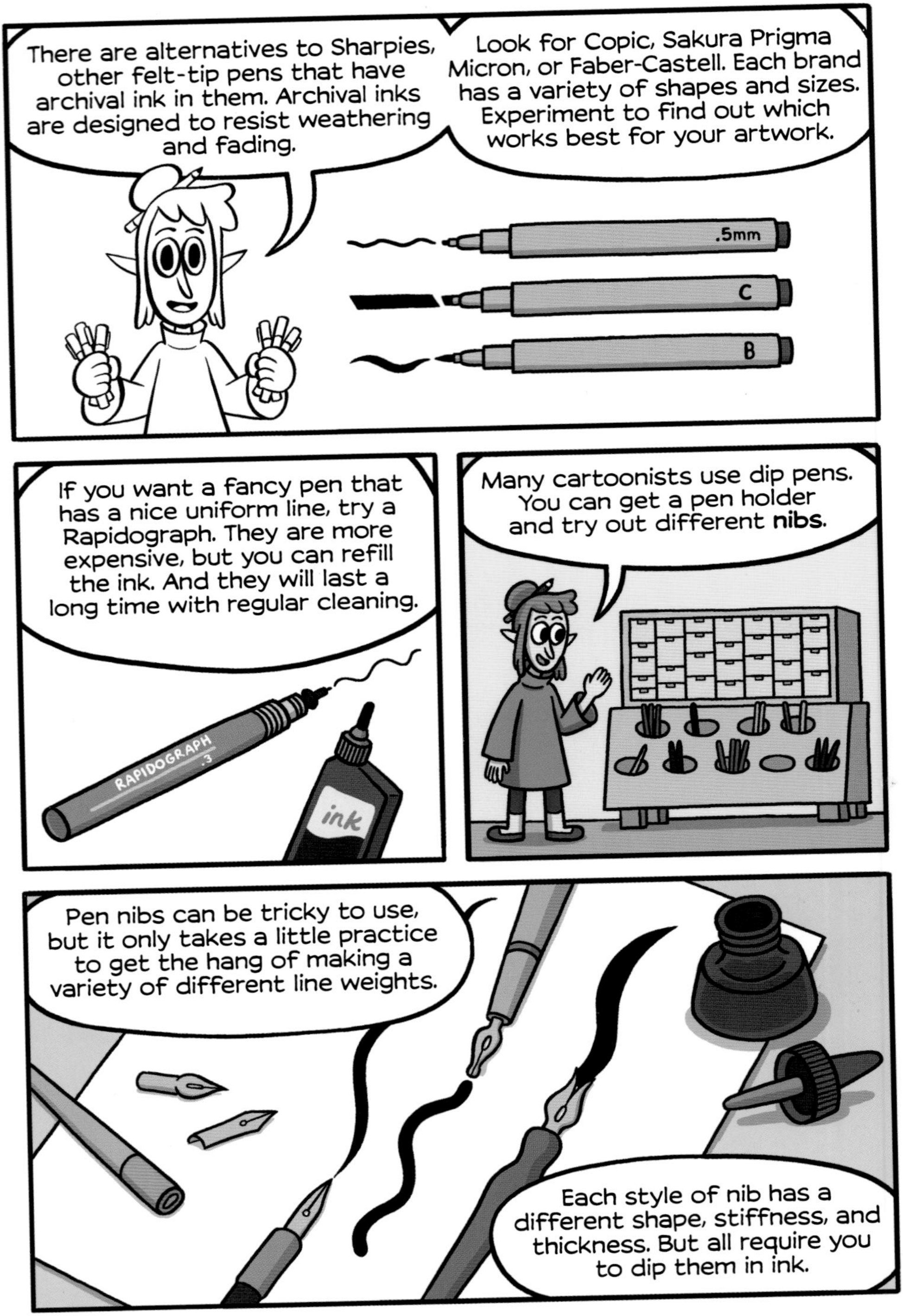
There are alternatives to Sharpies, other felt-tip pens that have archival ink in them. Archival inks are designed to resist weathering and fading.
Look for Copic, Sakura Prigma Micron, or Faber-Castell. Each brand has a variety of shapes and sizes. Experiment to find out which works best for your artwork.
.5mm
C
B
If you want a fancy pen that has a nice uniform line, try a Rapidograph. They are more expensive, but you can refill the ink. And they will last a long time with regular cleaning.
RAPIDOGRAPH
.3
ink
Many cartoonists use dip pens. You can get a pen holder and try out different **nibs**.
Pen nibs can be tricky to use, but it only takes a little practice to get the hang of making a variety of different line weights.
Each style of nib has a different shape, stiffness, and thickness. But all require you to dip them in ink.

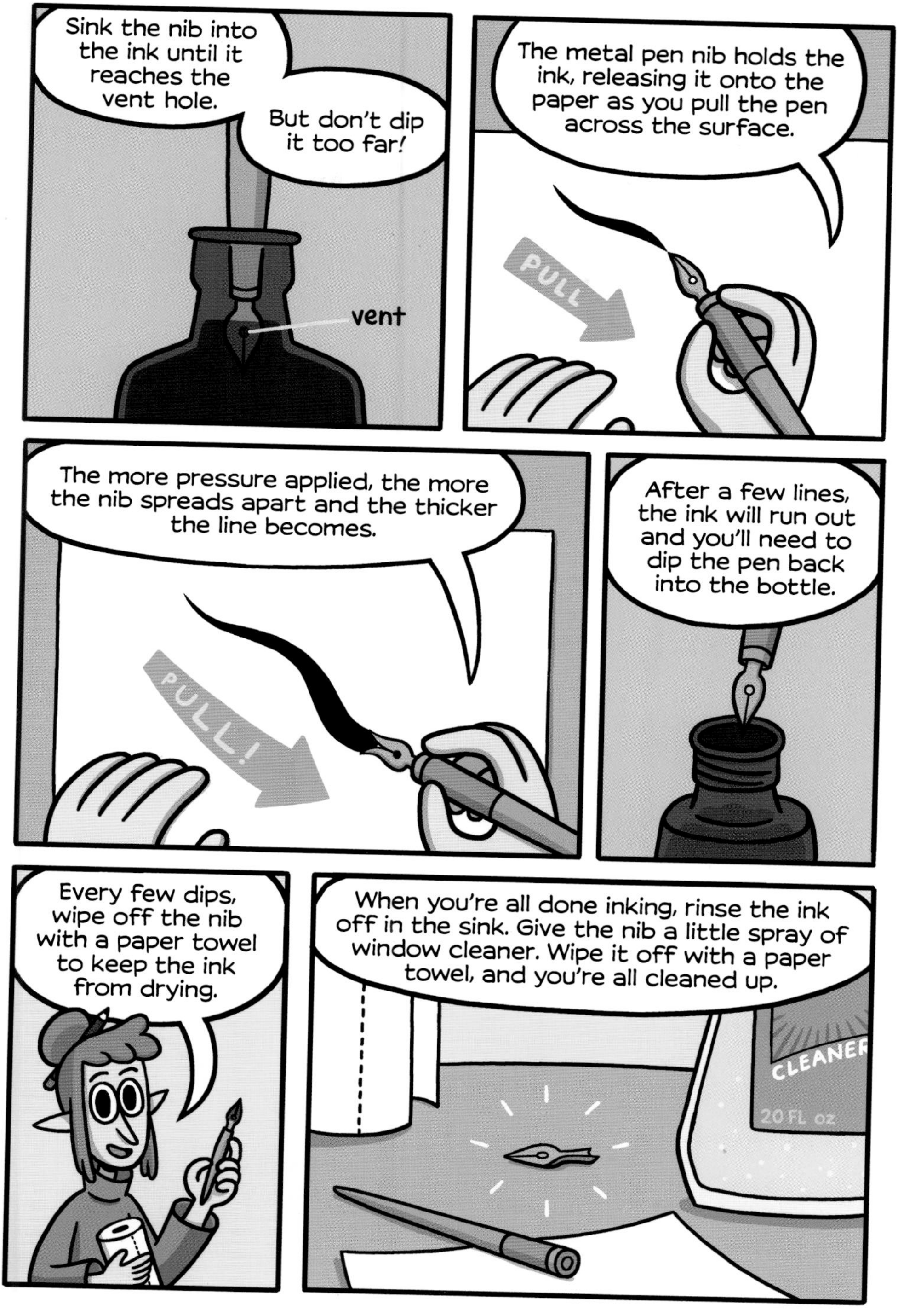
Sink the nib into the ink until it reaches the vent hole.
But don't dip it too far!
vent
The metal pen nib holds the ink, releasing it onto the paper as you pull the pen across the surface.
PULL
The more pressure applied, the more the nib spreads apart and the thicker the line becomes.
PULL!
After a few lines, the ink will run out and you'll need to dip the pen back into the bottle.
Every few dips, wipe off the nib with a paper towel to keep the ink from drying.
When you're all done inking, rinse the ink off in the sink. Give the nib a little spray of window cleaner. Wipe it off with a paper towel, and you're all cleaned up.
CLEANER
20 FL oz

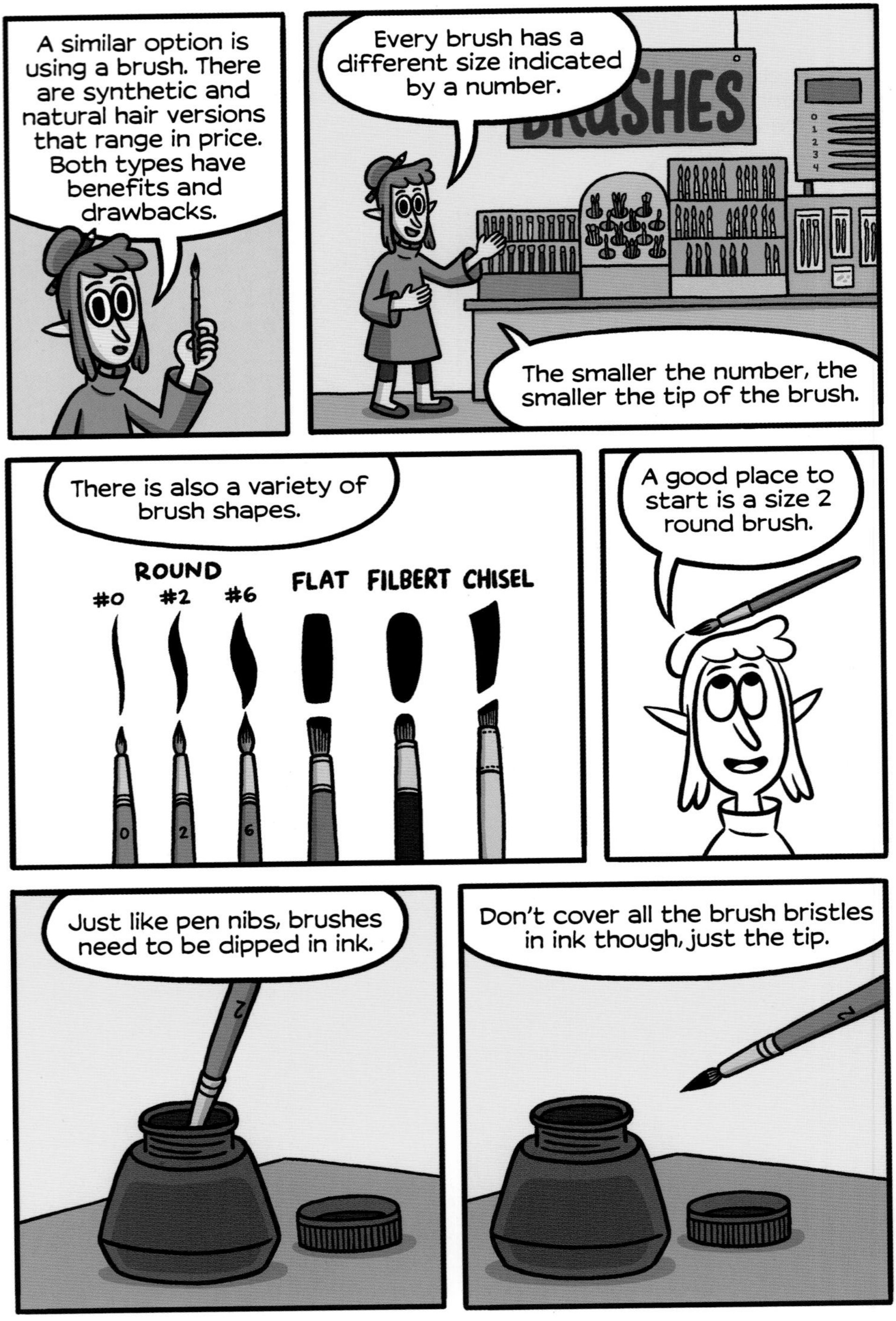

A similar option is using a brush. There are synthetic and natural hair versions that range in price. Both types have benefits and drawbacks.
Every brush has a different size indicated by a number.
The smaller the number, the smaller the tip of the brush.
There is also a variety of brush shapes.
ROUND
#0
#2
#6
FLAT
FILBERT
CHISEL
A good place to start is a size 2 round brush.
Just like pen nibs, brushes need to be dipped in ink.
Don't cover all the brush bristles in ink though, just the tip.

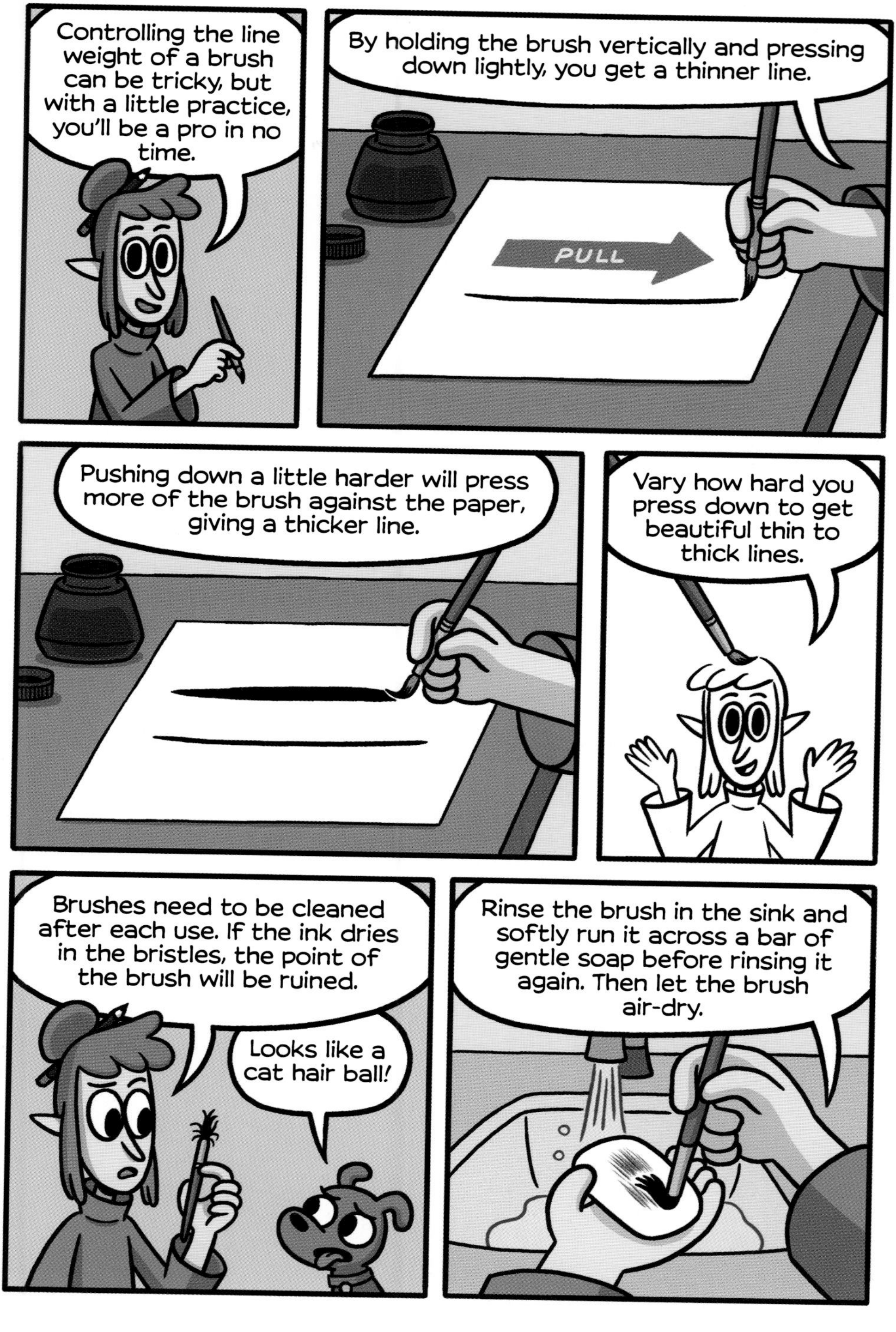
Controlling the line weight of a brush can be tricky, but with a little practice, you'll be a pro in no time.
By holding the brush vertically and pressing down lightly, you get a thinner line.
PULL
Pushing down a little harder will press more of the brush against the paper, giving a thicker line.
Vary how hard you press down to get beautiful thin to thick lines.
Brushes need to be cleaned after each use. If the ink dries in the bristles, the point of the brush will be ruined.
Looks like a cat hair ball!
Rinse the brush in the sink and softly run it across a bar of gentle soap before rinsing it again. Then let the brush air-dry.

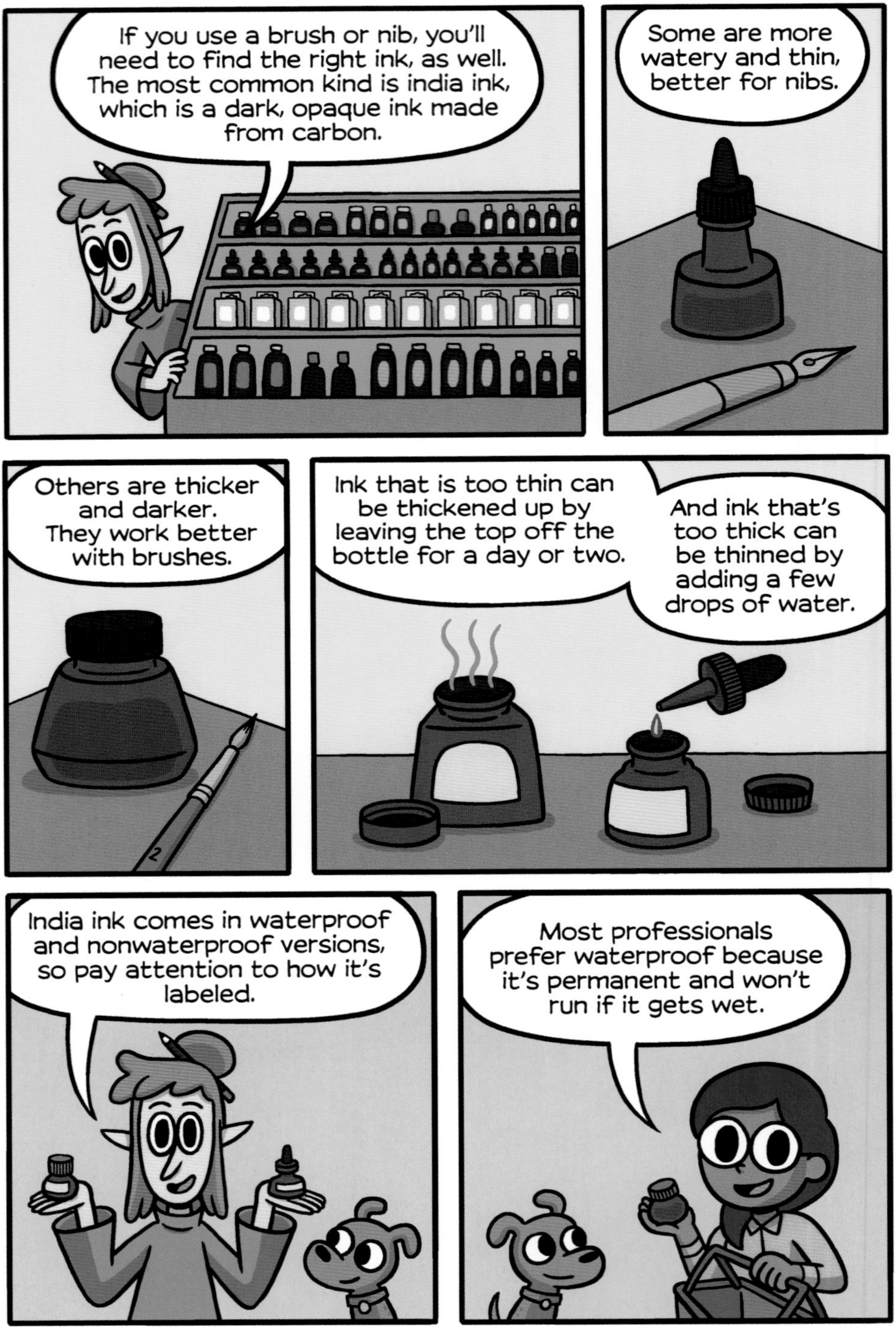
If you use a brush or nib, you'll need to find the right ink, as well. The most common kind is india ink, which is a dark, opaque ink made from carbon.
Some are more watery and thin, better for nibs.
Others are thicker and darker. They work better with brushes.
2
Ink that is too thin can be thickened up by leaving the top off the bottle for a day or two.
And ink that's too thick can be thinned by adding a few drops of water.
India ink comes in waterproof and nonwaterproof versions, so pay attention to how it's labeled.
Most professionals prefer waterproof because it's permanent and won't run if it gets wet.

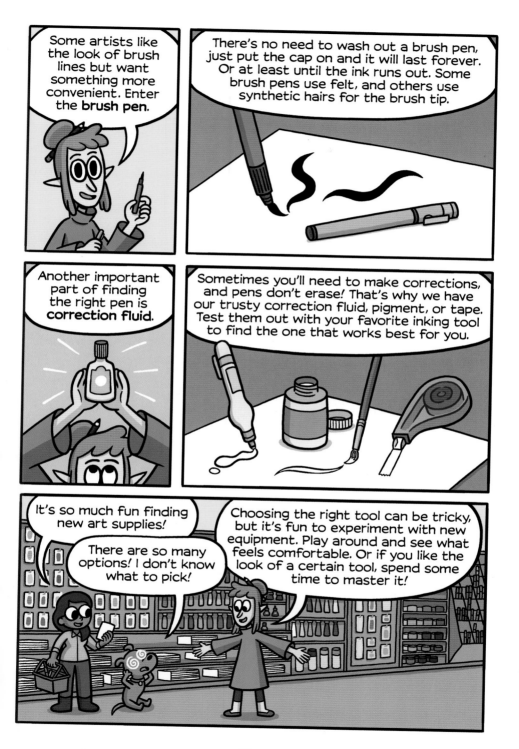

Some artists like the look of brush lines but want something more convenient. Enter the **brush pen**.

There's no need to wash out a brush pen, just put the cap on and it will last forever. Or at least until the ink runs out. Some brush pens use felt, and others use synthetic hairs for the brush tip.

Another important part of finding the right pen is **correction fluid**.

Sometimes you'll need to make corrections, and pens don't erase! That's why we have our trusty correction fluid, pigment, or tape. Test them out with your favorite inking tool to find the one that works best for you.

It's so much fun finding new art supplies!

There are so many options! I don't know what to pick!

Choosing the right tool can be tricky, but it's fun to experiment with new equipment. Play around and see what feels comfortable. Or if you like the look of a certain tool, spend some time to master it!

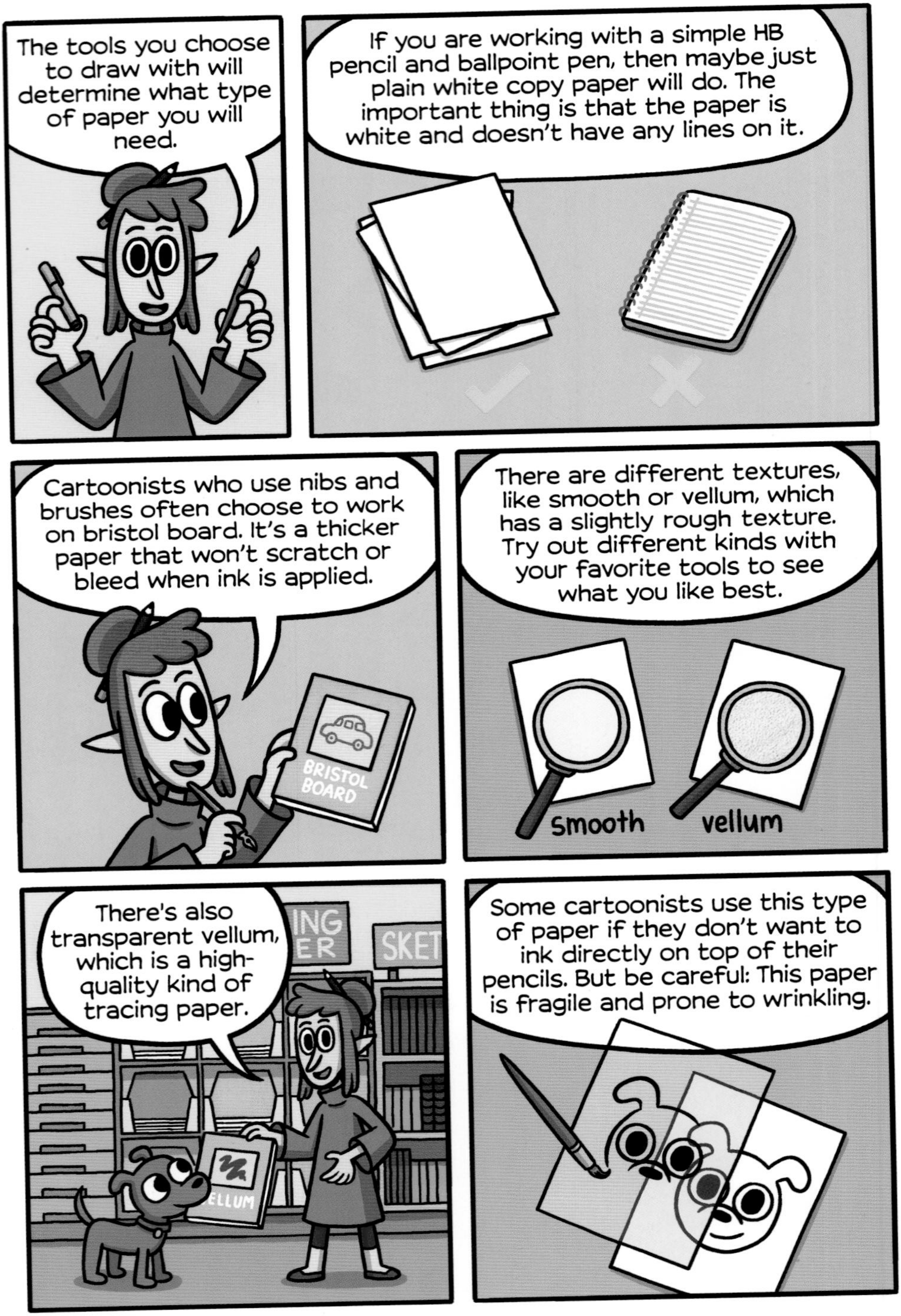
The tools you choose to draw with will determine what type of paper you will need.
If you are working with a simple HB pencil and ballpoint pen, then maybe just plain white copy paper will do. The important thing is that the paper is white and doesn't have any lines on it.
Cartoonists who use nibs and brushes often choose to work on bristol board. It's a thicker paper that won't scratch or bleed when ink is applied.
BRISTOL BOARD
There are different textures, like smooth or vellum, which has a slightly rough texture. Try out different kinds with your favorite tools to see what you like best.
smooth
vellum
There's also transparent vellum, which is a high-quality kind of tracing paper.
ING
ER
SKET
ELLUM
Some cartoonists use this type of paper if they don't want to ink directly on top of their pencils. But be careful: This paper is fragile and prone to wrinkling.

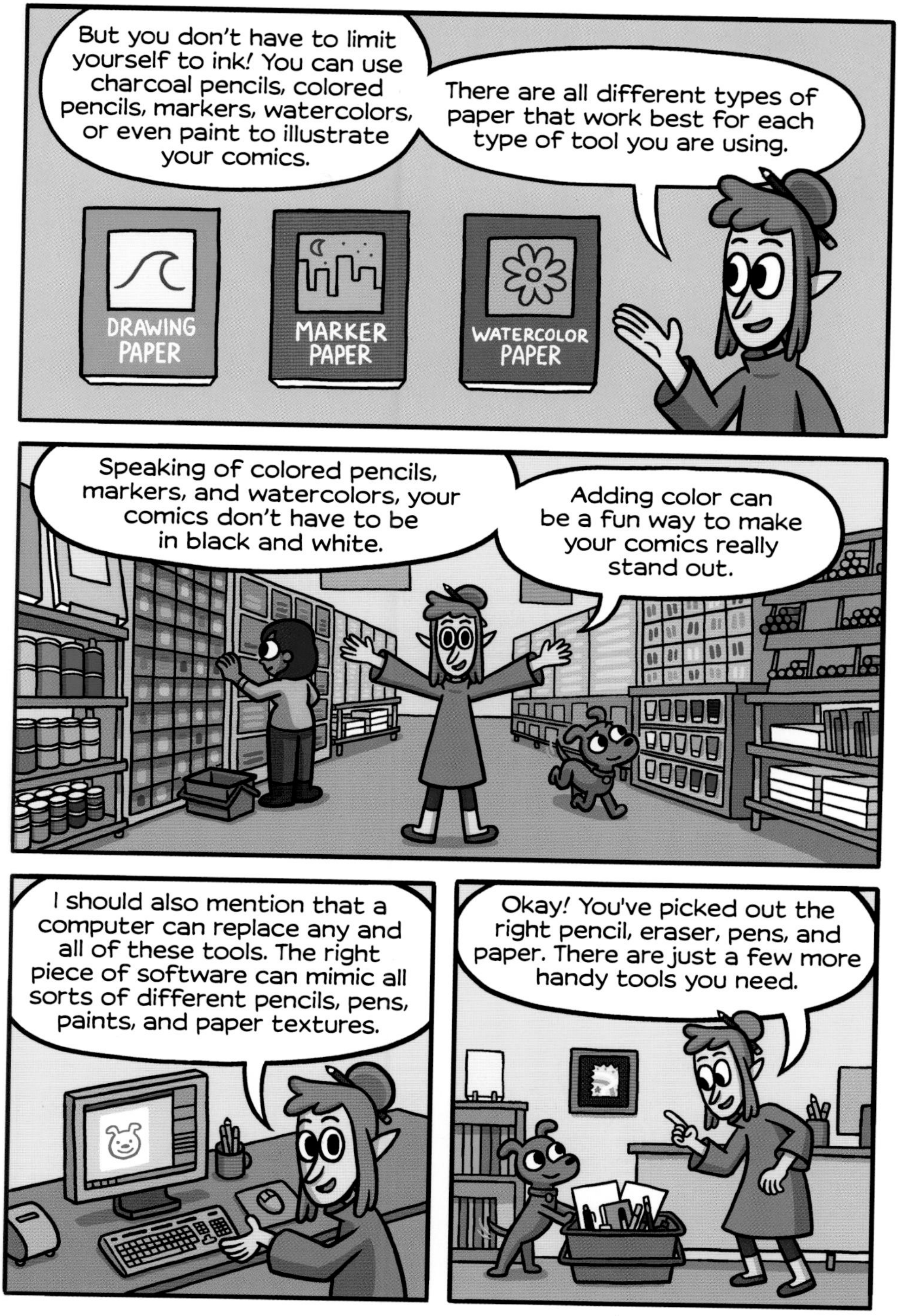
But you don't have to limit yourself to ink! You can use charcoal pencils, colored pencils, markers, watercolors, or even paint to illustrate your comics.
There are all different types of paper that work best for each type of tool you are using.
DRAWING PAPER
MARKER PAPER
WATERCOLOR PAPER
Speaking of colored pencils, markers, and watercolors, your comics don't have to be in black and white.
Adding color can be a fun way to make your comics really stand out.
I should also mention that a computer can replace any and all of these tools. The right piece of software can mimic all sorts of different pencils, pens, paints, and paper textures.
Okay! You've picked out the right pencil, eraser, pens, and paper. There are just a few more handy tools you need.

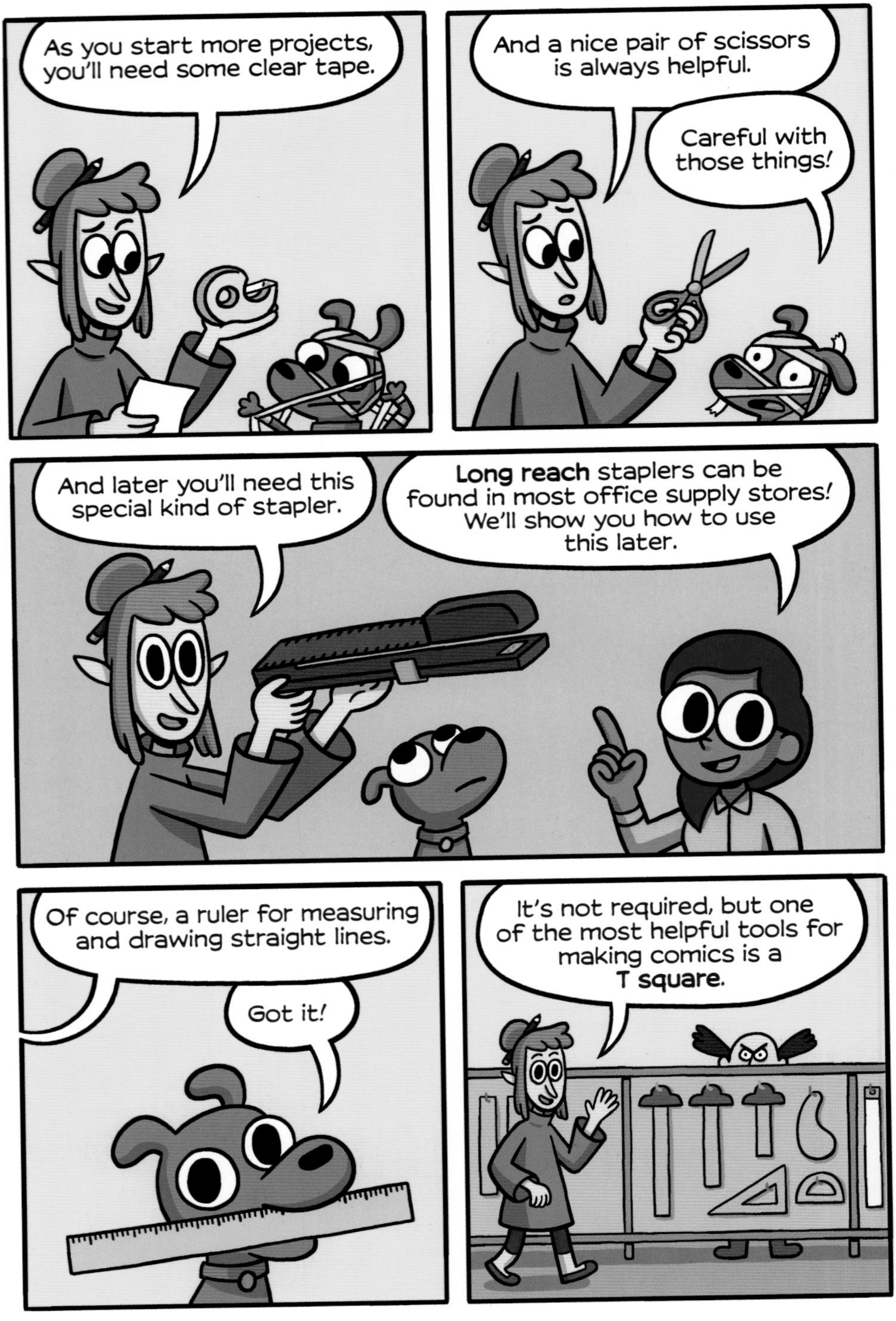
As you start more projects, you'll need some clear tape.
And a nice pair of scissors is always helpful.
Careful with those things!
And later you'll need this special kind of stapler.
Long reach staplers can be found in most office supply stores! We'll show you how to use this later.
Of course, a ruler for measuring and drawing straight lines.
Got it!
It's not required, but one of the most helpful tools for making comics is a **T square**.

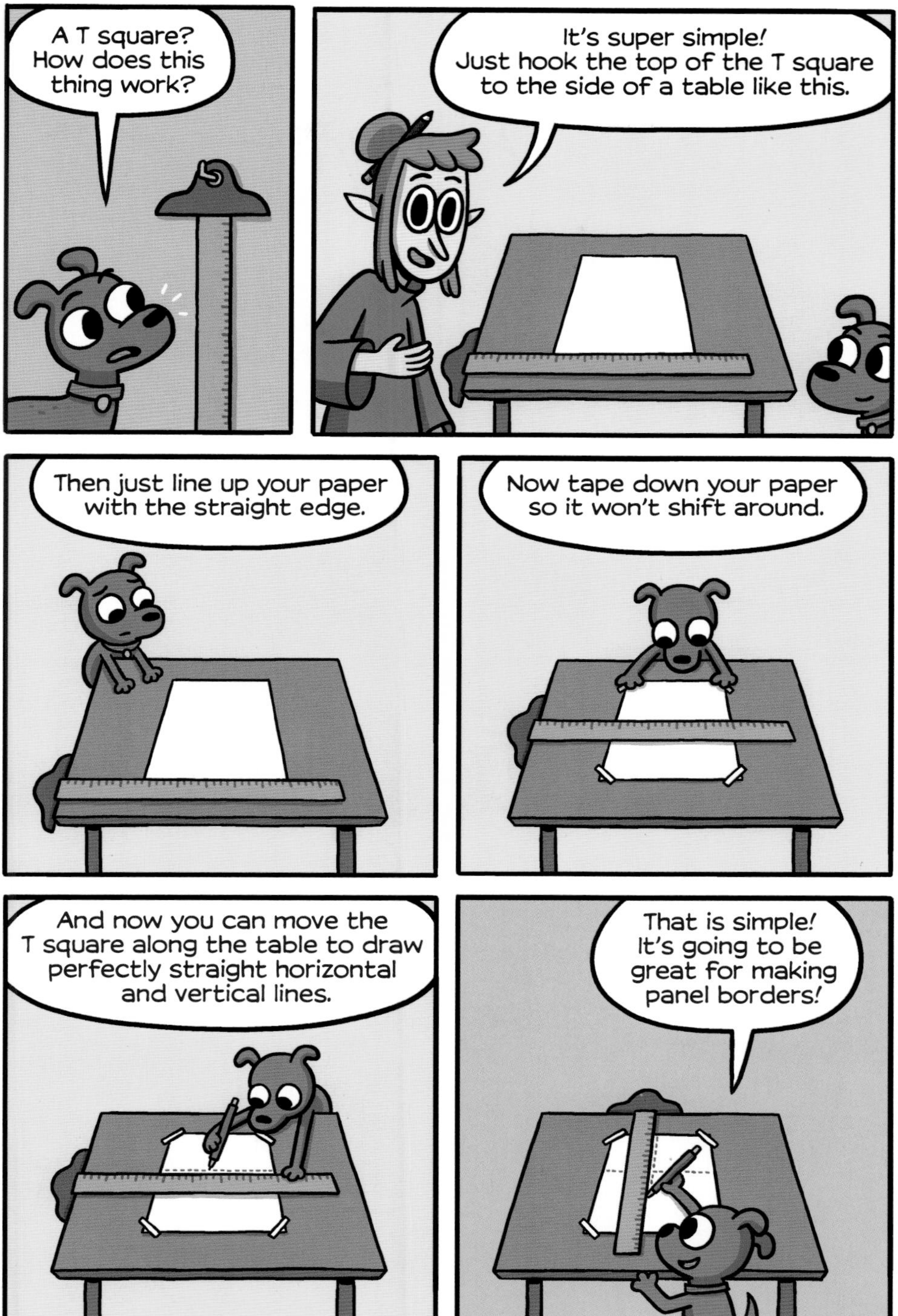
A T square? How does this thing work?
It's super simple! Just hook the top of the T square to the side of a table like this.
Then just line up your paper with the straight edge.
Now tape down your paper so it won't shift around.
And now you can move the T square along the table to draw perfectly straight horizontal and vertical lines.
That is simple! It's going to be great for making panel borders!

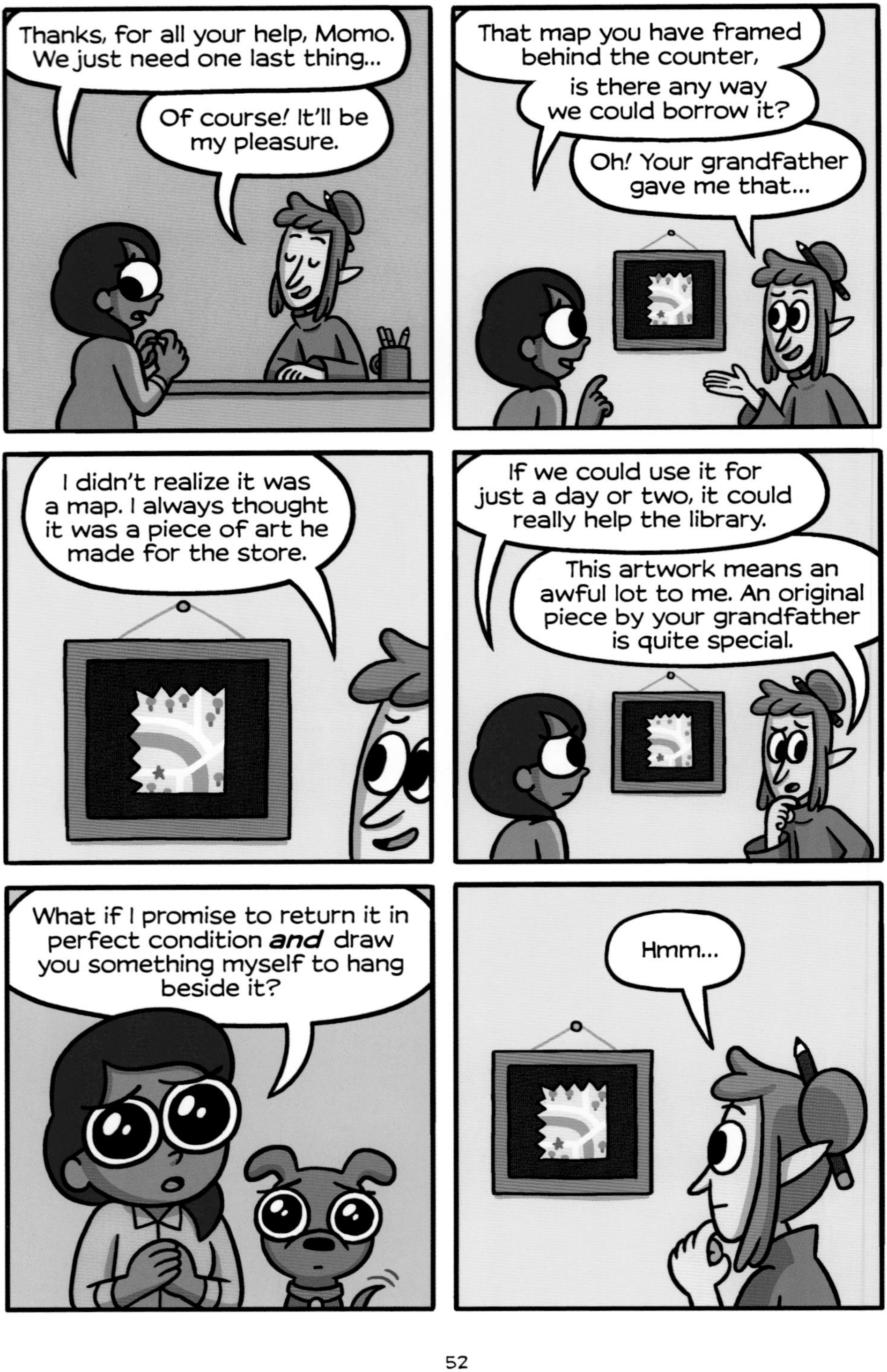
Thanks, for all your help, Momo. We just need one last thing...
Of course! It'll be my pleasure.
That map you have framed behind the counter,
is there any way we could borrow it?
Oh! Your grandfather gave me that...
I didn't realize it was a map. I always thought it was a piece of art he made for the store.
If we could use it for just a day or two, it could really help the library.
This artwork means an awful lot to me. An original piece by your grandfather is quite special.
What if I promise to return it in perfect condition *and* draw you something myself to hang beside it?
Hmm...

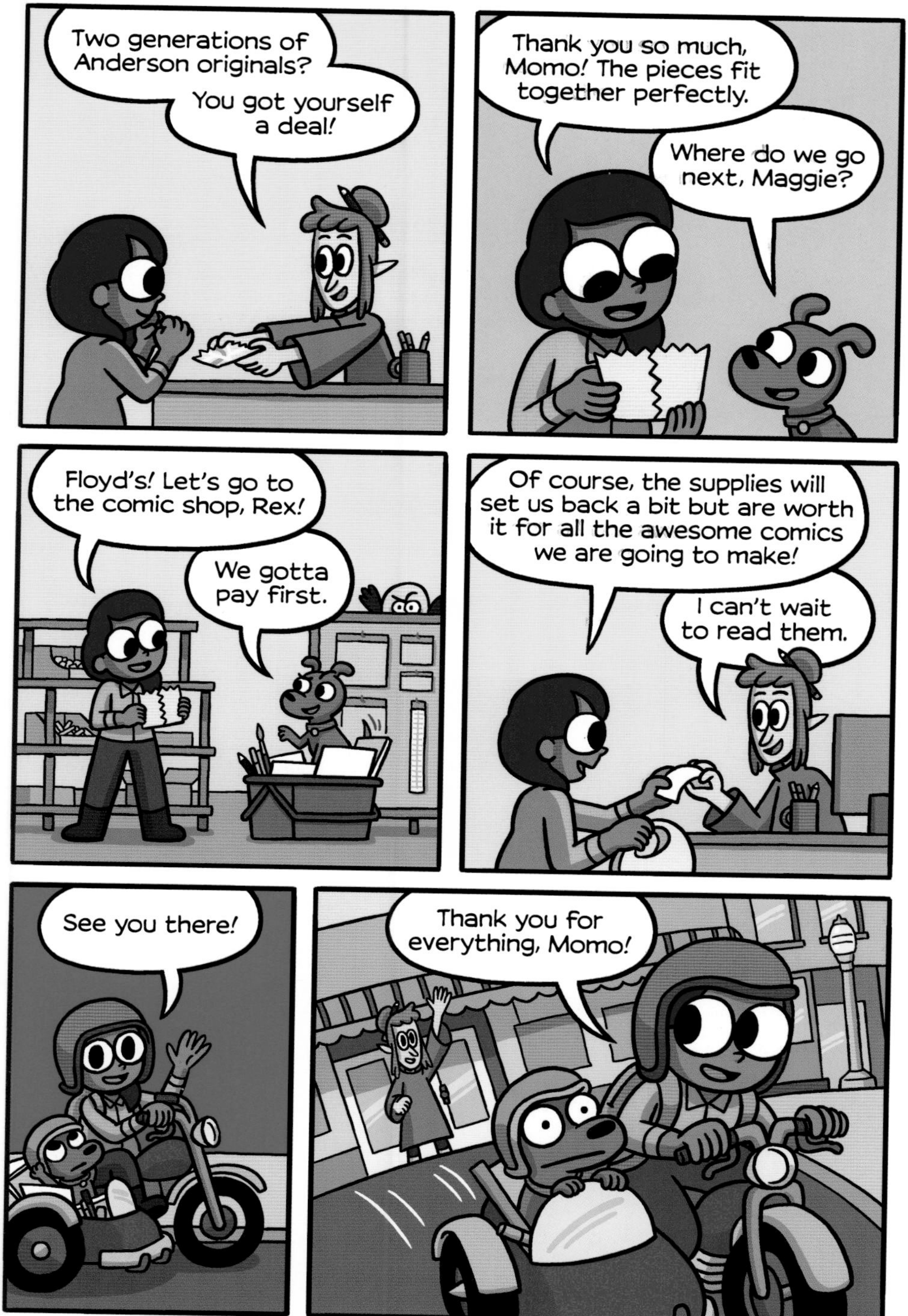

Two generations of Anderson originals?
You got yourself a deal!
Thank you so much, Momo! The pieces fit together perfectly.
Where do we go next, Maggie?
Floyd's! Let's go to the comic shop, Rex!
We gotta pay first.
Of course, the supplies will set us back a bit but are worth it for all the awesome comics we are going to make!
I can't wait to read them.
See you there!
Thank you for everything, Momo!

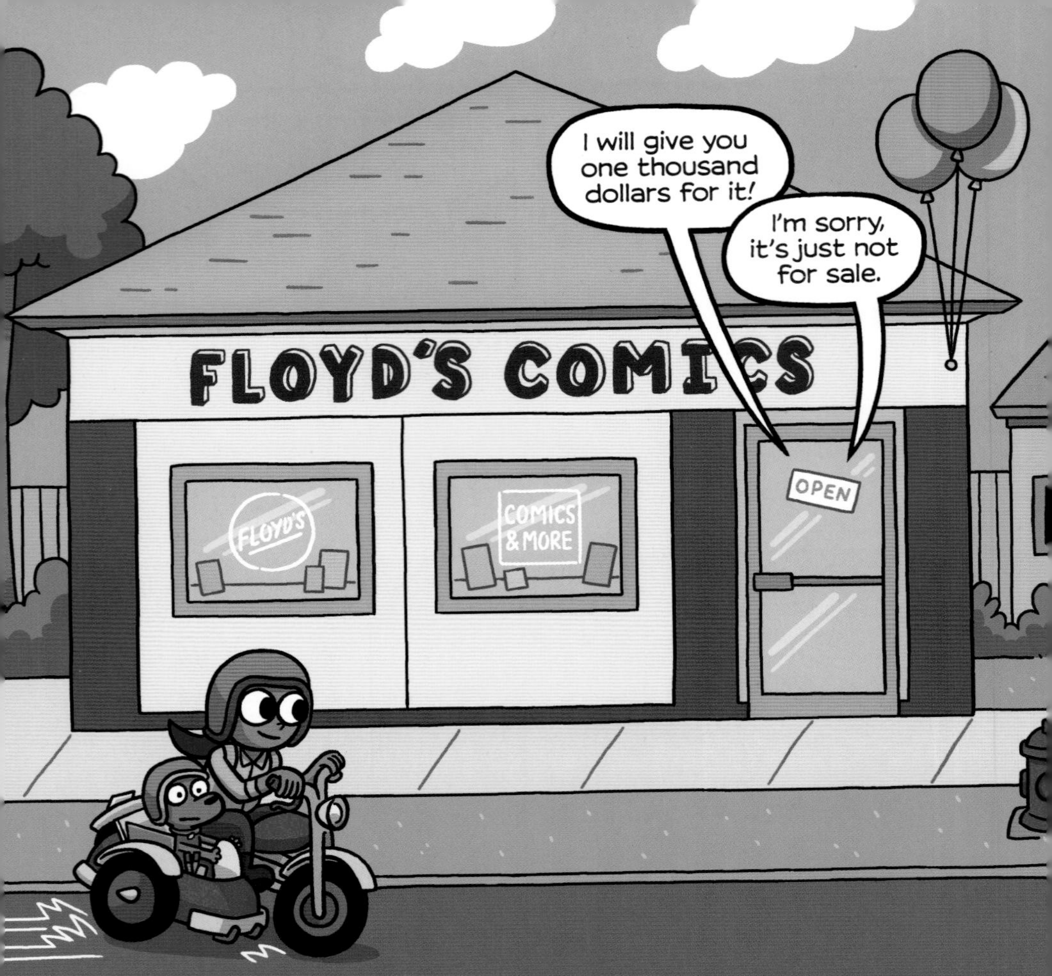
FLOYD'S COMICS
I will give you one thousand dollars for it!
I'm sorry, it's just not for sale.
FLOYD'S
COMICS & MORE
OPEN

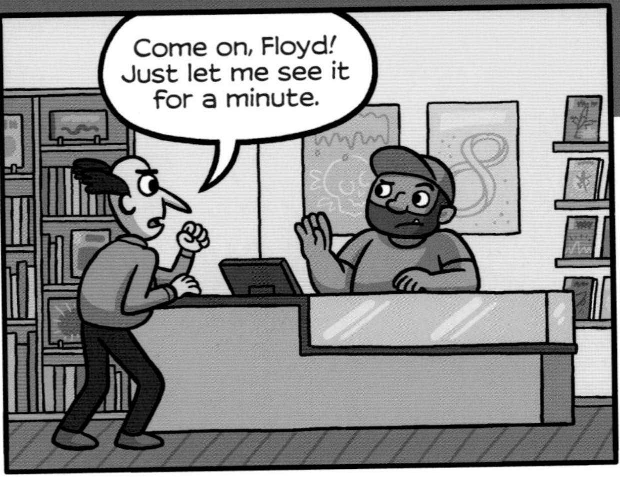
Come on, Floyd! Just let me see it for a minute.

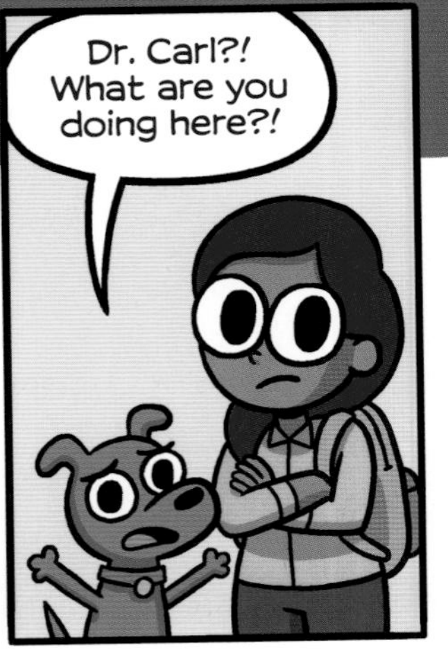
Dr. Carl?! What are you doing here?!

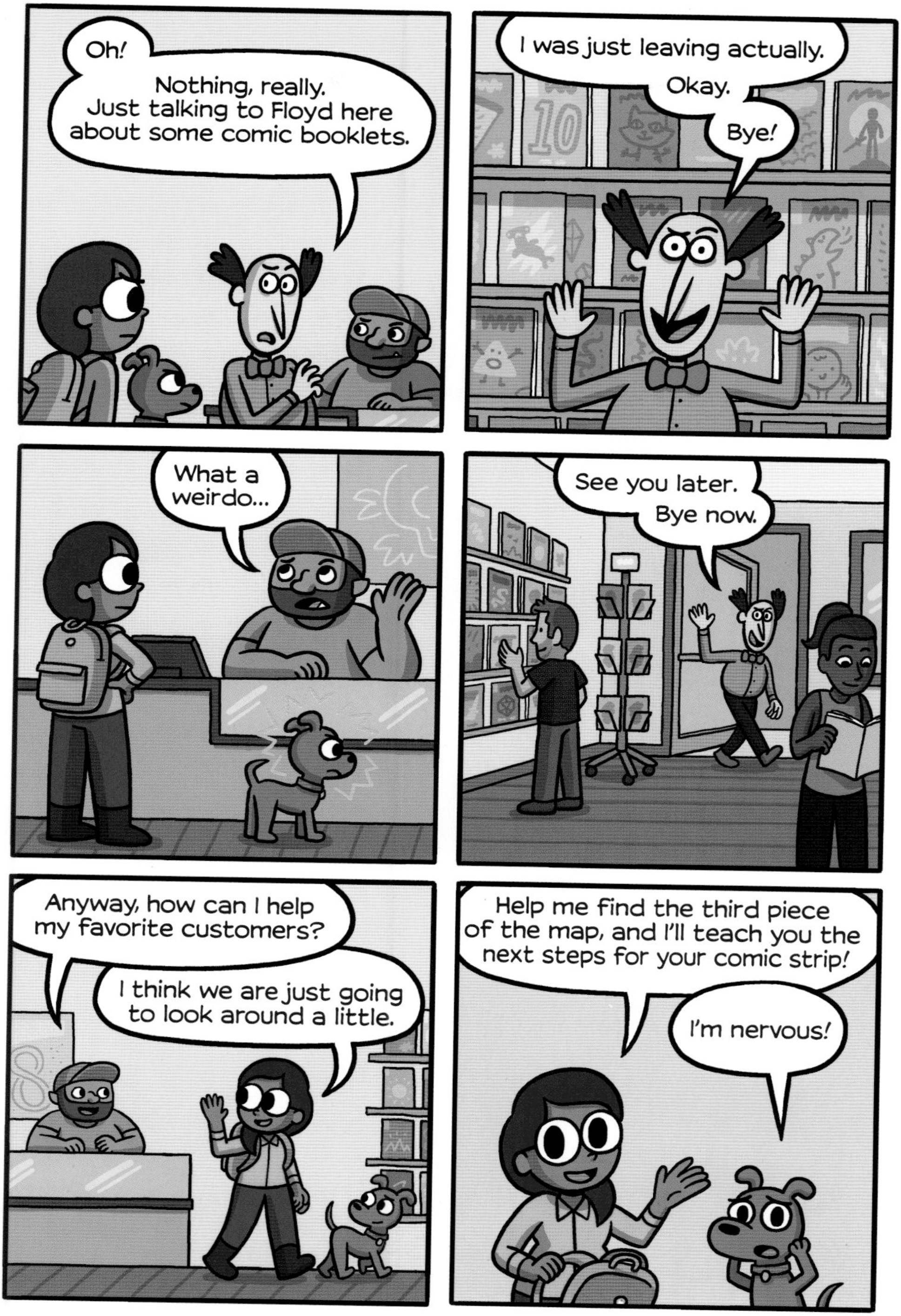
Oh!
Nothing, really. Just talking to Floyd here about some comic booklets.
I was just leaving actually.
Okay.
Bye!
What a weirdo...
See you later.
Bye now.
Anyway, how can I help my favorite customers?
I think we are just going to look around a little.
Help me find the third piece of the map, and I'll teach you the next steps for your comic strip!
I'm nervous!

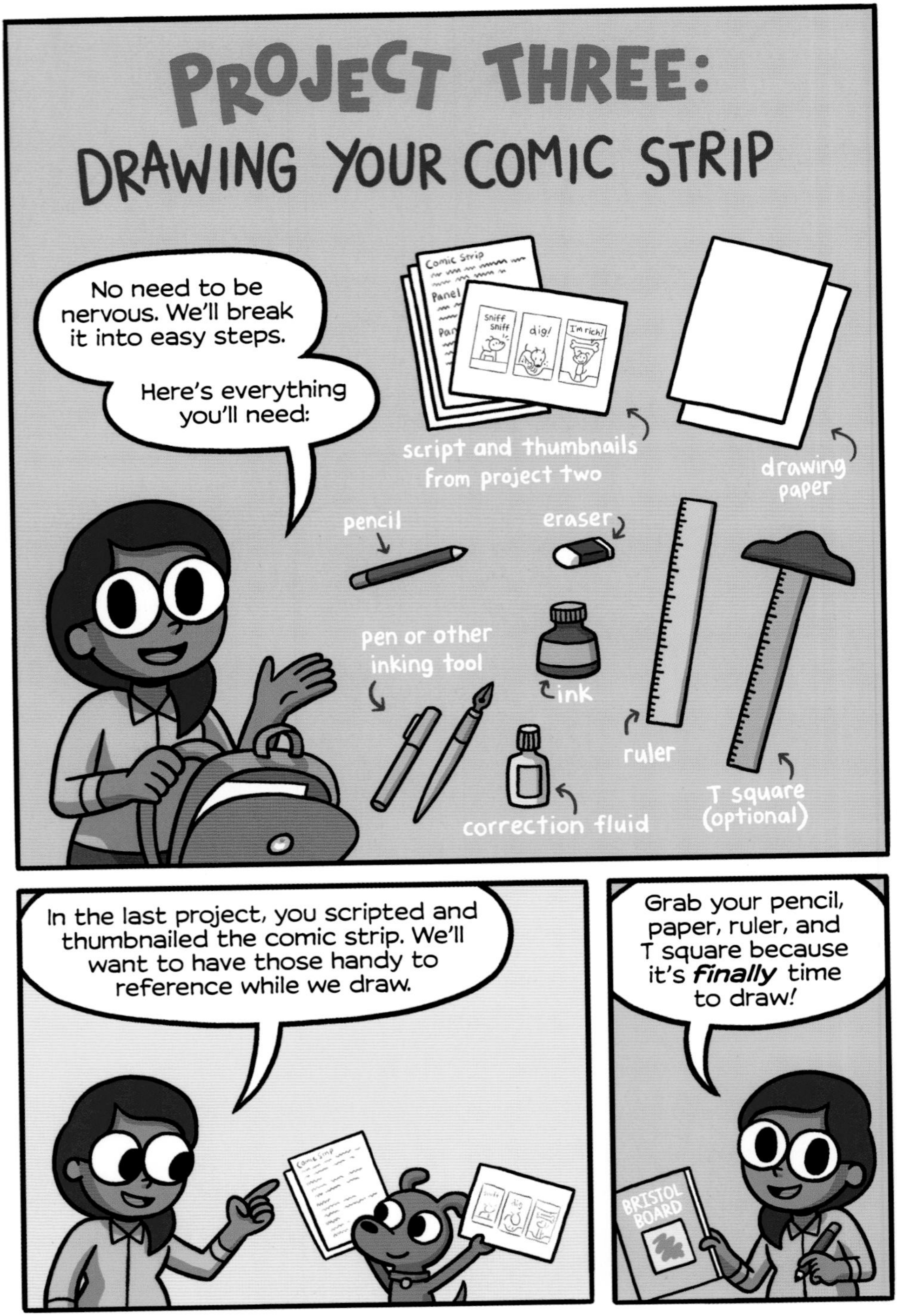
PROJECT THREE:
DRAWING YOUR COMIC STRIP
No need to be nervous. We'll break it into easy steps.
Here's everything you'll need:
Comic Strip
Panel
Sniff sniff
dig!
I'm rich!
script and thumbnails from project two
drawing paper
pencil
eraser
ruler
pen or other inking tool
ink
correction fluid
T square (optional)
In the last project, you scripted and thumbnailed the comic strip. We'll want to have those handy to reference while we draw.
Grab your pencil, paper, ruler, and T square because it's ***finally*** time to draw!
BRISTOL BOARD

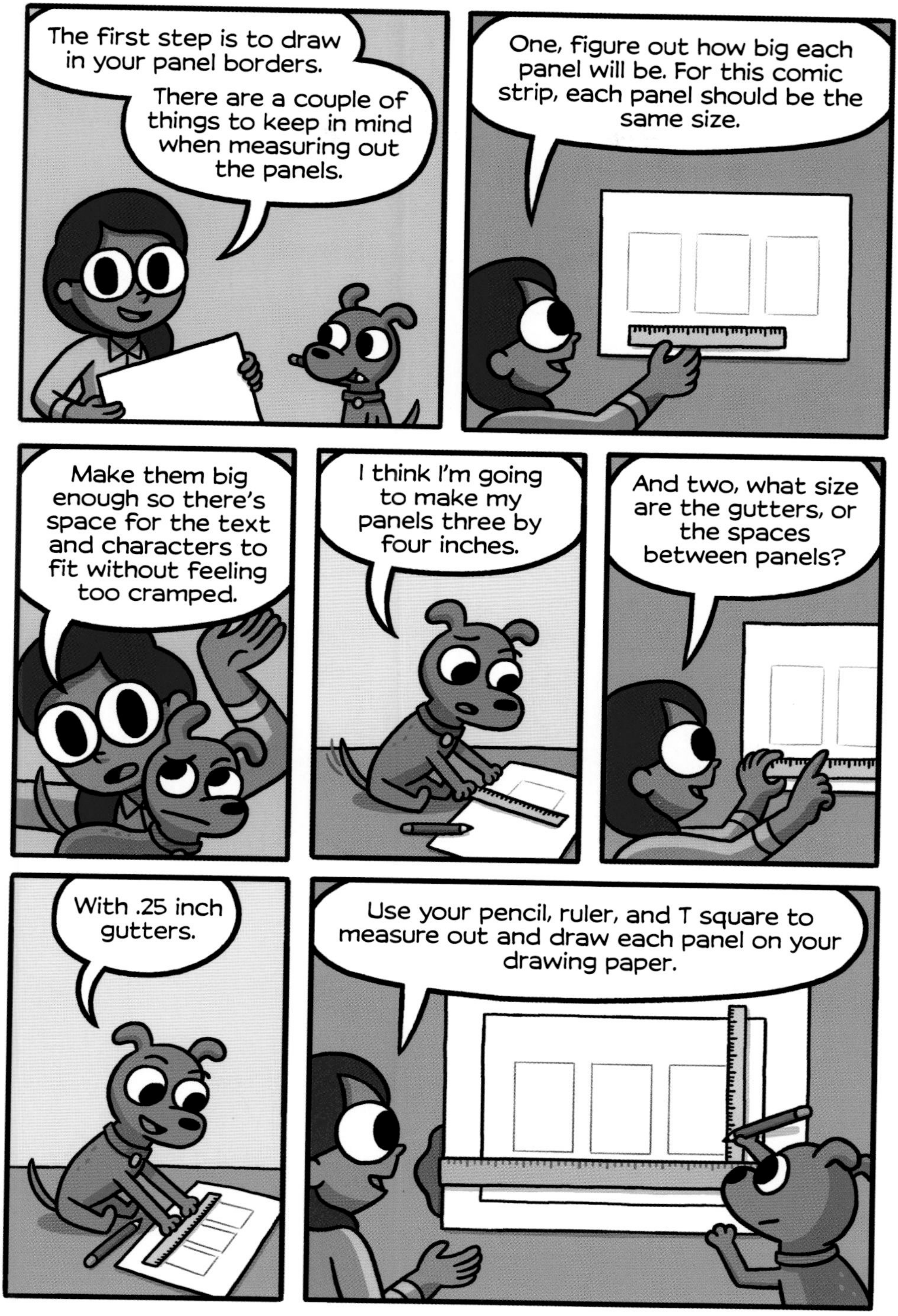
The first step is to draw in your panel borders.
There are a couple of things to keep in mind when measuring out the panels.
One, figure out how big each panel will be. For this comic strip, each panel should be the same size.
Make them big enough so there's space for the text and characters to fit without feeling too cramped.
I think I'm going to make my panels three by four inches.
And two, what size are the gutters, or the spaces between panels?
With .25 inch gutters.
Use your pencil, ruler, and T square to measure out and draw each panel on your drawing paper.

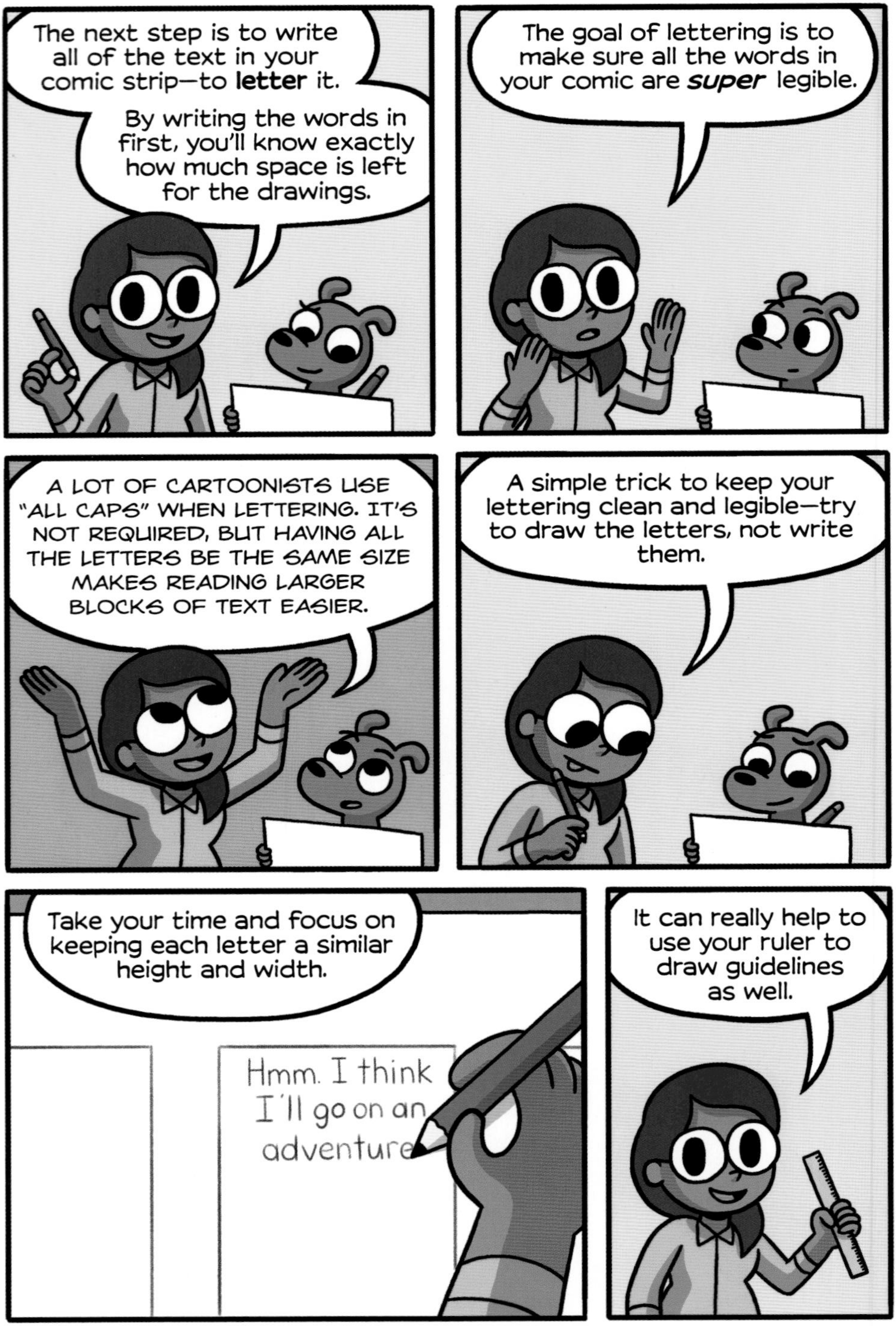
The next step is to write all of the text in your comic strip—to **letter** it.
By writing the words in first, you'll know exactly how much space is left for the drawings.
The goal of lettering is to make sure all the words in your comic are ***super*** legible.
A LOT OF CARTOONISTS USE "ALL CAPS" WHEN LETTERING. IT'S NOT REQUIRED, BUT HAVING ALL THE LETTERS BE THE SAME SIZE MAKES READING LARGER BLOCKS OF TEXT EASIER.
A simple trick to keep your lettering clean and legible—try to draw the letters, not write them.
Take your time and focus on keeping each letter a similar height and width.
Hmm. I think I'll go on an adventure
It can really help to use your ruler to draw guidelines as well.

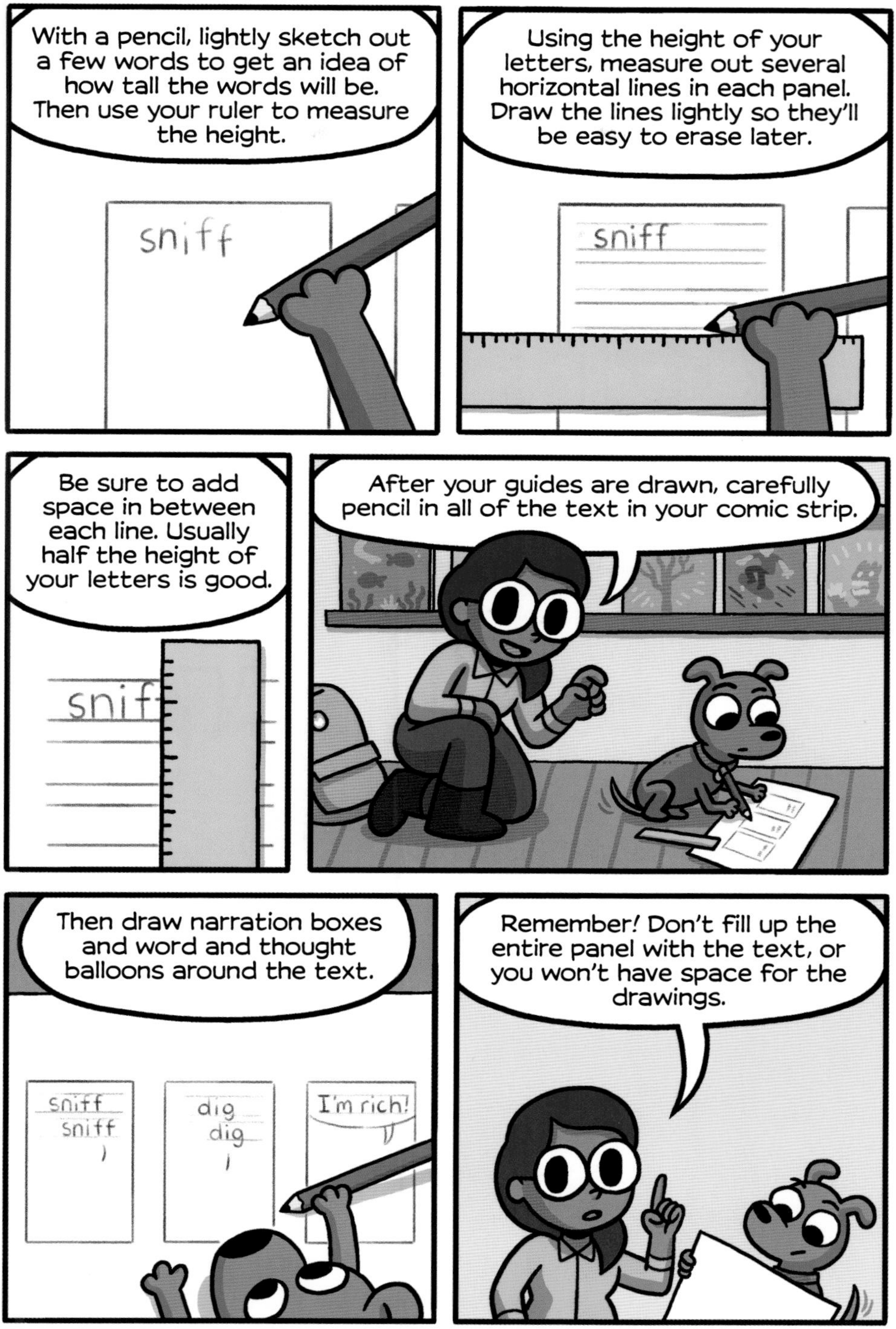

With a pencil, lightly sketch out a few words to get an idea of how tall the words will be. Then use your ruler to measure the height.
sniff
Using the height of your letters, measure out several horizontal lines in each panel. Draw the lines lightly so they'll be easy to erase later.
sniff
Be sure to add space in between each line. Usually half the height of your letters is good.
snif
After your guides are drawn, carefully pencil in all of the text in your comic strip.
Then draw narration boxes and word and thought balloons around the text.
sniff sniff
dig dig
I'm rich!
Remember! Don't fill up the entire panel with the text, or you won't have space for the drawings.

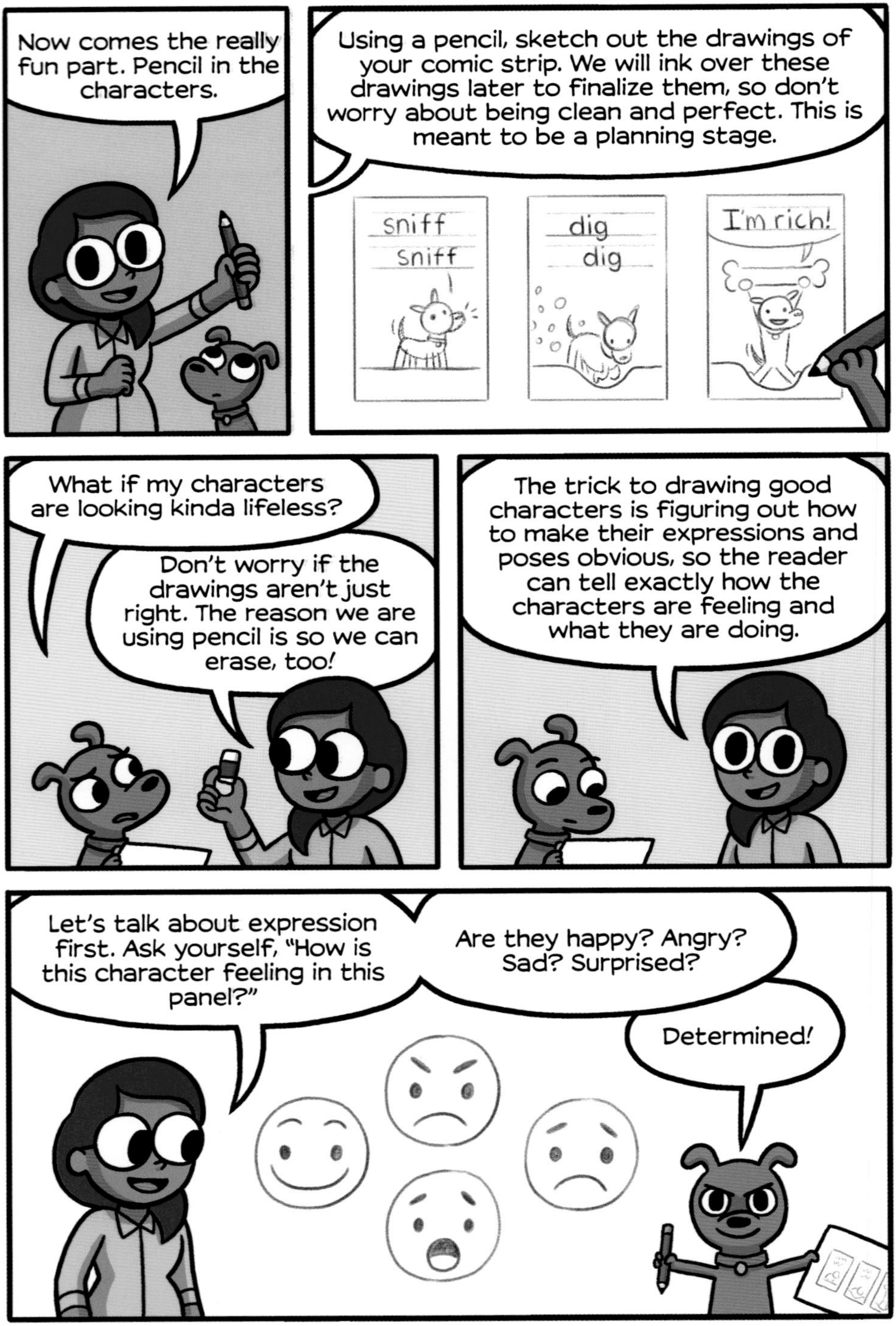
Now comes the really fun part. Pencil in the characters.
Using a pencil, sketch out the drawings of your comic strip. We will ink over these drawings later to finalize them, so don't worry about being clean and perfect. This is meant to be a planning stage.
sniff
sniff
dig
dig
I'm rich!
What if my characters are looking kinda lifeless?
Don't worry if the drawings aren't just right. The reason we are using pencil is so we can erase, too!
The trick to drawing good characters is figuring out how to make their expressions and poses obvious, so the reader can tell exactly how the characters are feeling and what they are doing.
Let's talk about expression first. Ask yourself, "How is this character feeling in this panel?"
Are they happy? Angry? Sad? Surprised?
Determined!

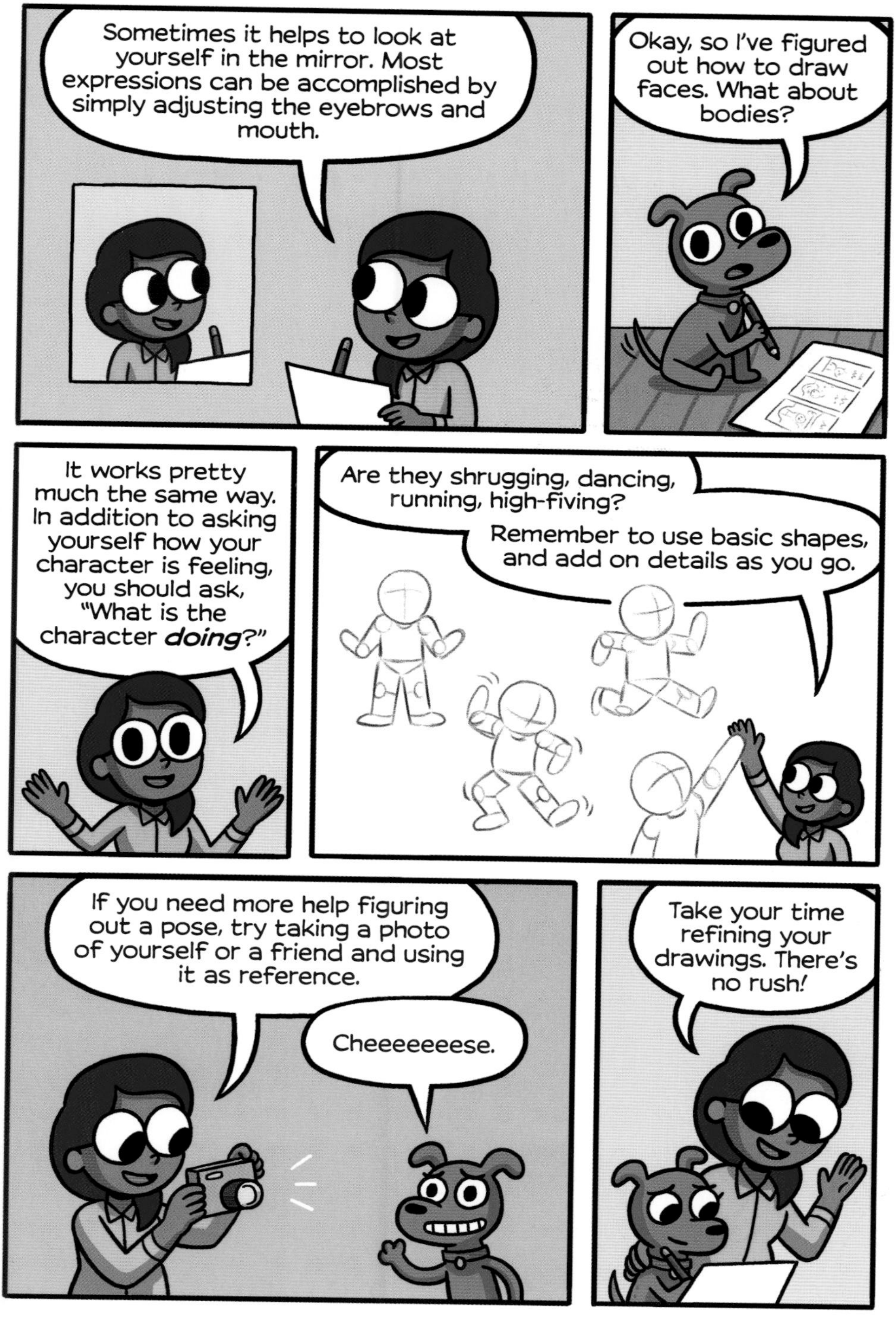
Sometimes it helps to look at yourself in the mirror. Most expressions can be accomplished by simply adjusting the eyebrows and mouth.
Okay, so I've figured out how to draw faces. What about bodies?
It works pretty much the same way. In addition to asking yourself how your character is feeling, you should ask, "What is the character *doing*?"
Are they shrugging, dancing, running, high-fiving?
Remember to use basic shapes, and add on details as you go.
If you need more help figuring out a pose, try taking a photo of yourself or a friend and using it as reference.
Cheeeeeeese.
Take your time refining your drawings. There's no rush!

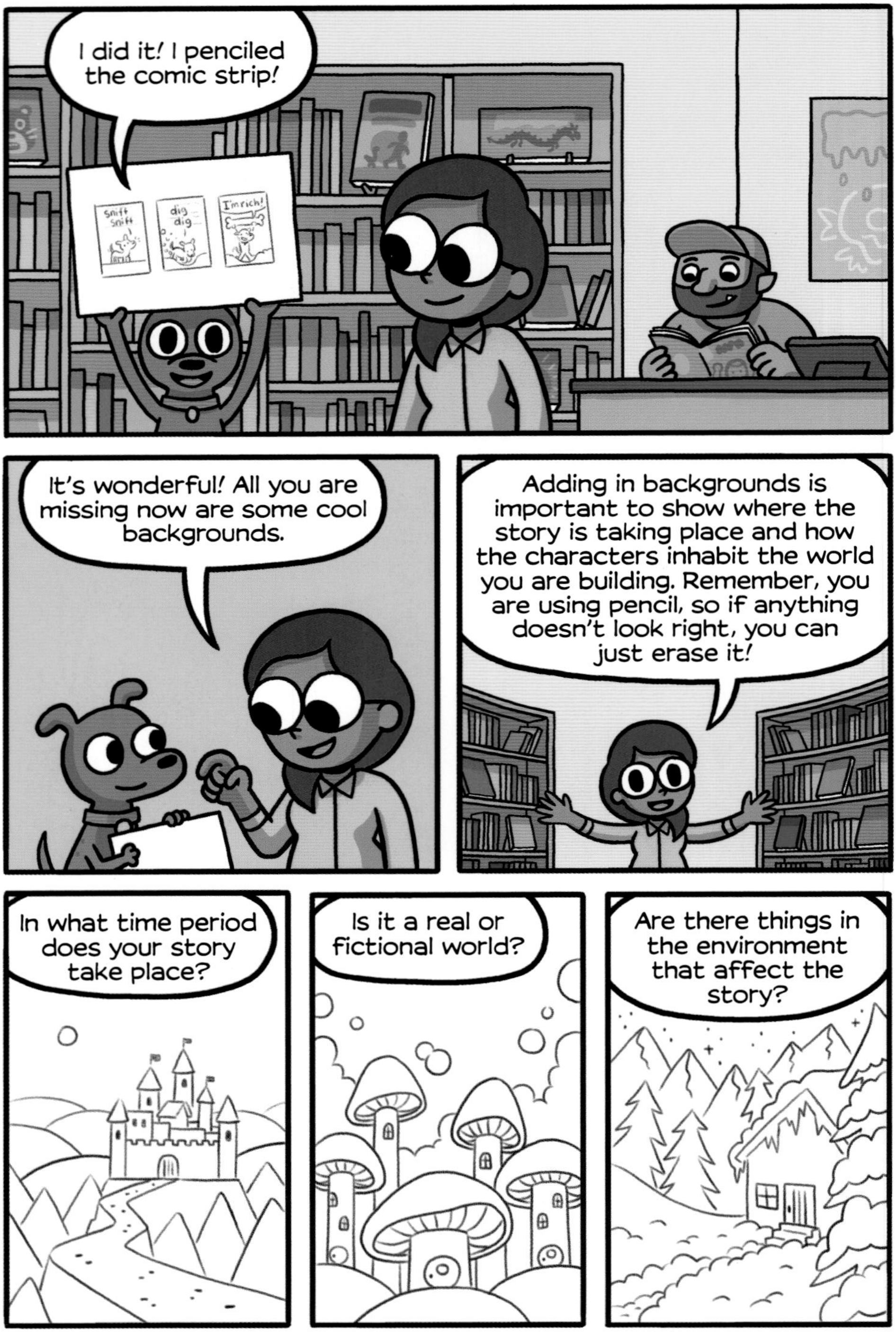

I did it! I penciled the comic strip!
Sniff Sniff
dig dig
I'm rich!
It's wonderful! All you are missing now are some cool backgrounds.
Adding in backgrounds is important to show where the story is taking place and how the characters inhabit the world you are building. Remember, you are using pencil, so if anything doesn't look right, you can just erase it!
In what time period does your story take place?
Is it a real or fictional world?
Are there things in the environment that affect the story?

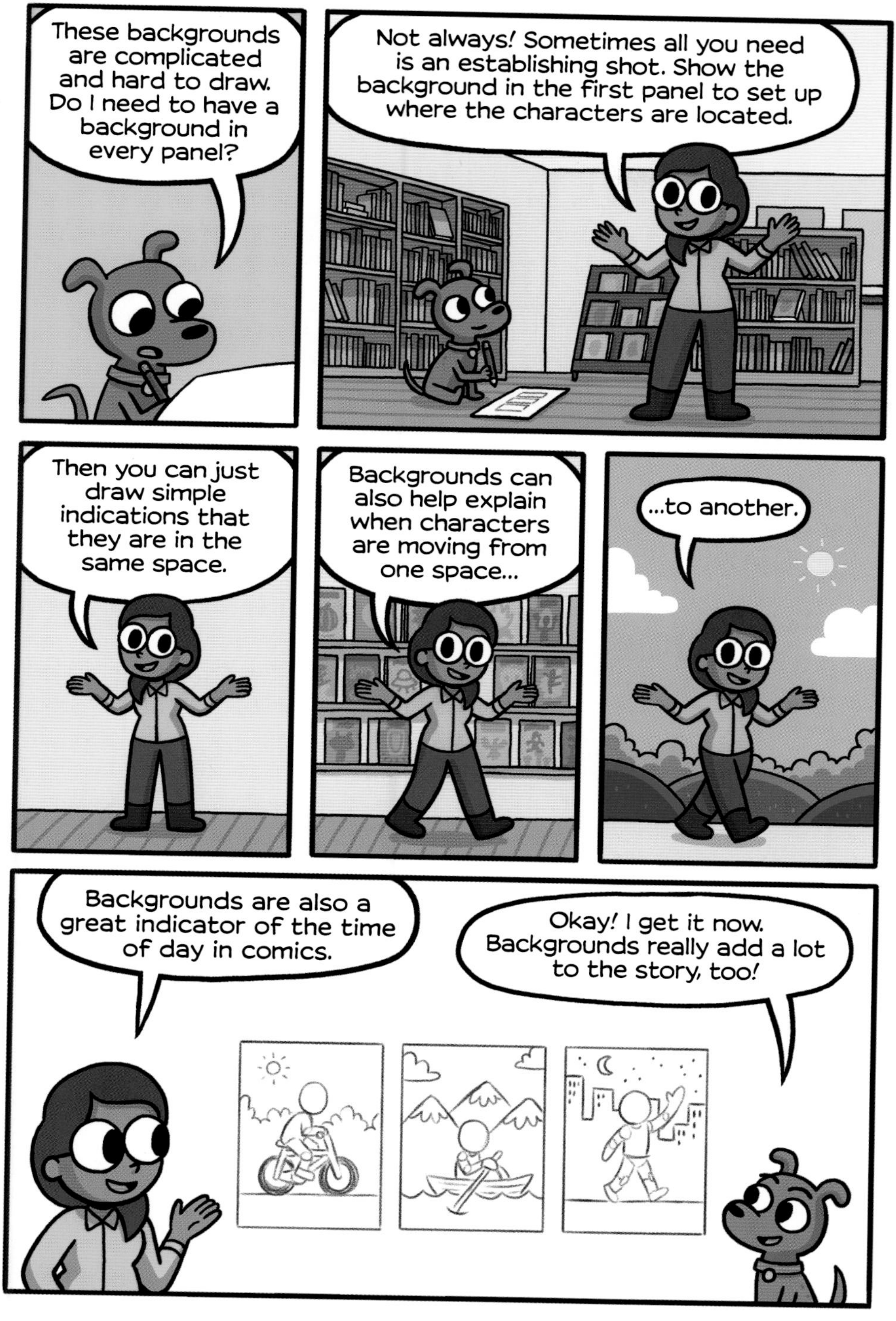
These backgrounds are complicated and hard to draw. Do I need to have a background in every panel?
Not always! Sometimes all you need is an establishing shot. Show the background in the first panel to set up where the characters are located.
Then you can just draw simple indications that they are in the same space.
Backgrounds can also help explain when characters are moving from one space...
...to another.
Backgrounds are also a great indicator of the time of day in comics.
Okay! I get it now. Backgrounds really add a lot to the story, too!

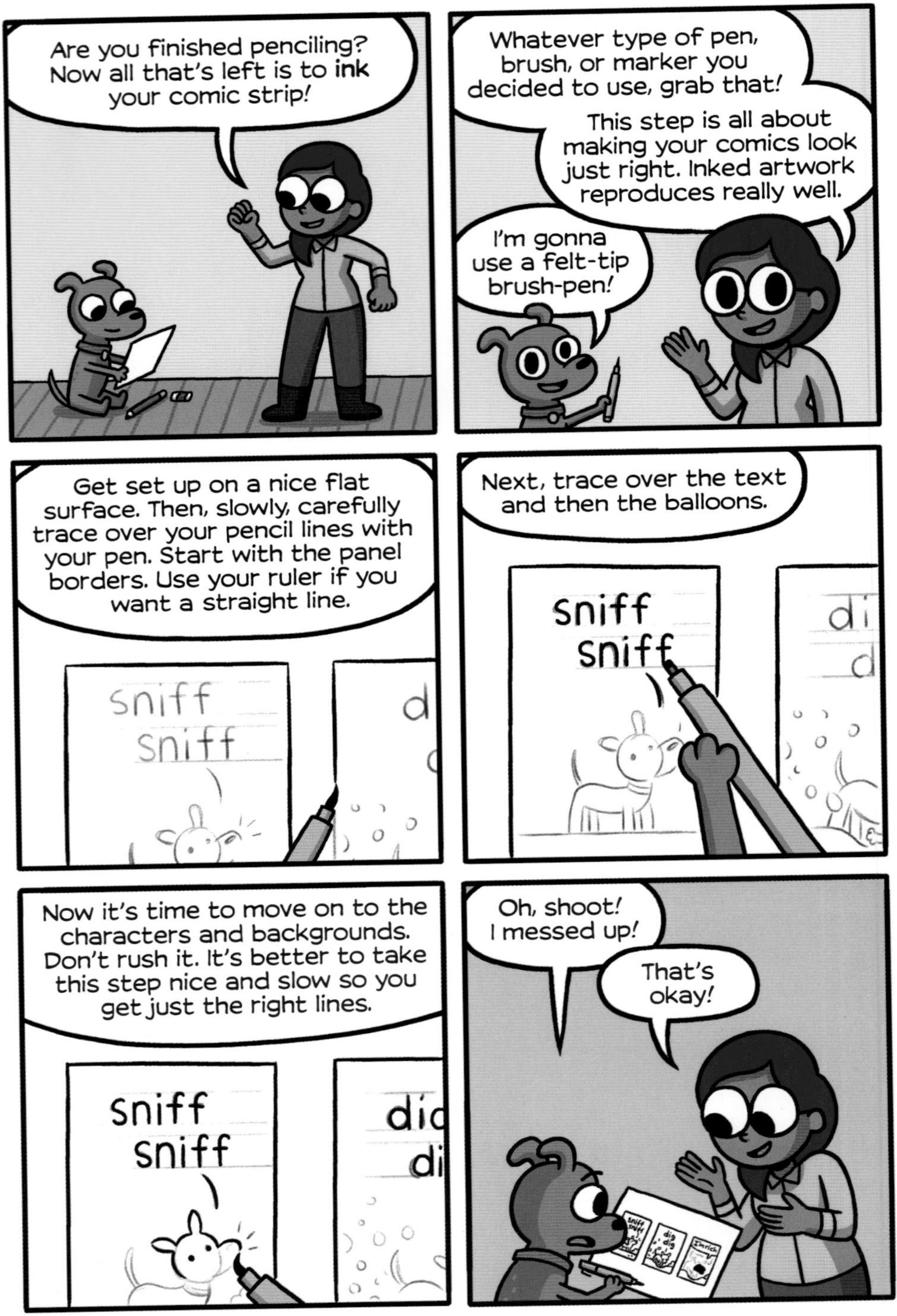
Are you finished penciling? Now all that's left is to **ink** your comic strip!
Whatever type of pen, brush, or marker you decided to use, grab that!
This step is all about making your comics look just right. Inked artwork reproduces really well.
I'm gonna use a felt-tip brush-pen!
Get set up on a nice flat surface. Then, slowly, carefully trace over your pencil lines with your pen. Start with the panel borders. Use your ruler if you want a straight line.
sniff
sniff
Next, trace over the text and then the balloons.
sniff
sniff
Now it's time to move on to the characters and backgrounds. Don't rush it. It's better to take this step nice and slow so you get just the right lines.
sniff
sniff
Oh, shoot! I messed up!
That's okay!

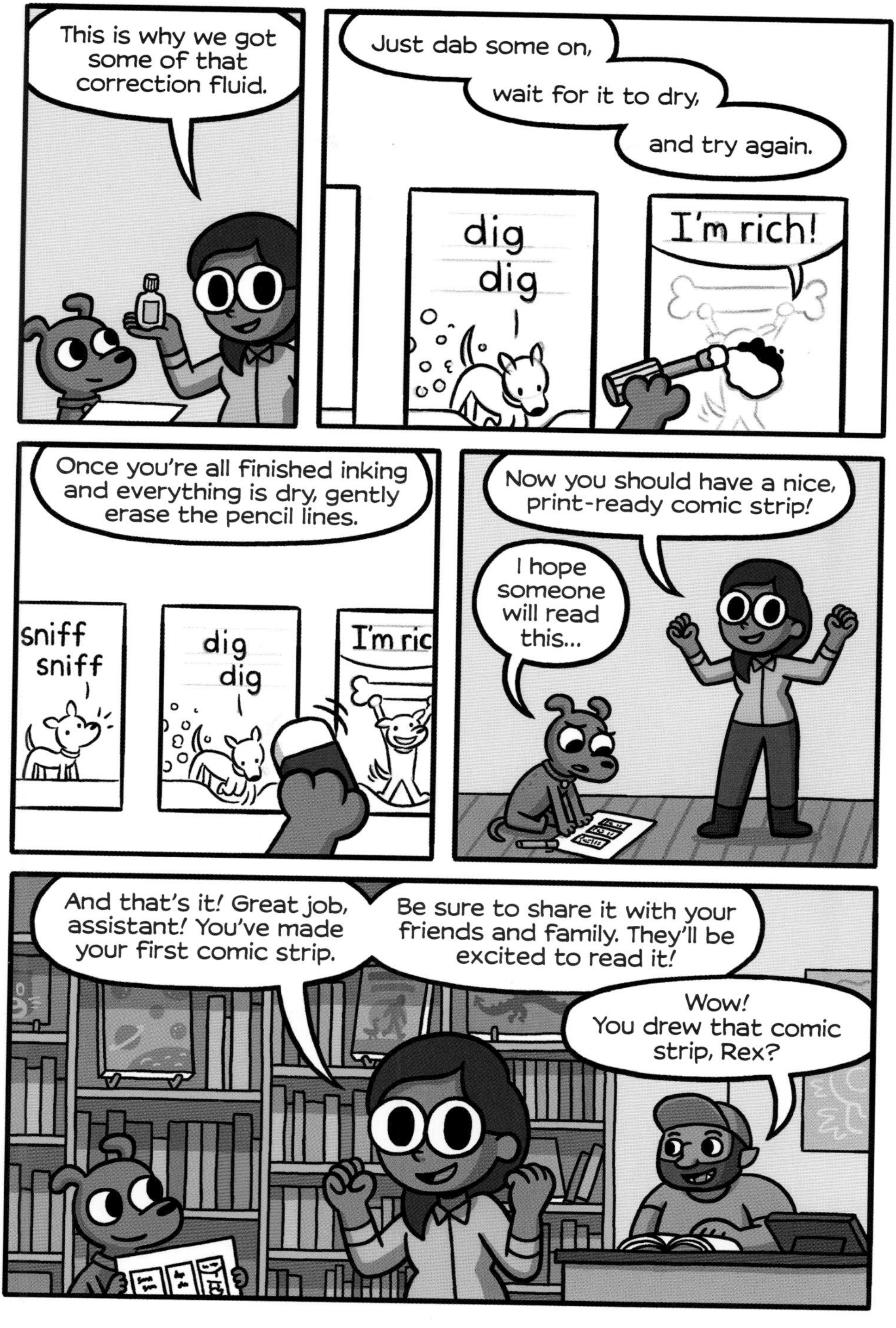
This is why we got some of that correction fluid.
Just dab some on,
wait for it to dry,
and try again.
dig dig
I'm rich!
Once you're all finished inking and everything is dry, gently erase the pencil lines.
sniff sniff
dig dig
I'm ric
Now you should have a nice, print-ready comic strip!
I hope someone will read this...
And that's it! Great job, assistant! You've made your first comic strip.
Be sure to share it with your friends and family. They'll be excited to read it!
Wow! You drew that comic strip, Rex?

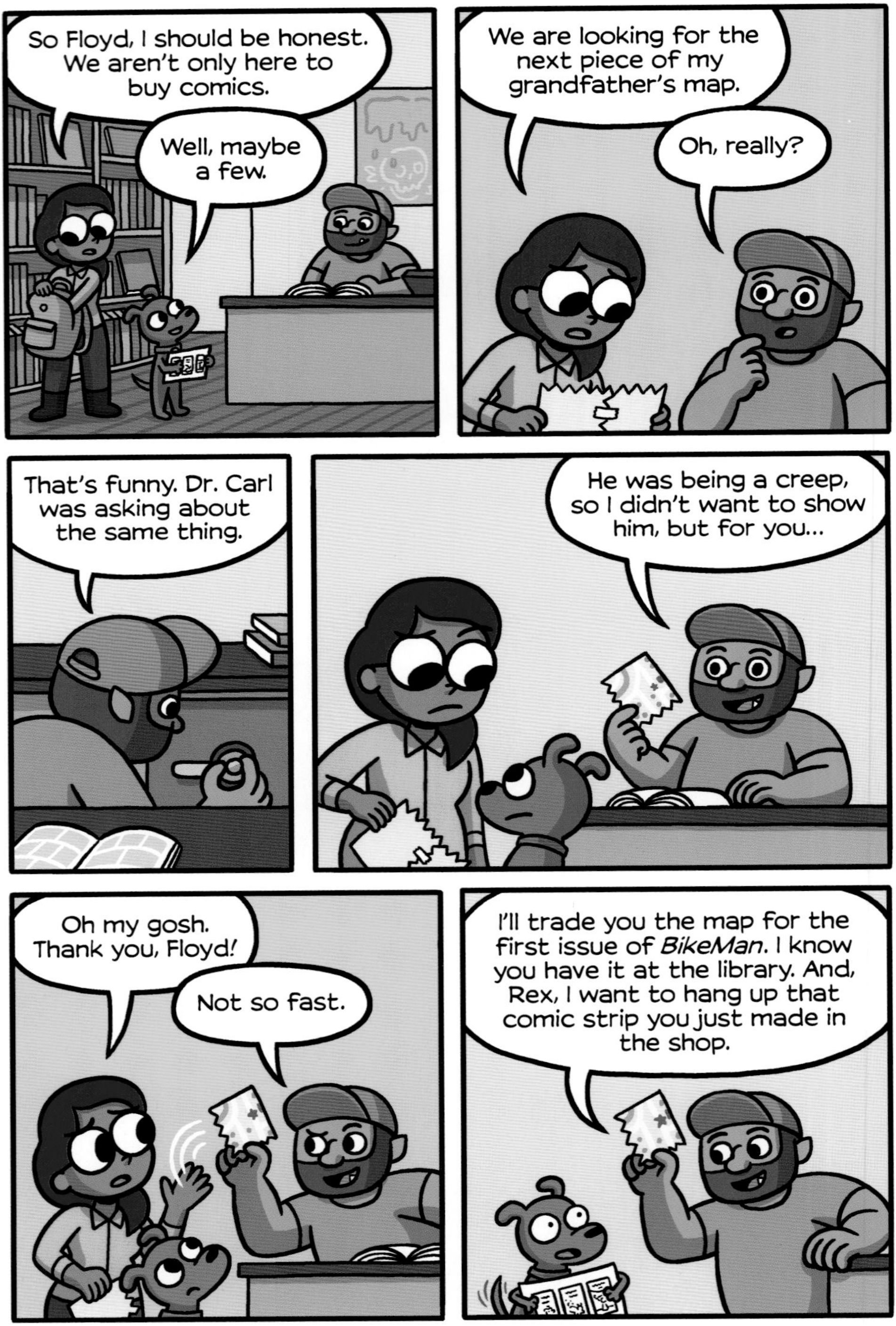
So Floyd, I should be honest. We aren't only here to buy comics.
Well, maybe a few.
We are looking for the next piece of my grandfather's map.
Oh, really?
That's funny. Dr. Carl was asking about the same thing.
He was being a creep, so I didn't want to show him, but for you...
Oh my gosh. Thank you, Floyd!
Not so fast.
I'll trade you the map for the first issue of *BikeMan*. I know you have it at the library. And, Rex, I want to hang up that comic strip you just made in the shop.

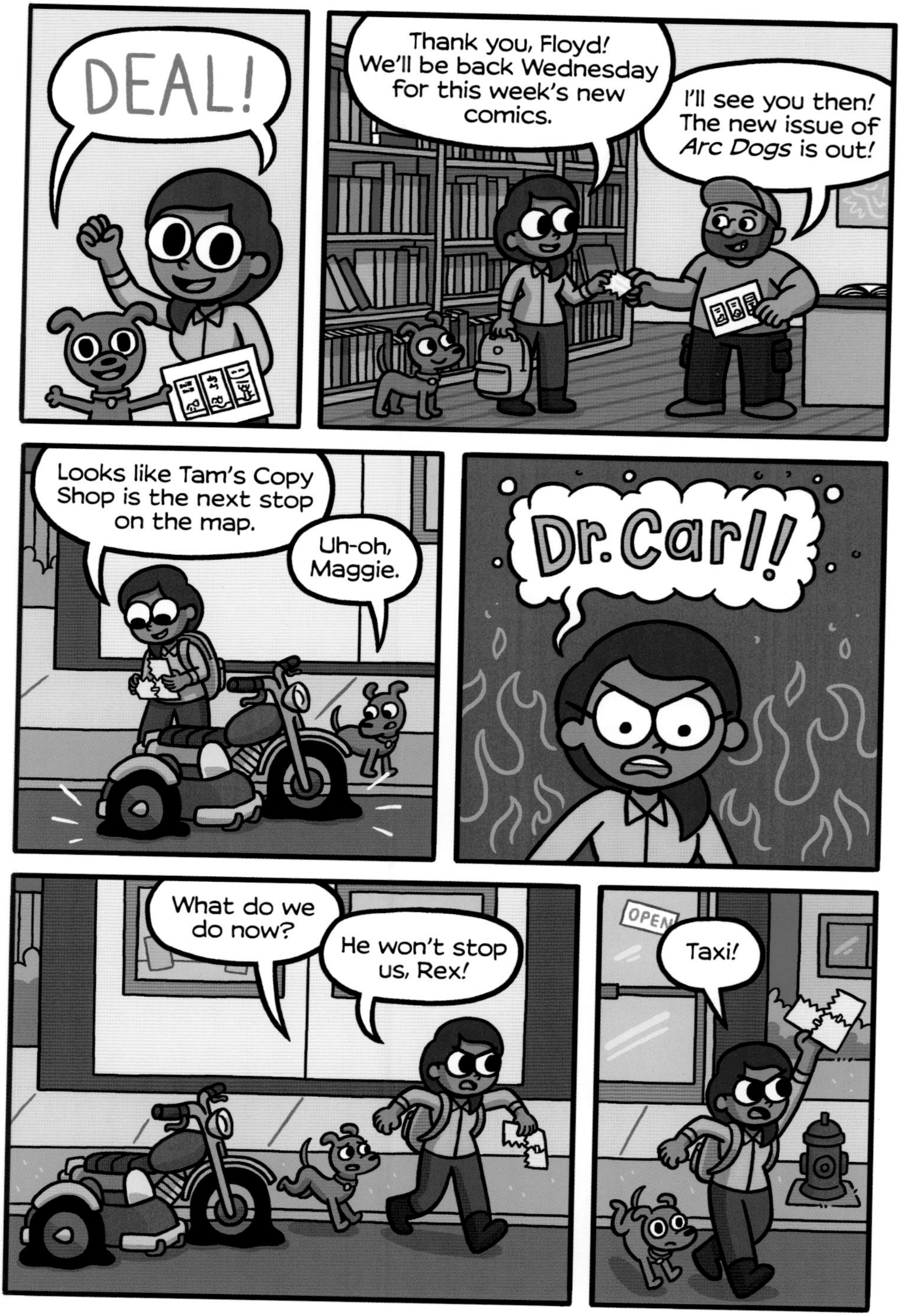
DEAL!
Thank you, Floyd! We'll be back Wednesday for this week's new comics.
I'll see you then! The new issue of *Arc Dogs* is out!
Looks like Tam's Copy Shop is the next stop on the map.
Uh-oh, Maggie.
Dr. Carl!!
What do we do now?
He won't stop us, Rex!
OPEN
Taxi!

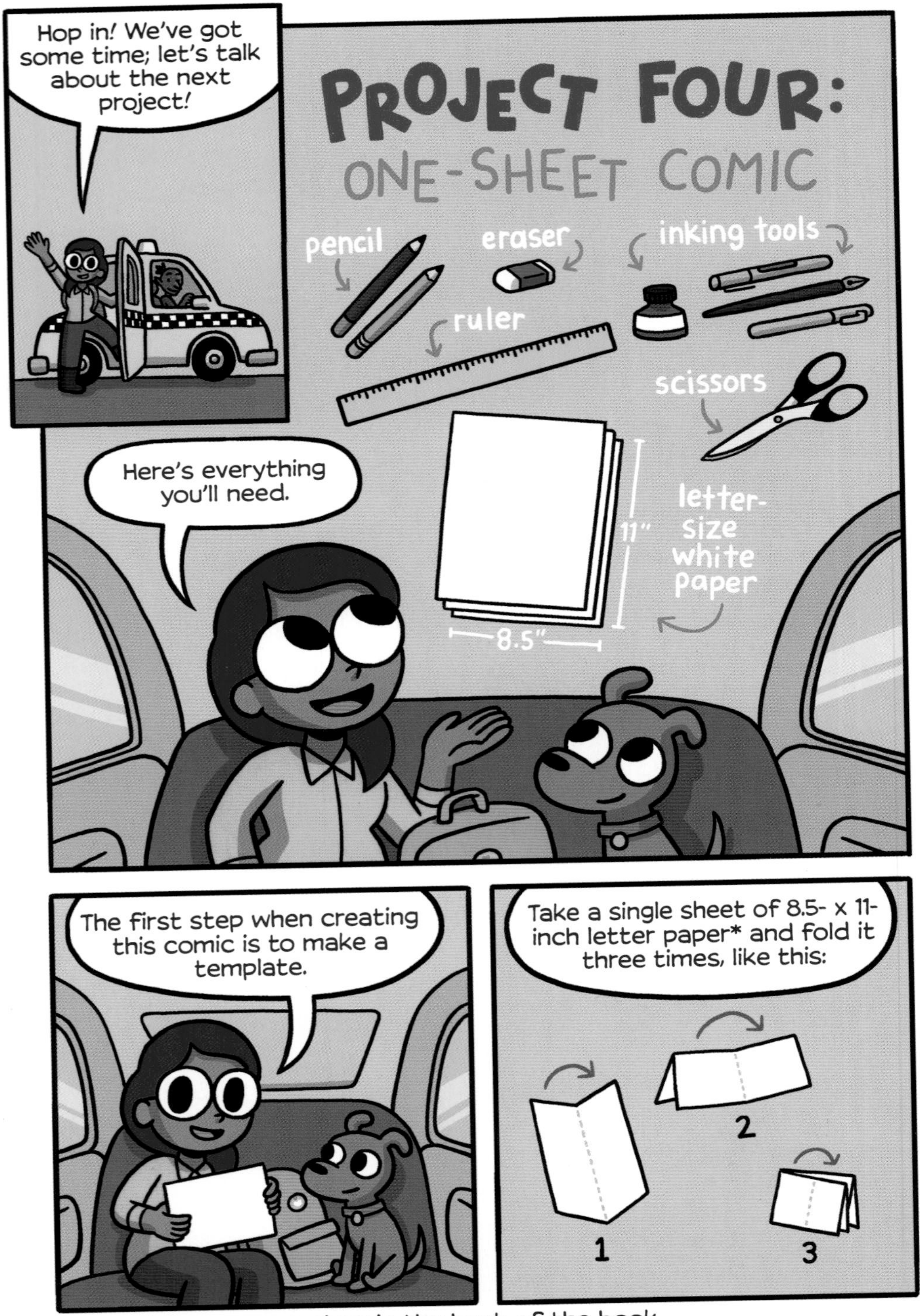
Hop in! We've got some time; let's talk about the next project!
PROJECT FOUR:
ONE-SHEET COMIC
pencil
eraser
inking tools
ruler
scissors
Here's everything you'll need.
11"
letter-size white paper
8.5"
The first step when creating this comic is to make a template.
Take a single sheet of 8.5- x 11-inch letter paper* and fold it three times, like this:
1
2
3

* More info on paper sizes in the back of the book.

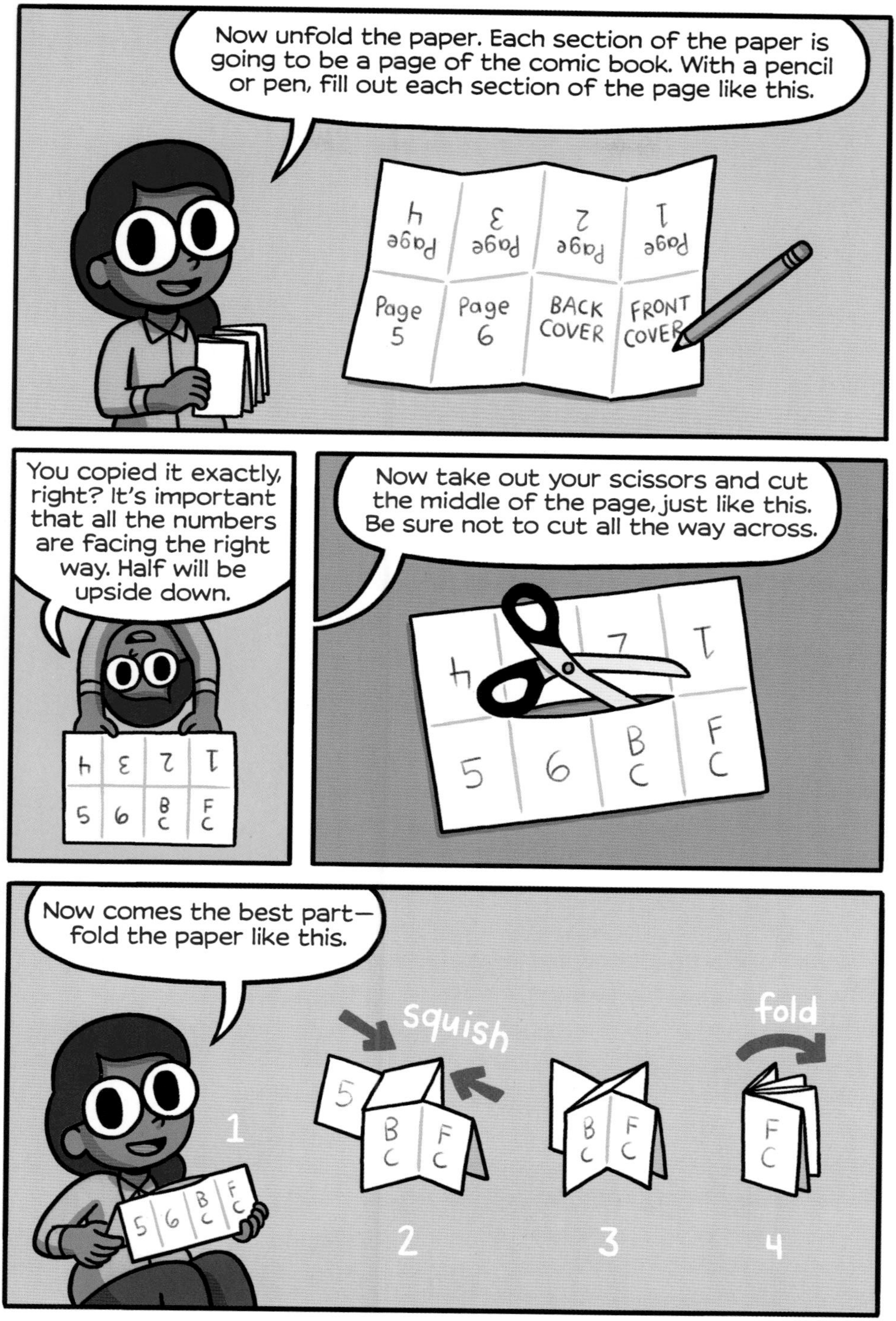
Now unfold the paper. Each section of the paper is going to be a page of the comic book. With a pencil or pen, fill out each section of the page like this.
Page 5
Page 6
BACK COVER
FRONT COVER
You copied it exactly, right? It's important that all the numbers are facing the right way. Half will be upside down.
Now take out your scissors and cut the middle of the page, just like this. Be sure not to cut all the way across.
Now comes the best part— fold the paper like this.
squish
fold
1
2
3
4

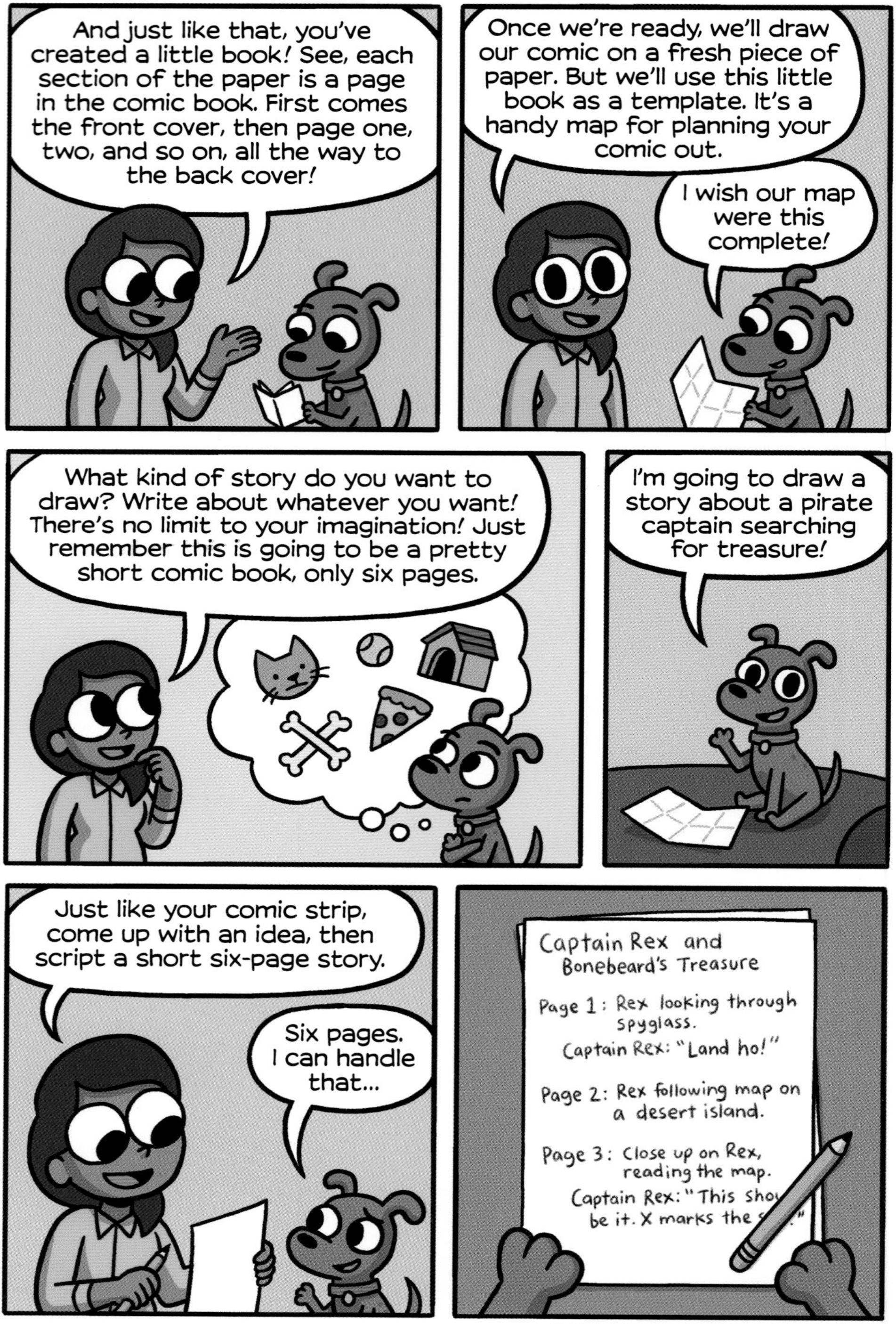
And just like that, you've created a little book! See, each section of the paper is a page in the comic book. First comes the front cover, then page one, two, and so on, all the way to the back cover!
Once we're ready, we'll draw our comic on a fresh piece of paper. But we'll use this little book as a template. It's a handy map for planning your comic out.
I wish our map were this complete!
What kind of story do you want to draw? Write about whatever you want! There's no limit to your imagination! Just remember this is going to be a pretty short comic book, only six pages.
I'm going to draw a story about a pirate captain searching for treasure!
Just like your comic strip, come up with an idea, then script a short six-page story.
Six pages. I can handle that...
Captain Rex and Bonebeard's Treasure
Page 1: Rex looking through spyglass.
Captain Rex: "Land ho!"
Page 2: Rex following map on a desert island.
Page 3: Close up on Rex, reading the map.
Captain Rex: "This sho
be it. X marks the

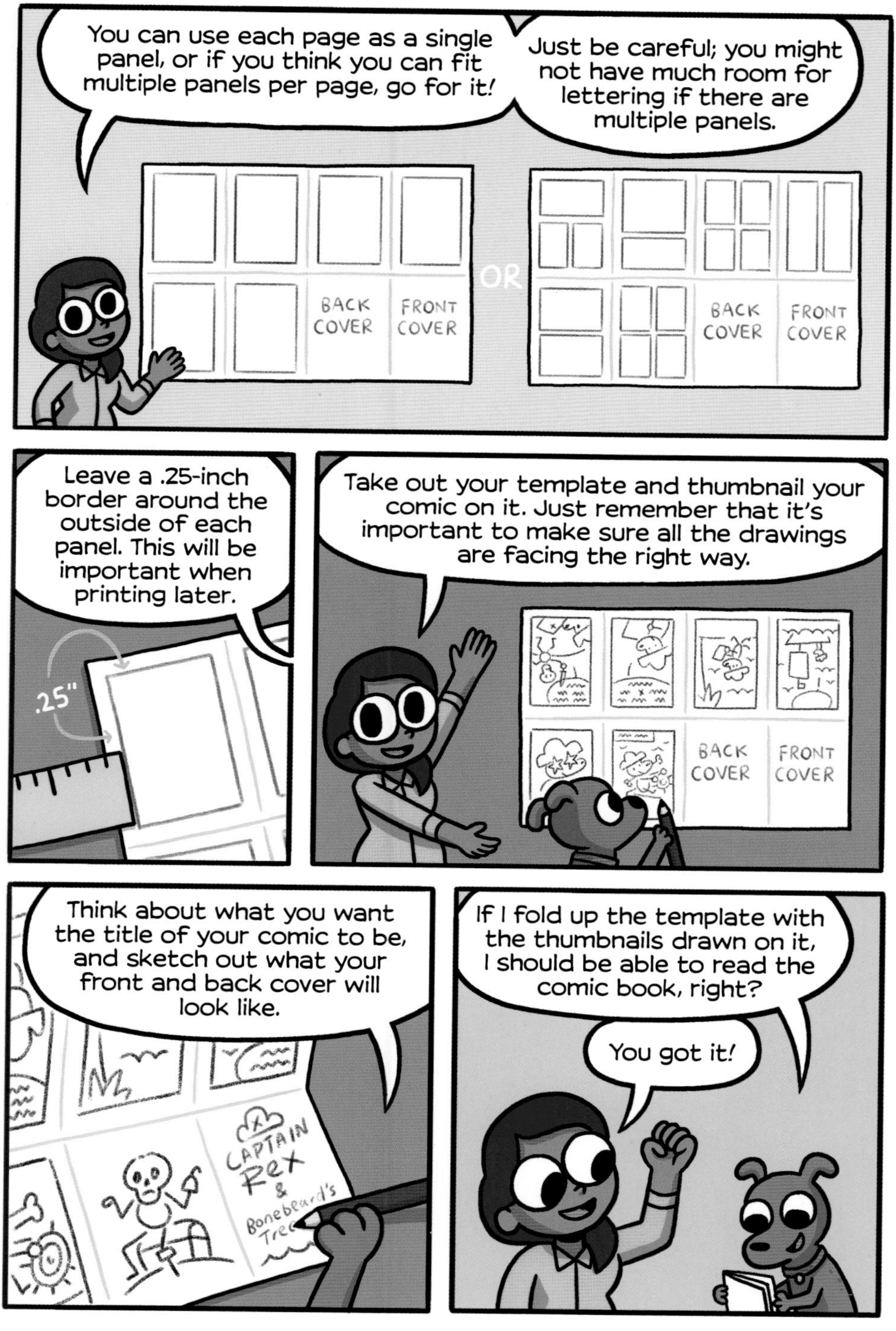
You can use each page as a single panel, or if you think you can fit multiple panels per page, go for it!
Just be careful; you might not have much room for lettering if there are multiple panels.
BACK COVER
FRONT COVER
OR
BACK COVER
FRONT COVER
Leave a .25-inch border around the outside of each panel. This will be important when printing later.
.25"
Take out your template and thumbnail your comic on it. Just remember that it's important to make sure all the drawings are facing the right way.
BACK COVER
FRONT COVER
Think about what you want the title of your comic to be, and sketch out what your front and back cover will look like.
CAPTAIN
Rex
&
Bonebeard's
If I fold up the template with the thumbnails drawn on it, I should be able to read the comic book, right?
You got it!

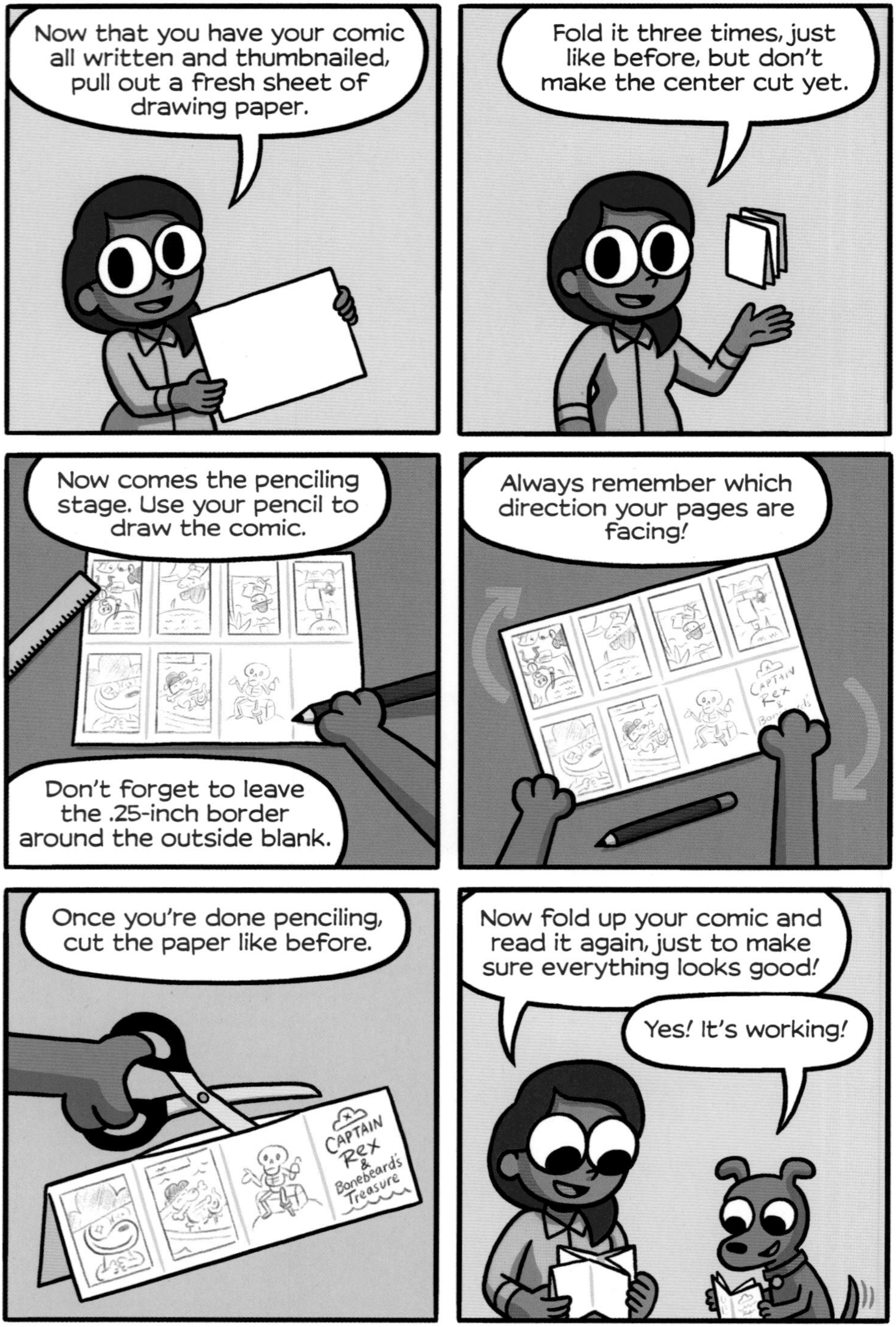
Now that you have your comic all written and thumbnailed, pull out a fresh sheet of drawing paper.
Fold it three times, just like before, but don't make the center cut yet.
Now comes the penciling stage. Use your pencil to draw the comic.
Don't forget to leave the .25-inch border around the outside blank.
Always remember which direction your pages are facing!
Once you're done penciling, cut the paper like before.
CAPTAIN Rex & Bonebeard's Treasure
Now fold up your comic and read it again, just to make sure everything looks good!
Yes! It's working!

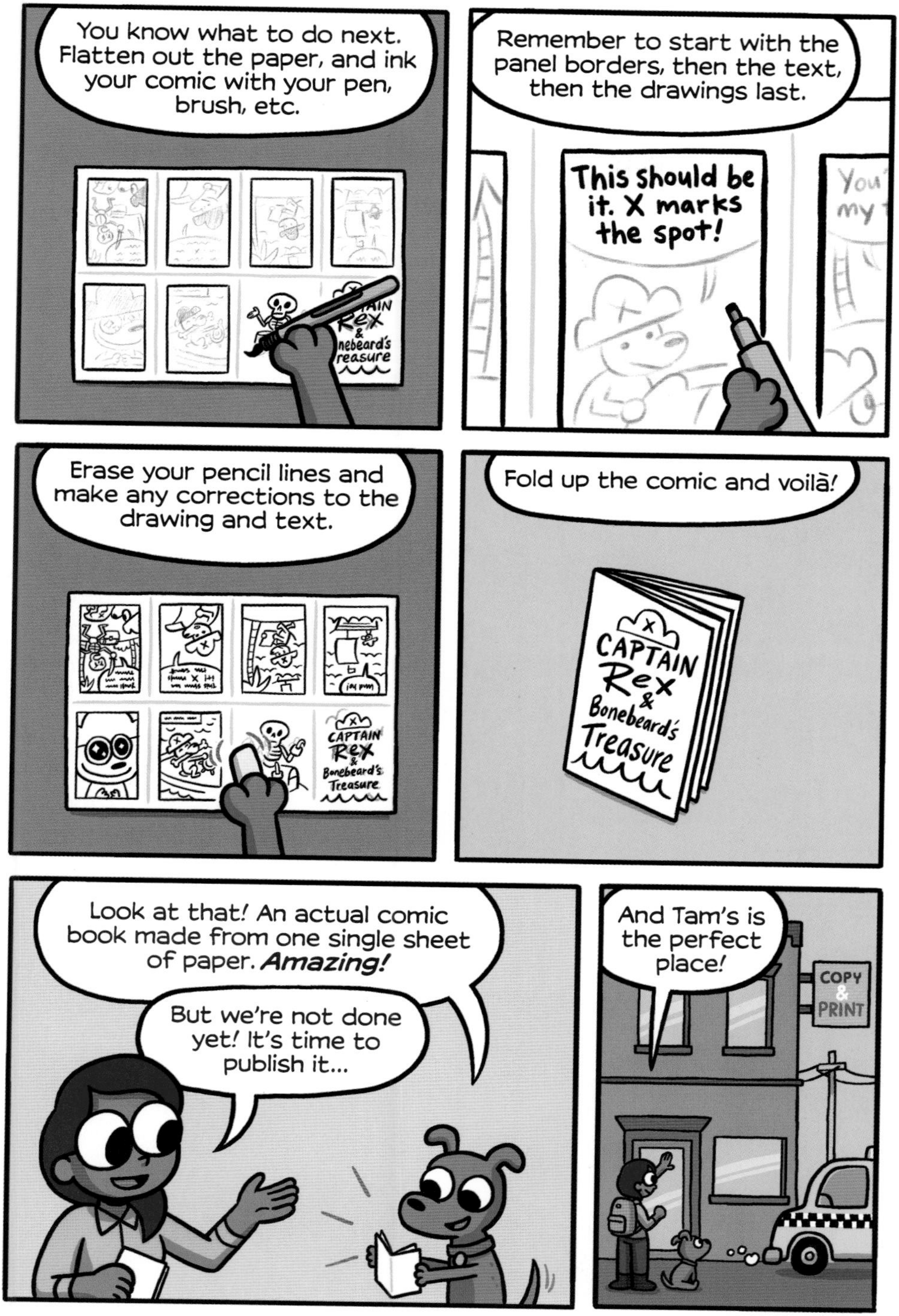
You know what to do next. Flatten out the paper, and ink your comic with your pen, brush, etc.
Remember to start with the panel borders, then the text, then the drawings last.
This should be it. X marks the spot!
Erase your pencil lines and make any corrections to the drawing and text.
CAPTAIN Rex & Bonebeard's Treasure
Fold up the comic and voilà!
CAPTAIN Rex & Bonebeard's Treasure
Look at that! An actual comic book made from one single sheet of paper. ***Amazing!***
But we're not done yet! It's time to publish it...
And Tam's is the perfect place!
COPY & PRINT

PROJECT FIVE:
PRINTING YOUR ONE-PAGE COMIC

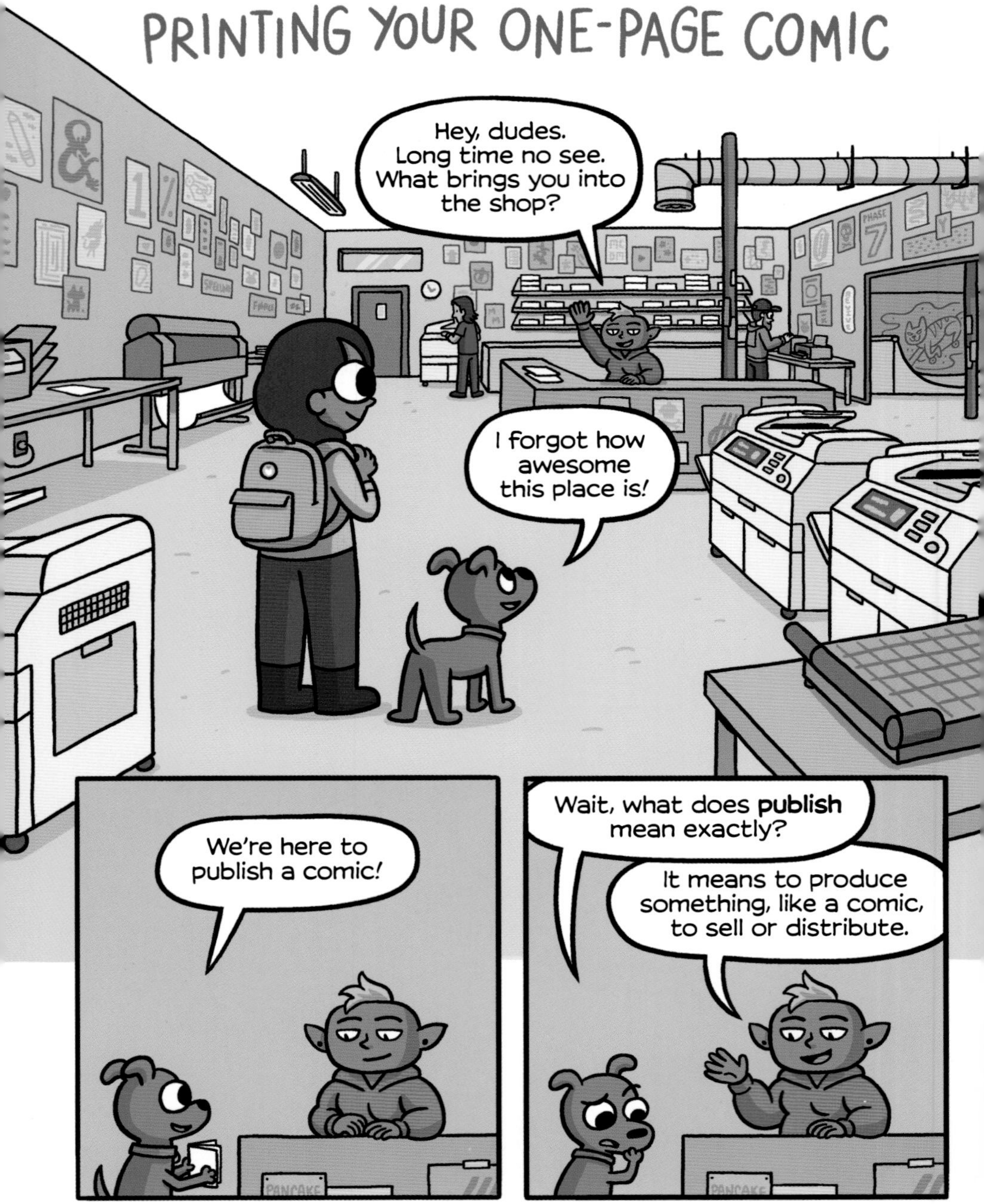
Hey, dudes. Long time no see. What brings you into the shop?
I forgot how awesome this place is!
We're here to publish a comic!
Wait, what does **publish** mean exactly?
It means to produce something, like a comic, to sell or distribute.

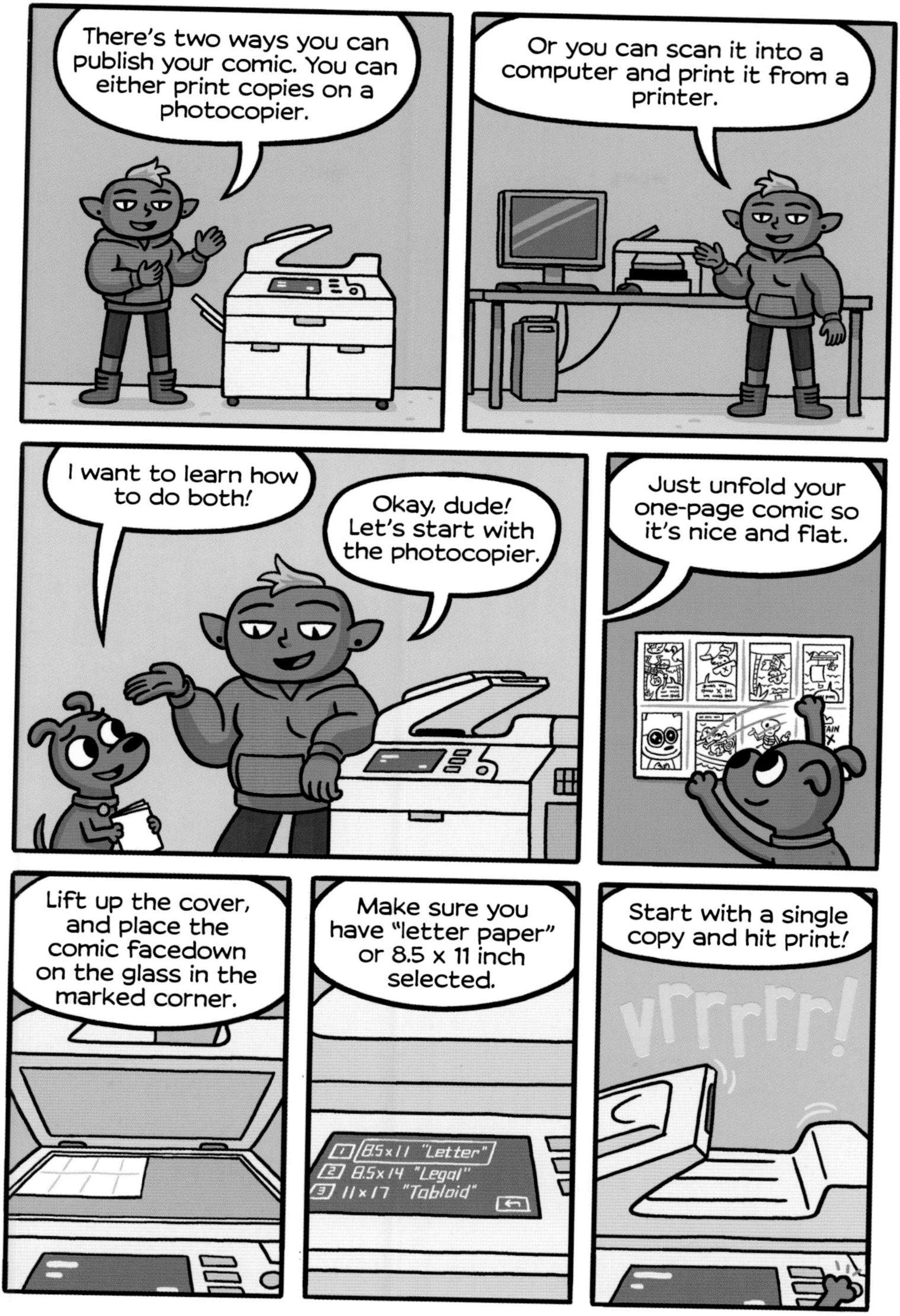

There's two ways you can publish your comic. You can either print copies on a photocopier.
Or you can scan it into a computer and print it from a printer.
I want to learn how to do both!
Okay, dude! Let's start with the photocopier.
Just unfold your one-page comic so it's nice and flat.
Lift up the cover, and place the comic facedown on the glass in the marked corner.
Make sure you have "letter paper" or 8.5 x 11 inch selected.
1 8.5x11 "Letter"
2 8.5x14 "Legal"
3 11x17 "Tabloid"
Start with a single copy and hit print!
vrrrrr!

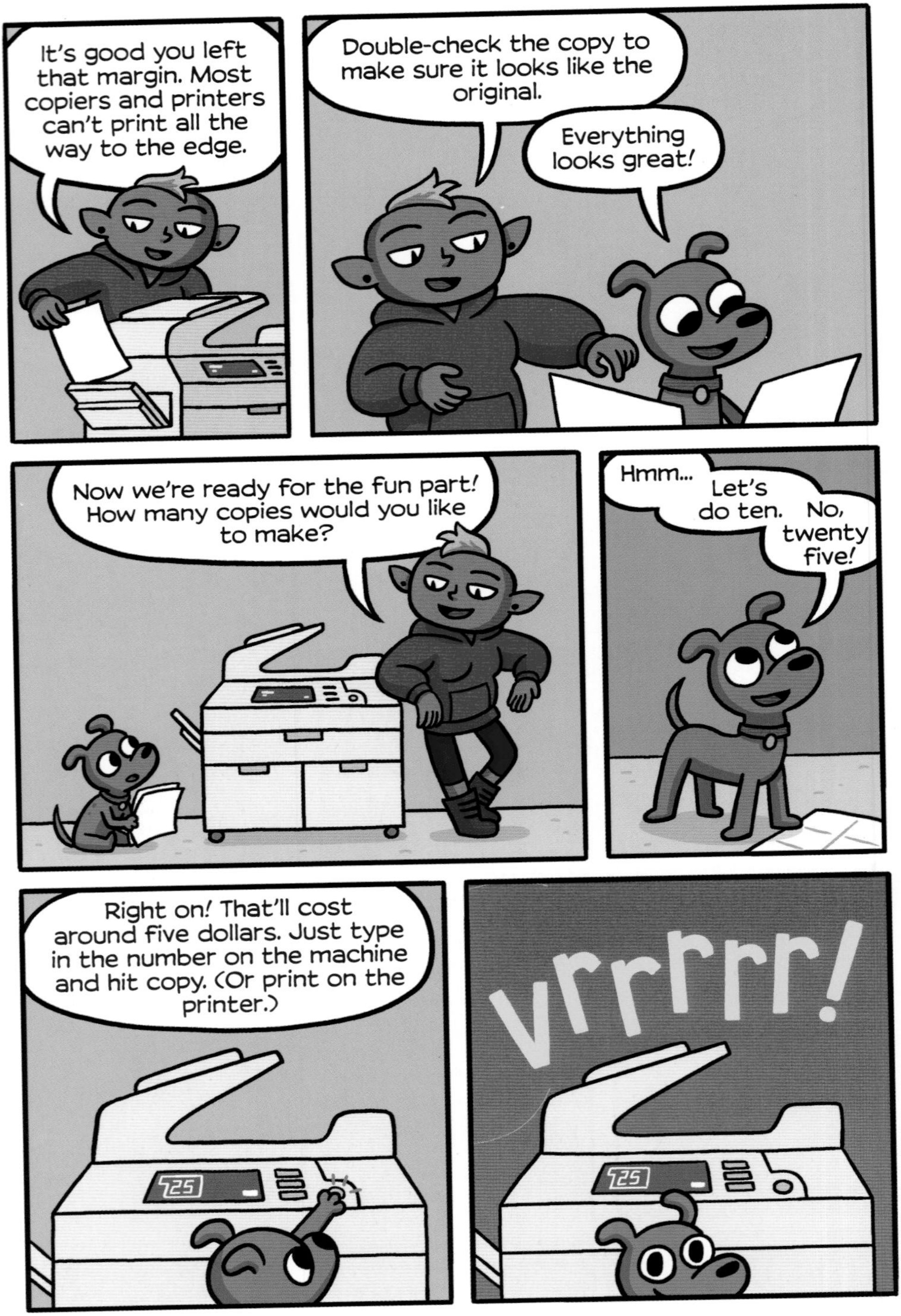

It's good you left that margin. Most copiers and printers can't print all the way to the edge.
Double-check the copy to make sure it looks like the original.
Everything looks great!
Now we're ready for the fun part! How many copies would you like to make?
Hmm...
Let's do ten.
No, twenty five!
Right on! That'll cost around five dollars. Just type in the number on the machine and hit copy. (Or print on the printer.)
25
25
vrrrrr!

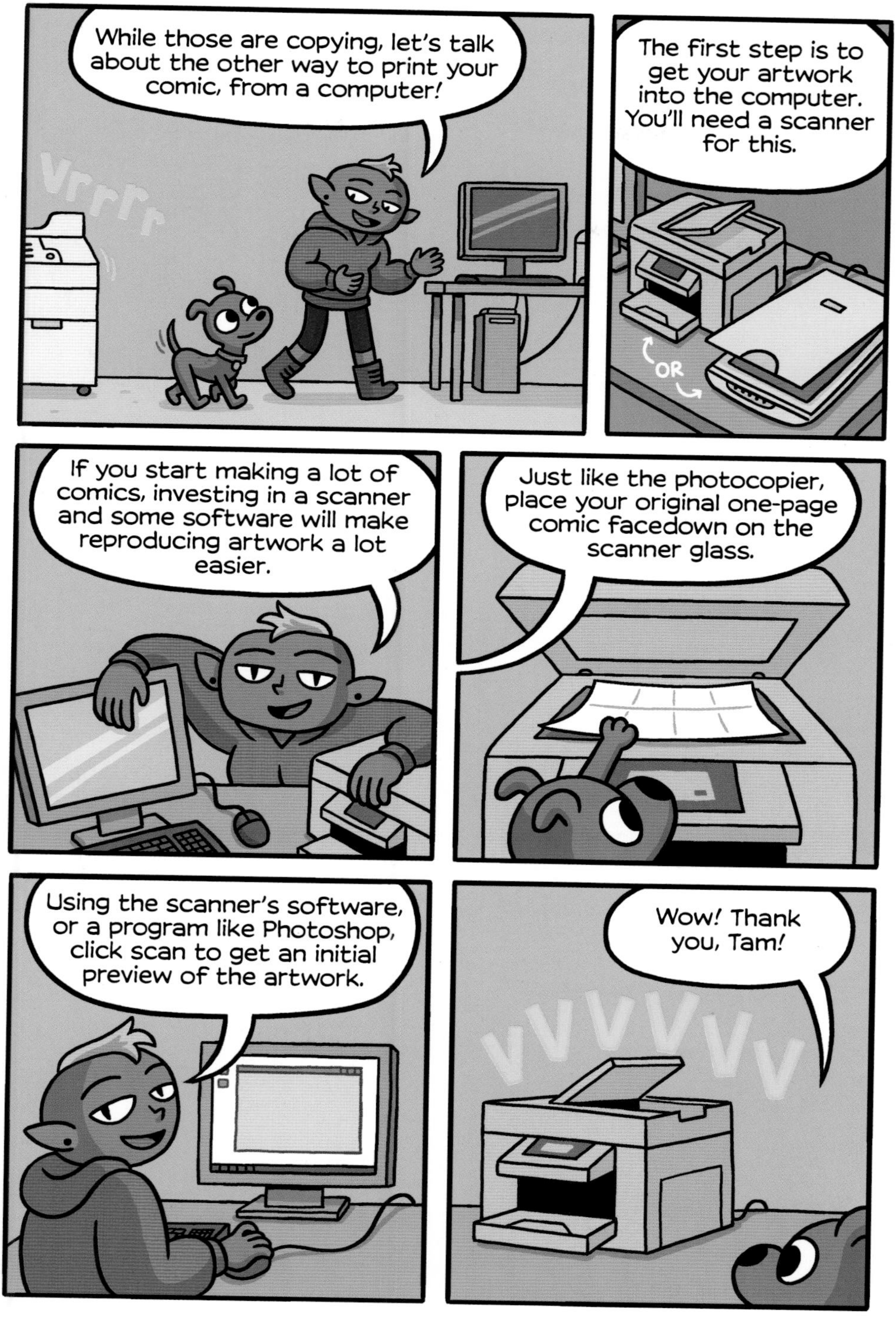
While those are copying, let's talk about the other way to print your comic, from a computer!
VRRRR
The first step is to get your artwork into the computer. You'll need a scanner for this.
OR
If you start making a lot of comics, investing in a scanner and some software will make reproducing artwork a lot easier.
Just like the photocopier, place your original one-page comic facedown on the scanner glass.
Using the scanner's software, or a program like Photoshop, click scan to get an initial preview of the artwork.
Wow! Thank you, Tam!
VVVVVVV

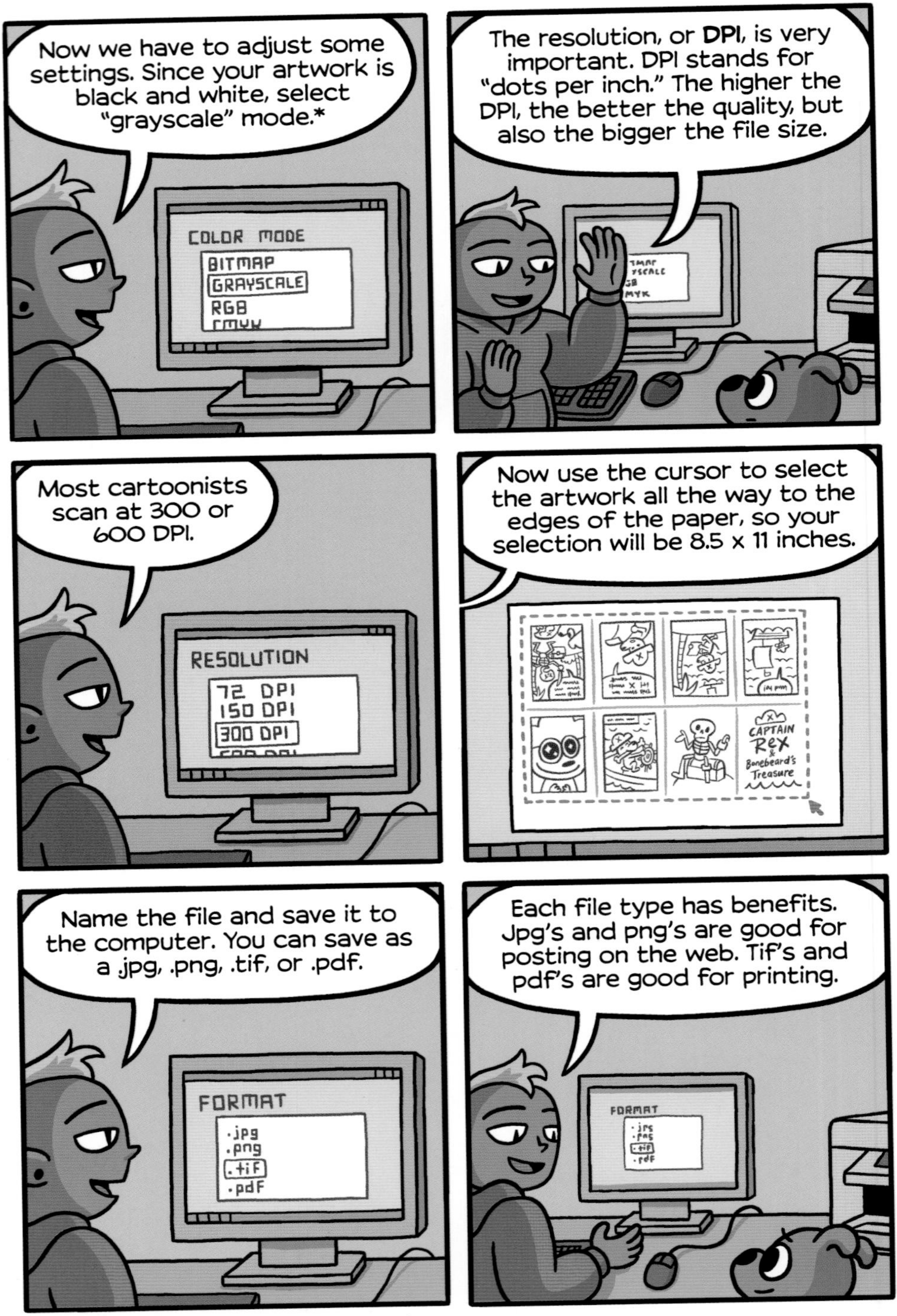
Now we have to adjust some settings. Since your artwork is black and white, select "grayscale" mode.*
COLOR MODE
BITMAP
GRAYSCALE
RGB
The resolution, or **DPI**, is very important. DPI stands for "dots per inch." The higher the DPI, the better the quality, but also the bigger the file size.
Most cartoonists scan at 300 or 600 DPI.
RESOLUTION
72 DPI
150 DPI
300 DPI
Now use the cursor to select the artwork all the way to the edges of the paper, so your selection will be 8.5 x 11 inches.
CAPTAIN
Rex
&
Bonebeard's
Treasure
Name the file and save it to the computer. You can save as a .jpg, .png, .tif, or .pdf.
FORMAT
.jpg
.png
.tif
.pdf
Each file type has benefits. Jpg's and png's are good for posting on the web. Tif's and pdf's are good for printing.
FORMAT

*More info on scanning in the glossary.

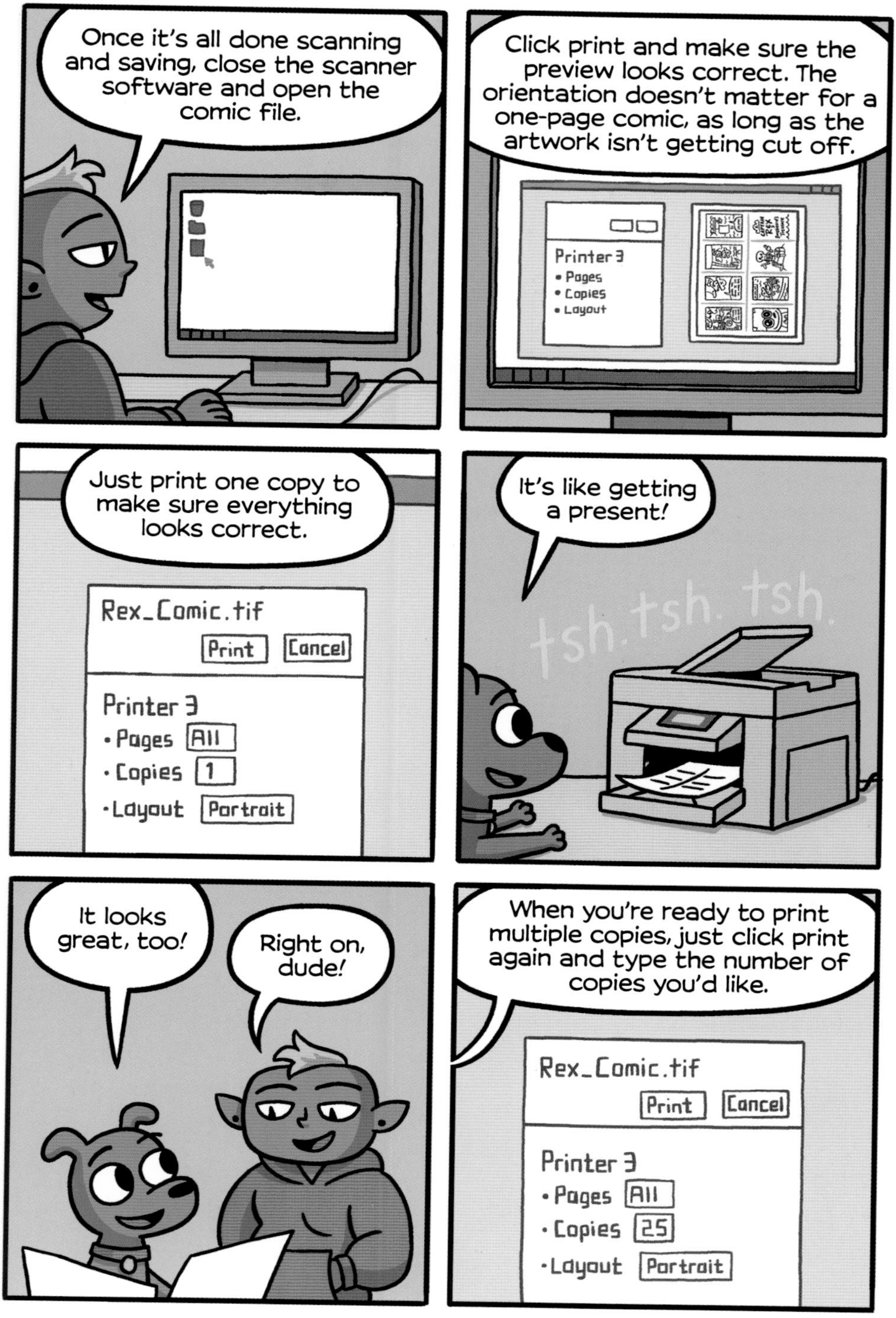
Once it's all done scanning and saving, close the scanner software and open the comic file.
Click print and make sure the preview looks correct. The orientation doesn't matter for a one-page comic, as long as the artwork isn't getting cut off.
Printer 3
• Pages
• Copies
• Layout
Just print one copy to make sure everything looks correct.
Rex_Comic.tif
Print
Cancel
Printer 3
• Pages All
• Copies 1
• Layout Portrait
It's like getting a present!
tsh. tsh. tsh.
It looks great, too!
Right on, dude!
When you're ready to print multiple copies, just click print again and type the number of copies you'd like.
Rex_Comic.tif
Print
Cancel
Printer 3
• Pages All
• Copies 25
• Layout Portrait

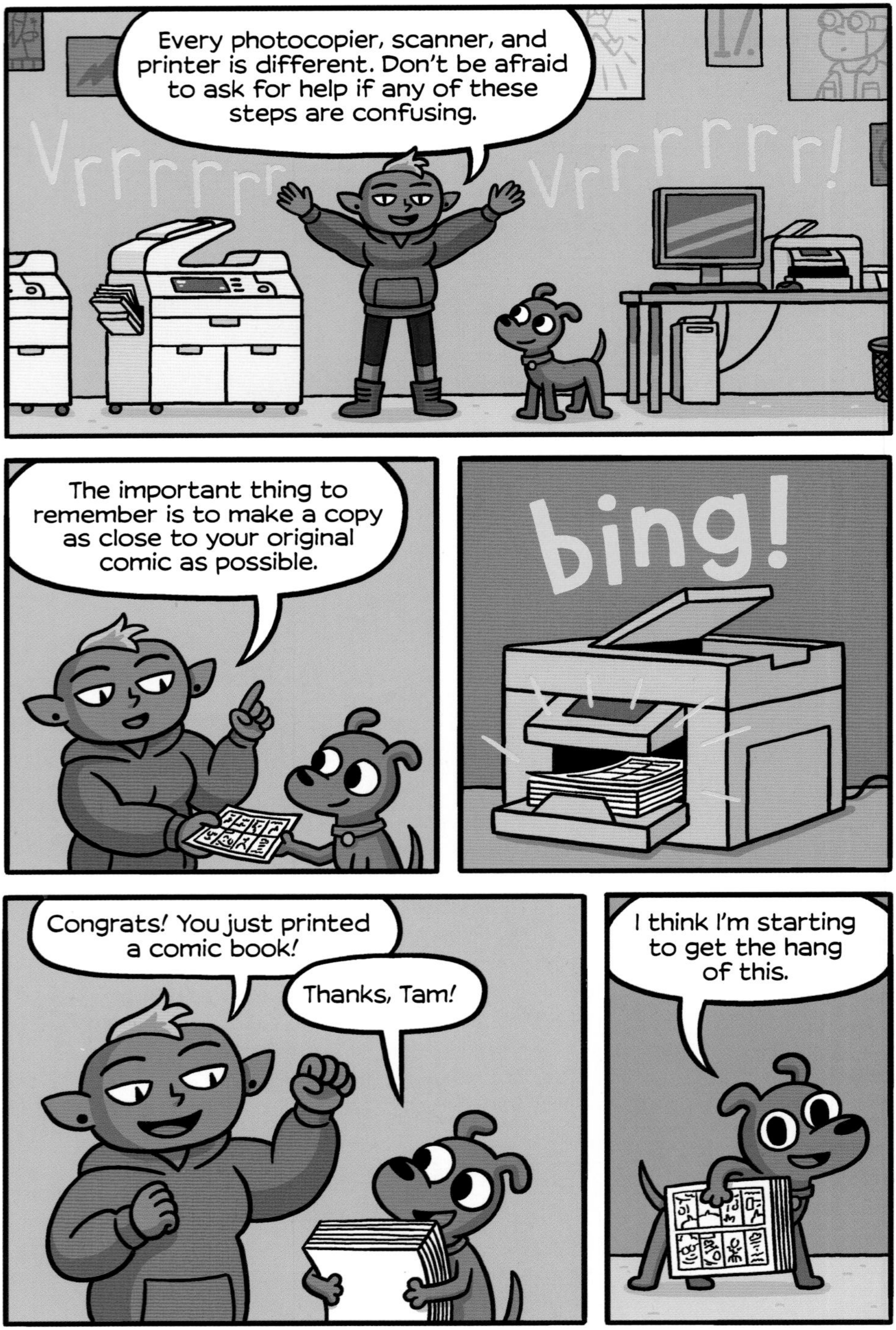

Every photocopier, scanner, and printer is different. Don't be afraid to ask for help if any of these steps are confusing.
Vrrrrrr
Vrrrrrrr!
The important thing to remember is to make a copy as close to your original comic as possible.
bing!
Congrats! You just printed a comic book!
Thanks, Tam!
I think I'm starting to get the hang of this.

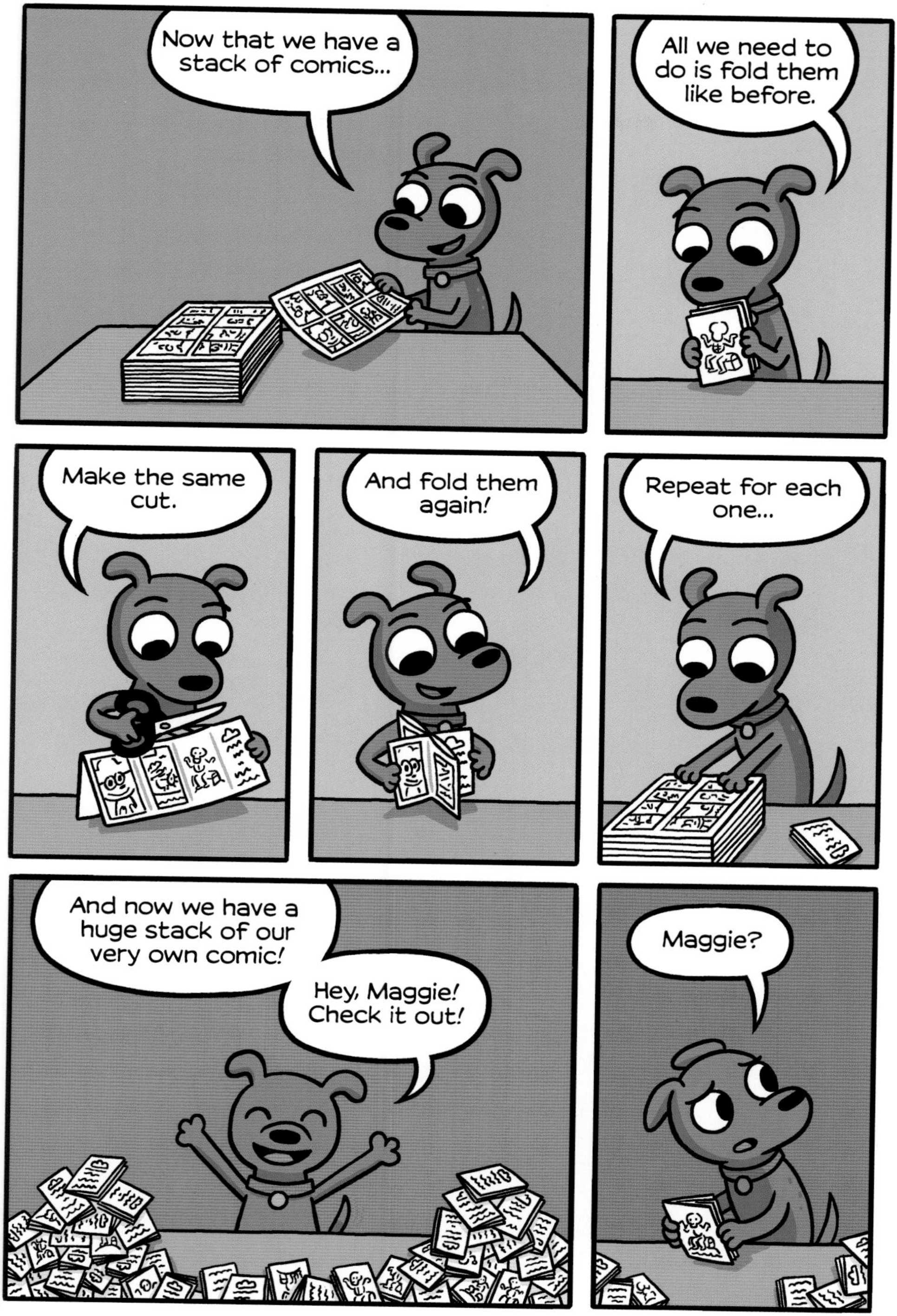
Now that we have a stack of comics...
All we need to do is fold them like before.
Make the same cut.
And fold them again!
Repeat for each one...
And now we have a huge stack of our very own comic!
Hey, Maggie! Check it out!
Maggie?

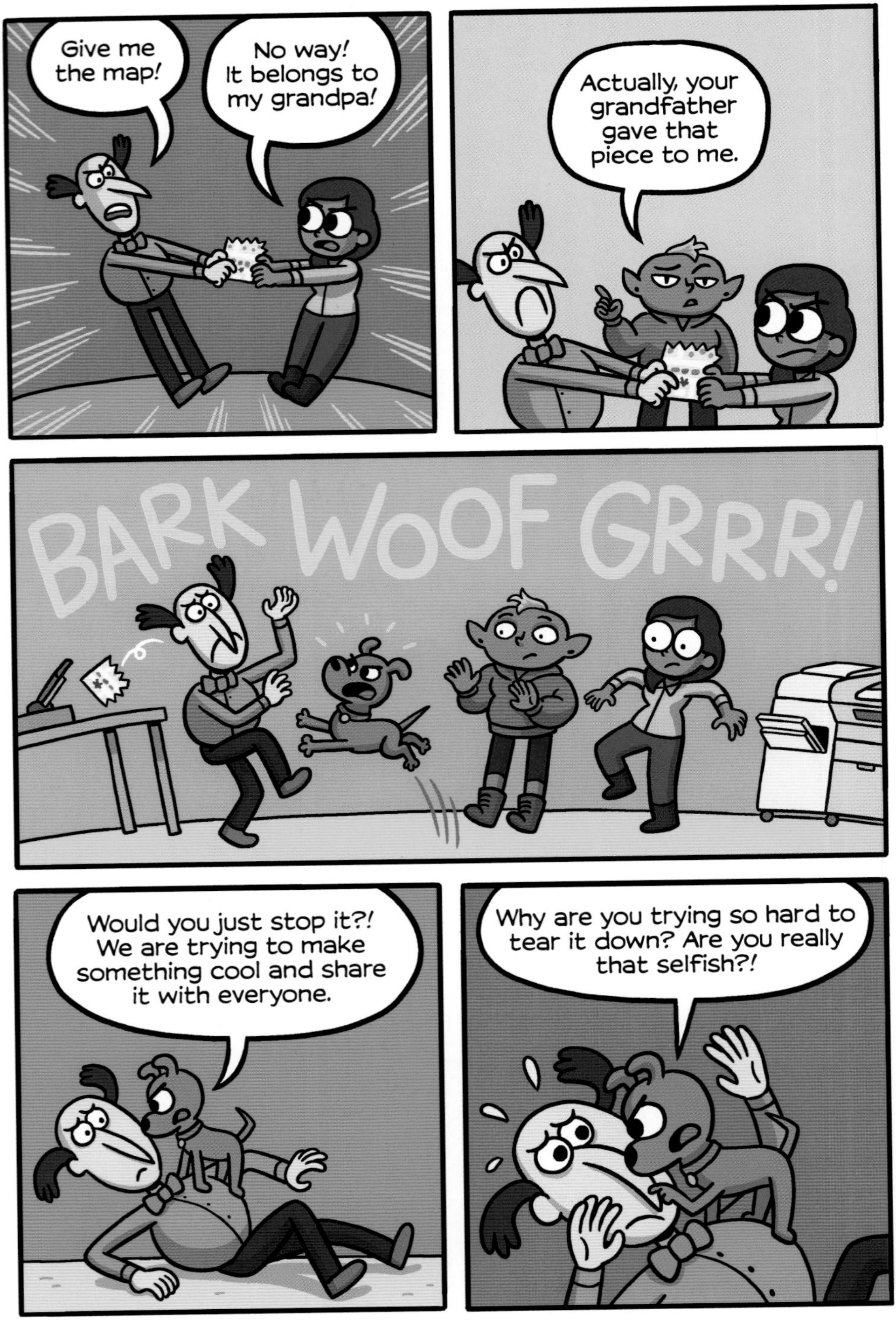
Give me the map!
No way! It belongs to my grandpa!
Actually, your grandfather gave that piece to me.
BARK WOOF GRRR!
Would you just stop it?! We are trying to make something cool and share it with everyone.
Why are you trying so hard to tear it down? Are you really that selfish?!

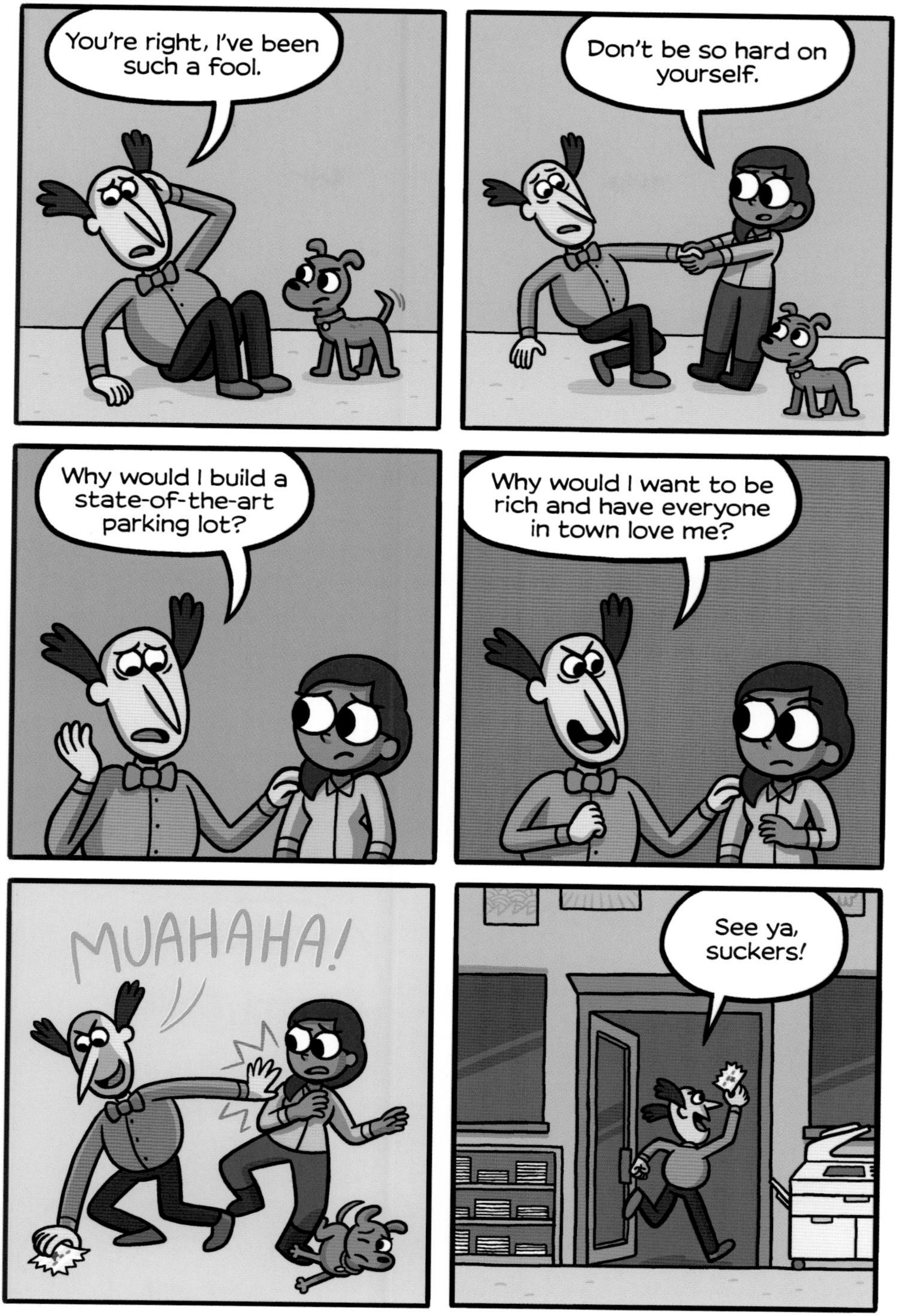
You're right, I've been such a fool.
Don't be so hard on yourself.
Why would I build a state-of-the-art parking lot?
Why would I want to be rich and have everyone in town love me?
MUAHAHA!
See ya, suckers!

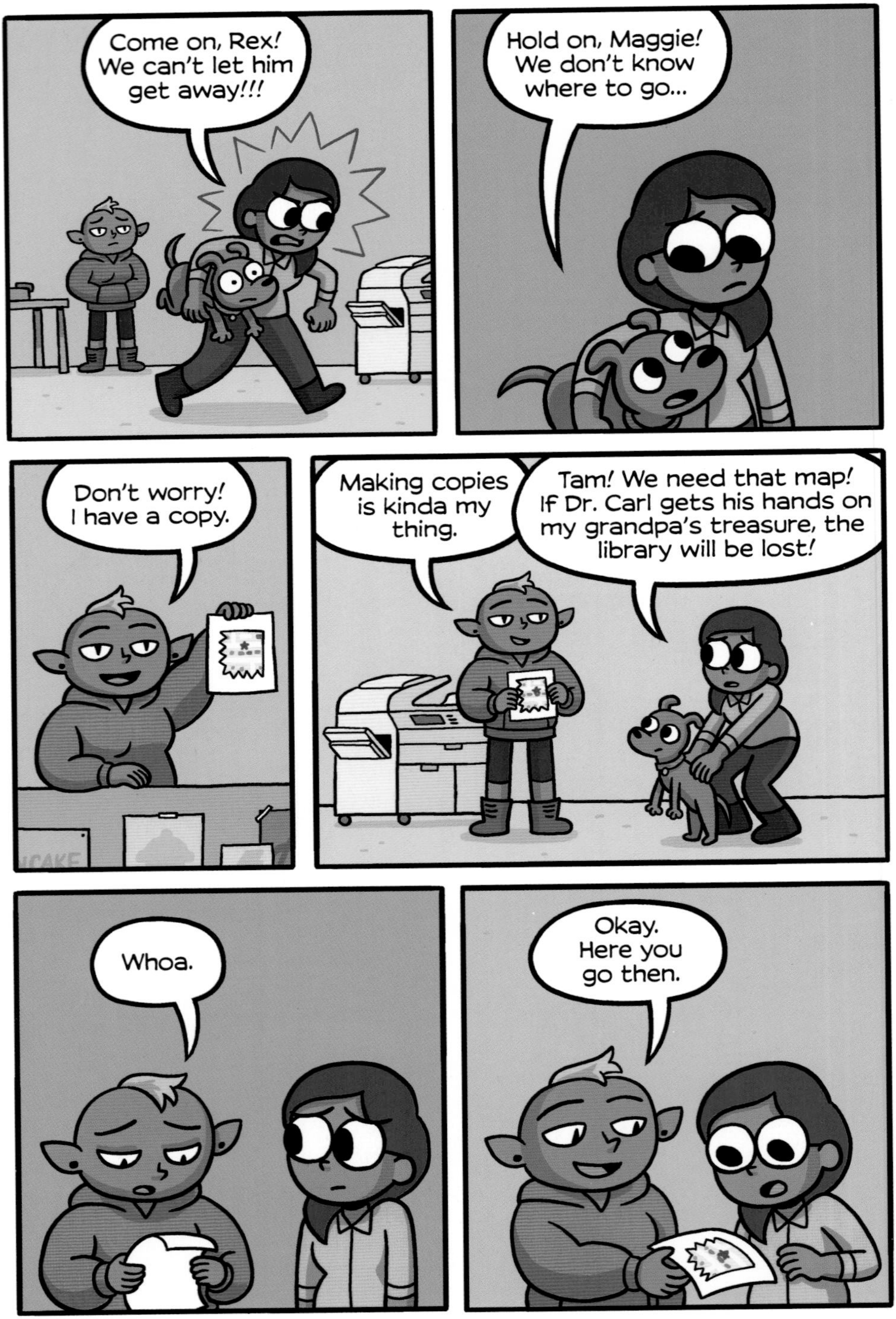
Come on, Rex! We can't let him get away!!!
Hold on, Maggie! We don't know where to go...
Don't worry! I have a copy.
Making copies is kinda my thing.
Tam! We need that map! If Dr. Carl gets his hands on my grandpa's treasure, the library will be lost!
Whoa.
Okay. Here you go then.

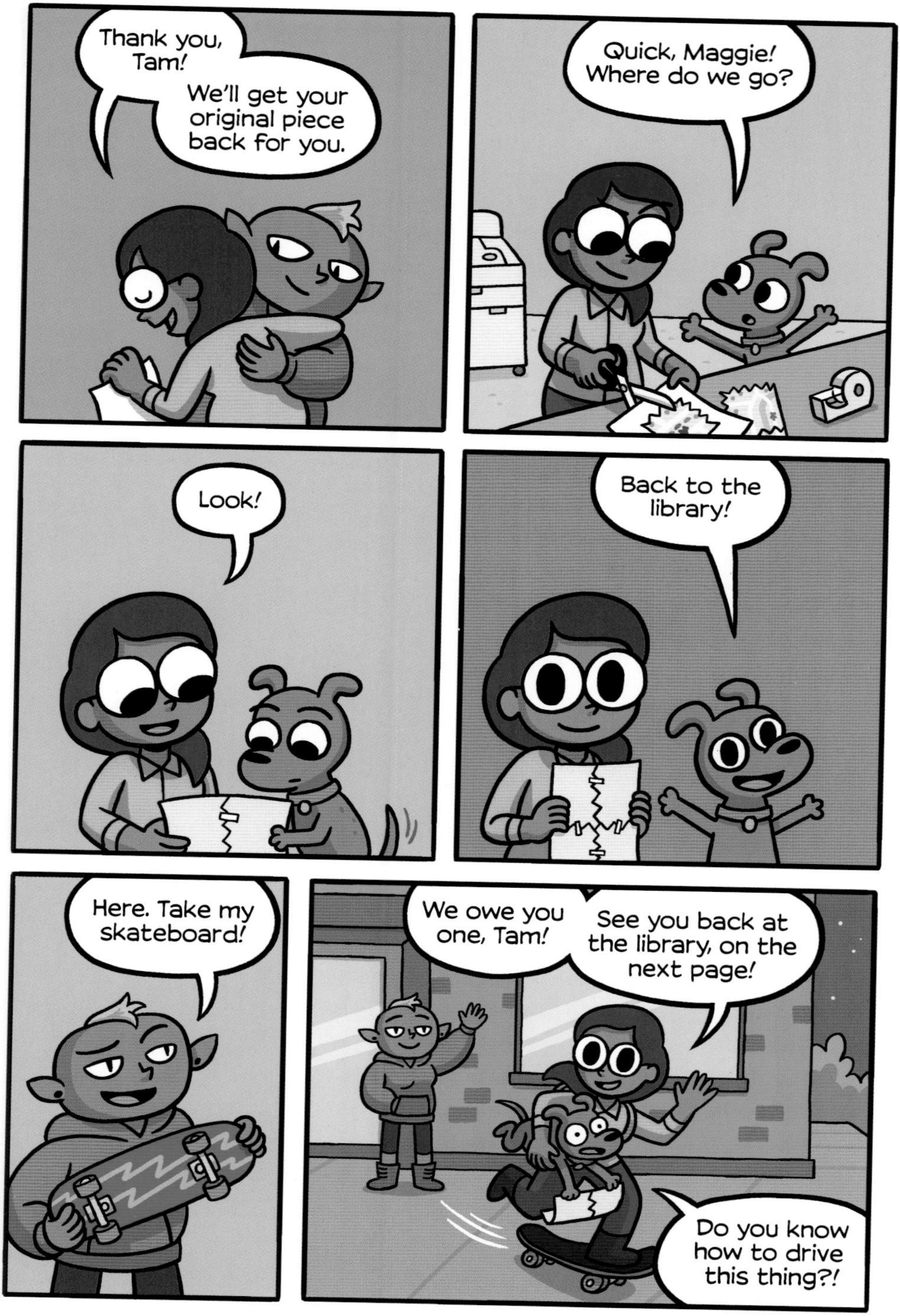
Thank you, Tam!
We'll get your original piece back for you.
Quick, Maggie! Where do we go?
Look!
Back to the library!
Here. Take my skateboard!
We owe you one, Tam!
See you back at the library, on the next page!
Do you know how to drive this thing?!

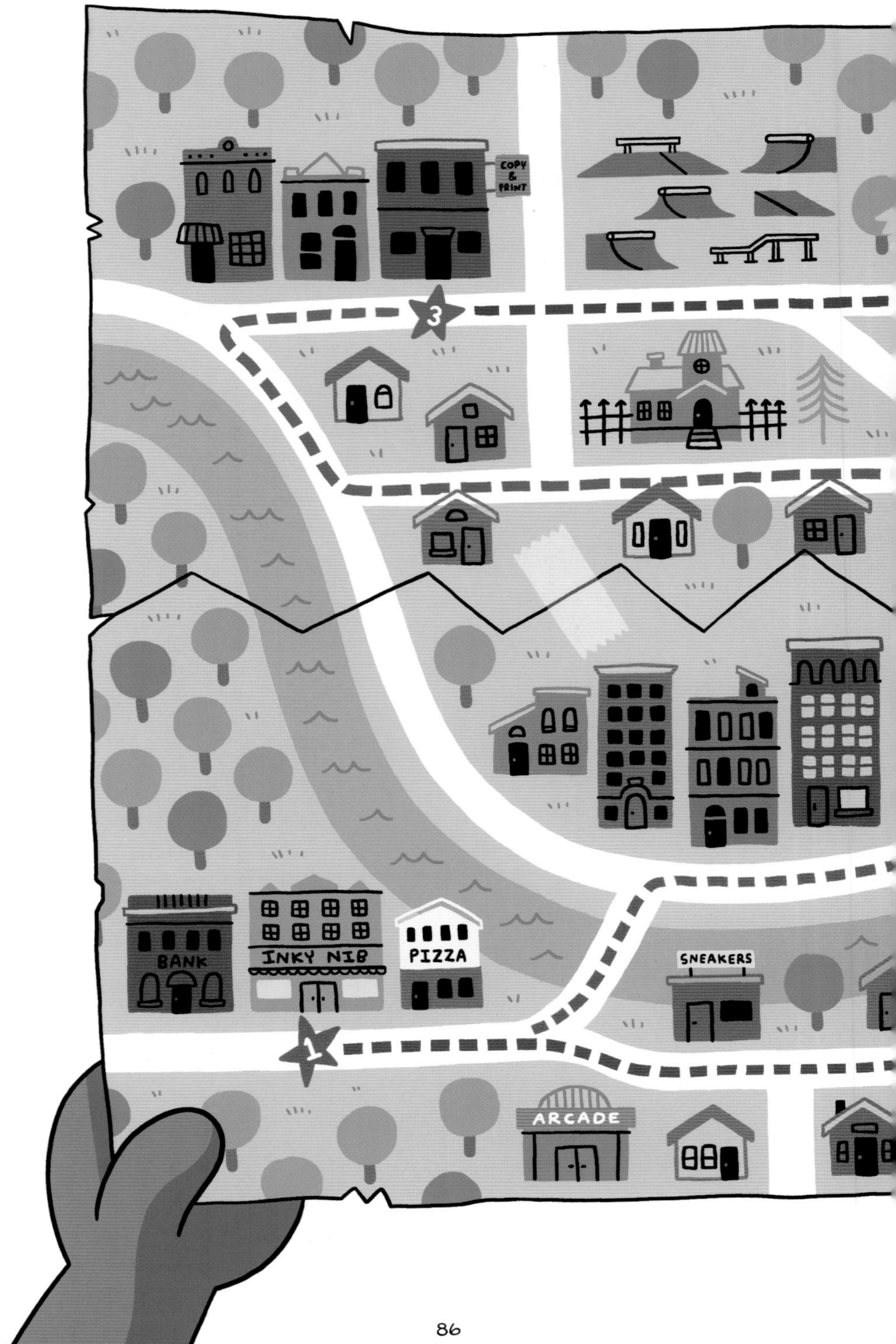
COPY & PRINT
3
BANK
INKY NIB
PIZZA
SNEAKERS
1
ARCADE

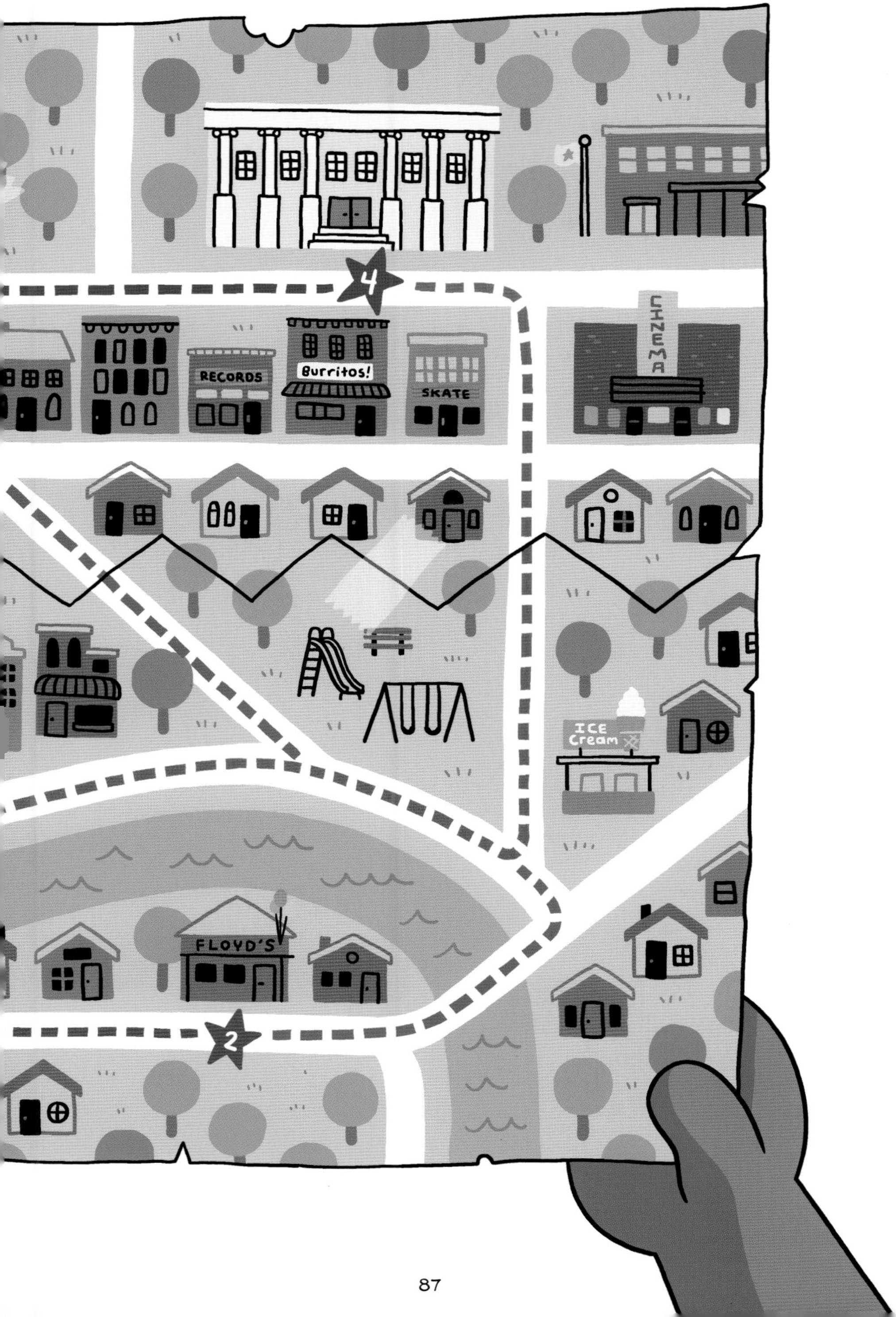

4
CINEMA
RECORDS
Burritos!
SKATE
ICE Cream
FLOYD'S
2

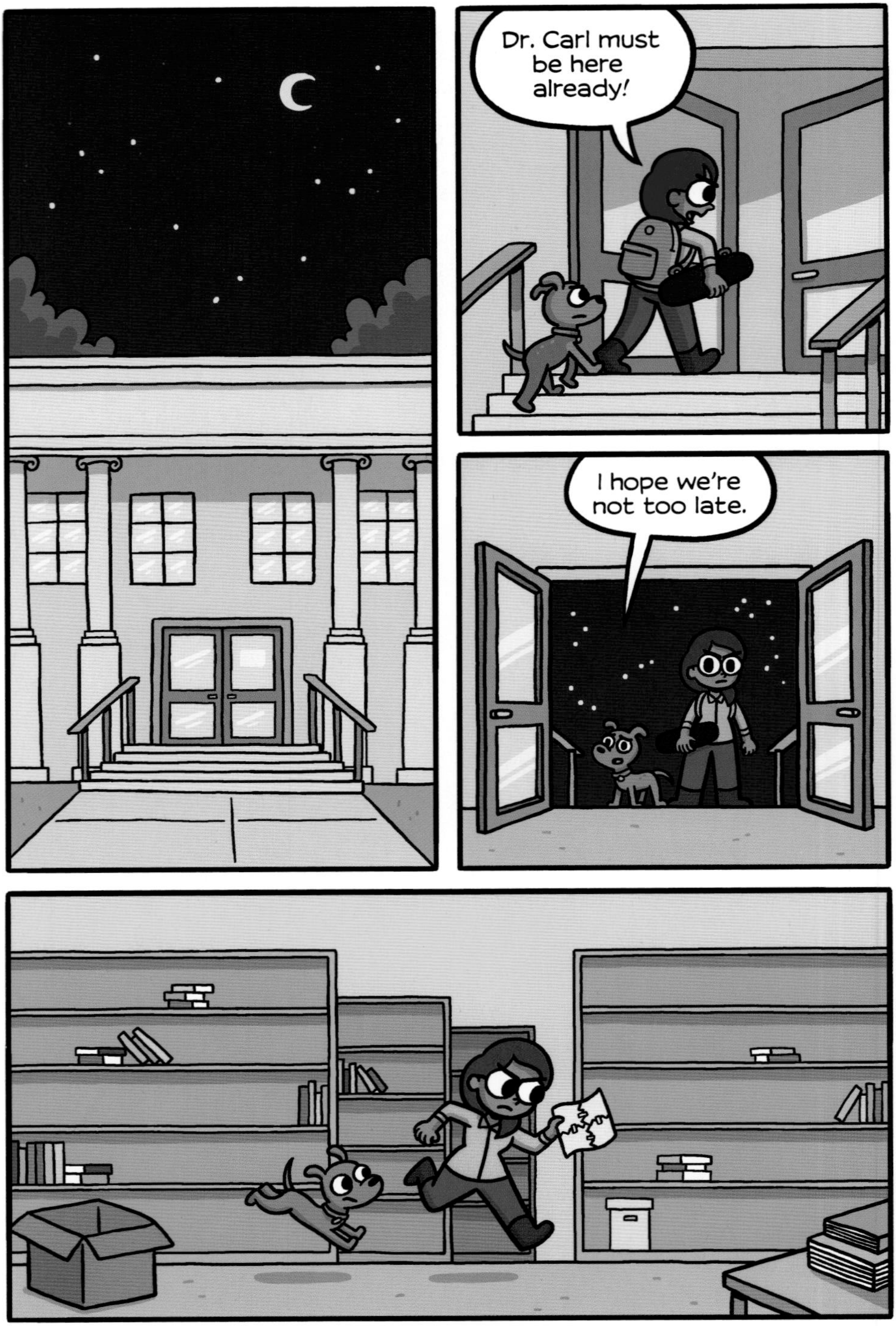
Dr. Carl must be here already!
I hope we're not too late.

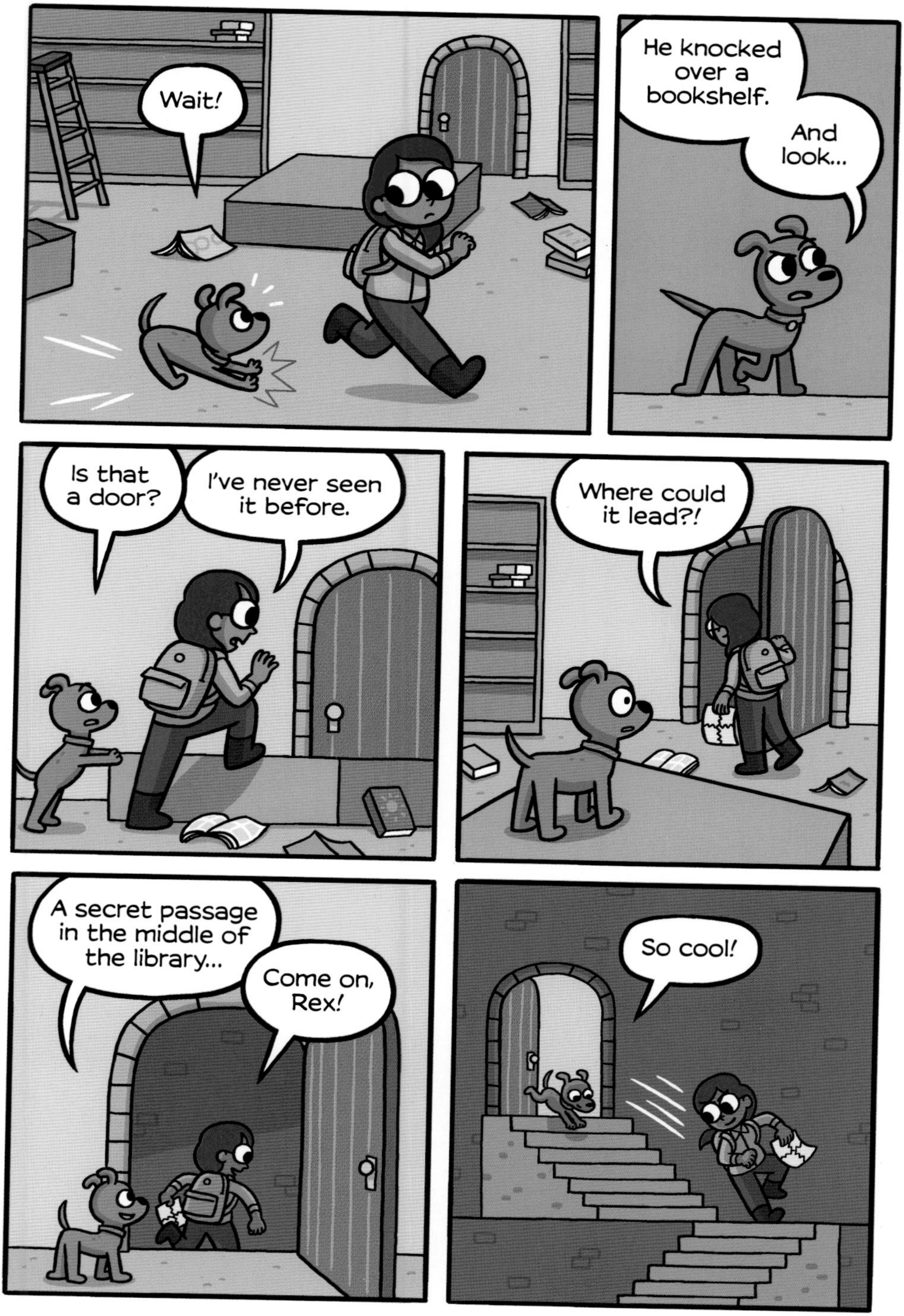
Wait!
He knocked over a bookshelf.
And look...
Is that a door?
I've never seen it before.
Where could it lead?!
A secret passage in the middle of the library...
Come on, Rex!
So cool!

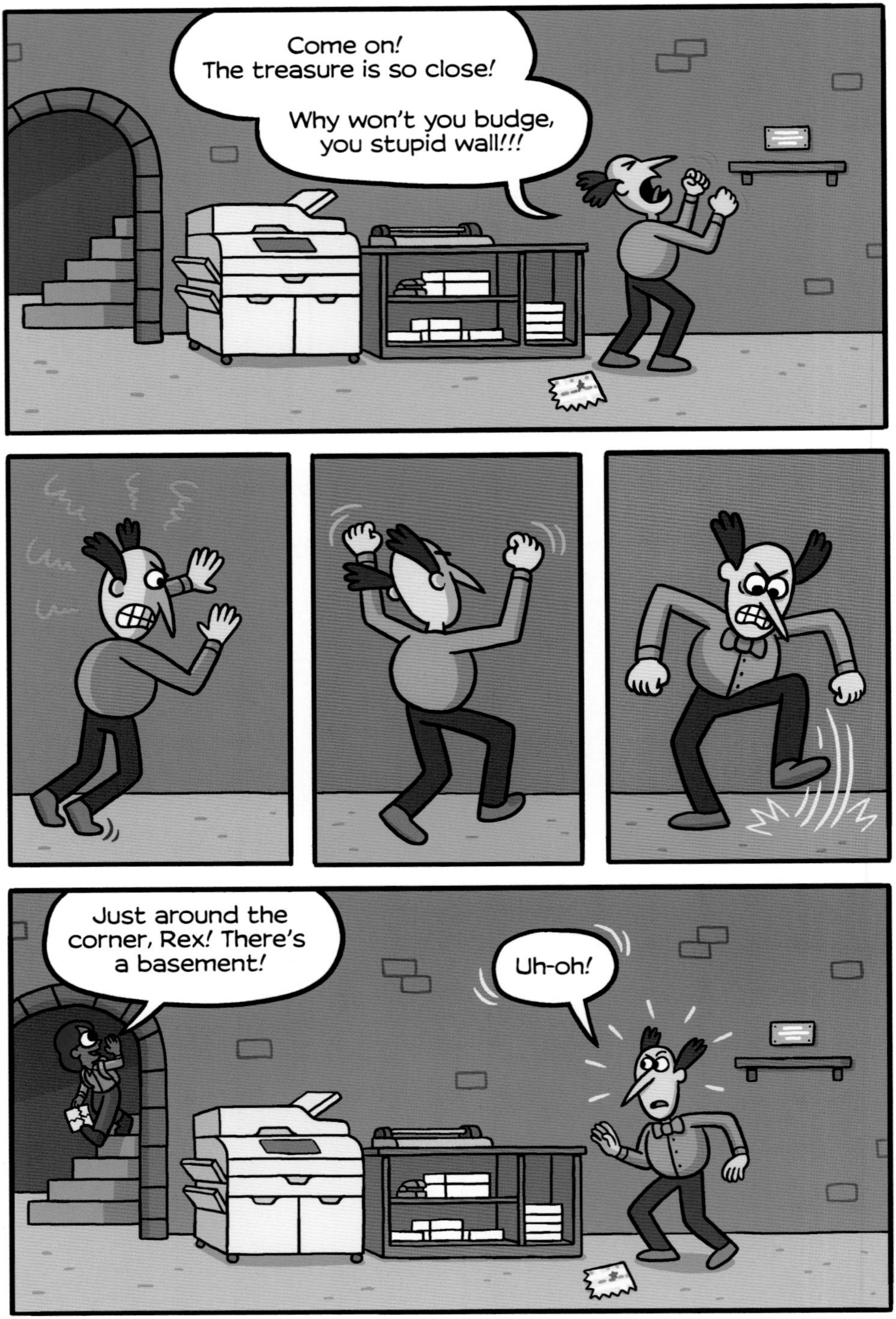
Come on!
The treasure is so close!
Why won't you budge,
you stupid wall!!!
Just around the corner, Rex! There's a basement!
Uh-oh!

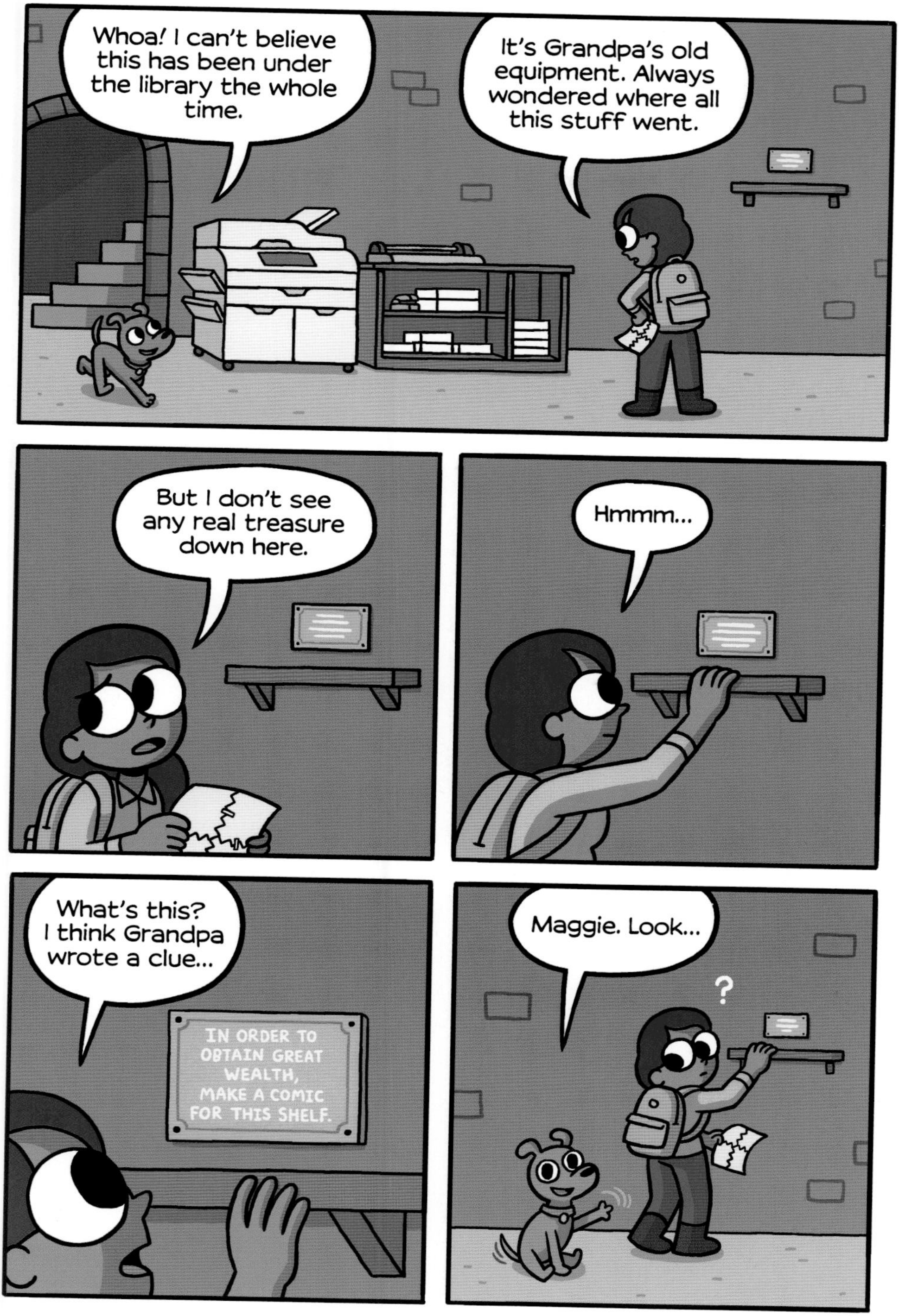
Whoa! I can't believe this has been under the library the whole time.
It's Grandpa's old equipment. Always wondered where all this stuff went.
But I don't see any real treasure down here.
Hmmm...
What's this? I think Grandpa wrote a clue...
IN ORDER TO OBTAIN GREAT WEALTH, MAKE A COMIC FOR THIS SHELF.
Maggie. Look...
?

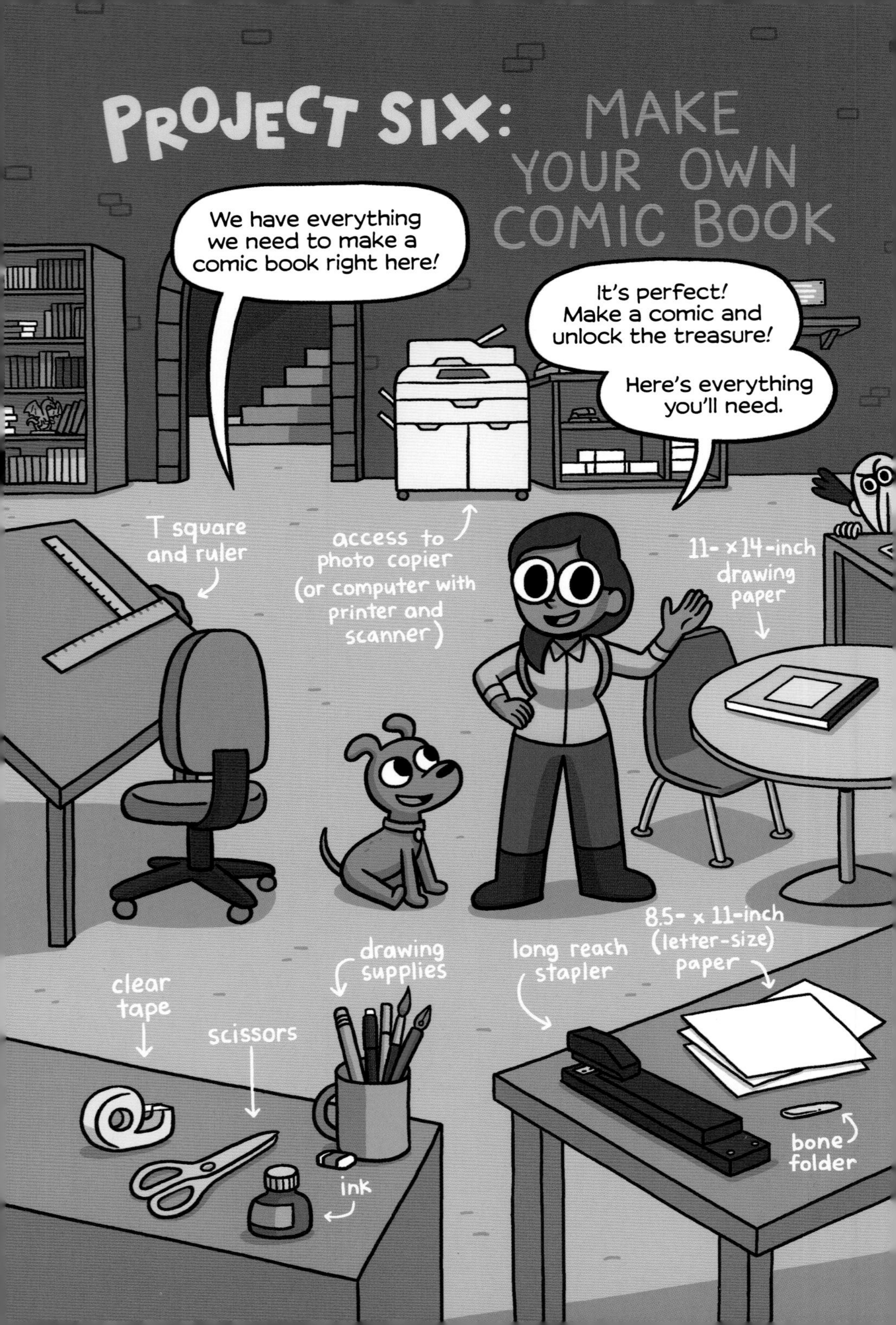

PROJECT SIX: MAKE YOUR OWN COMIC BOOK
We have everything we need to make a comic book right here!
It's perfect! Make a comic and unlock the treasure!
Here's everything you'll need.
T square and ruler
access to photo copier (or computer with printer and scanner)
11- x 14-inch drawing paper
clear tape
scissors
drawing supplies
ink
long reach stapler
8.5- x 11-inch (letter-size) paper
bone folder

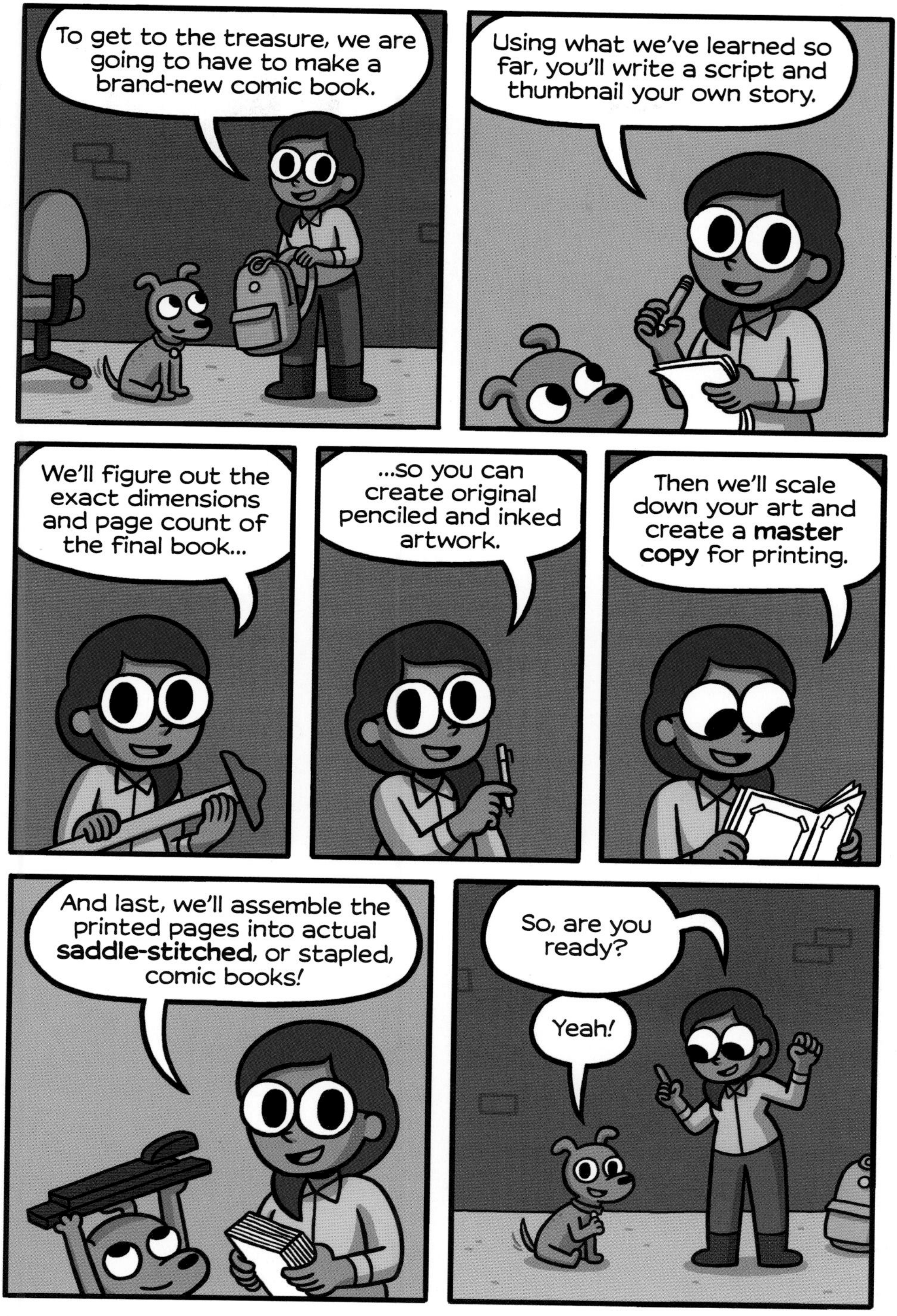
To get to the treasure, we are going to have to make a brand-new comic book.
Using what we've learned so far, you'll write a script and thumbnail your own story.
We'll figure out the exact dimensions and page count of the final book...
...so you can create original penciled and inked artwork.
Then we'll scale down your art and create a **master copy** for printing.
And last, we'll assemble the printed pages into actual **saddle-stitched**, or stapled, comic books!
So, are you ready?
Yeah!

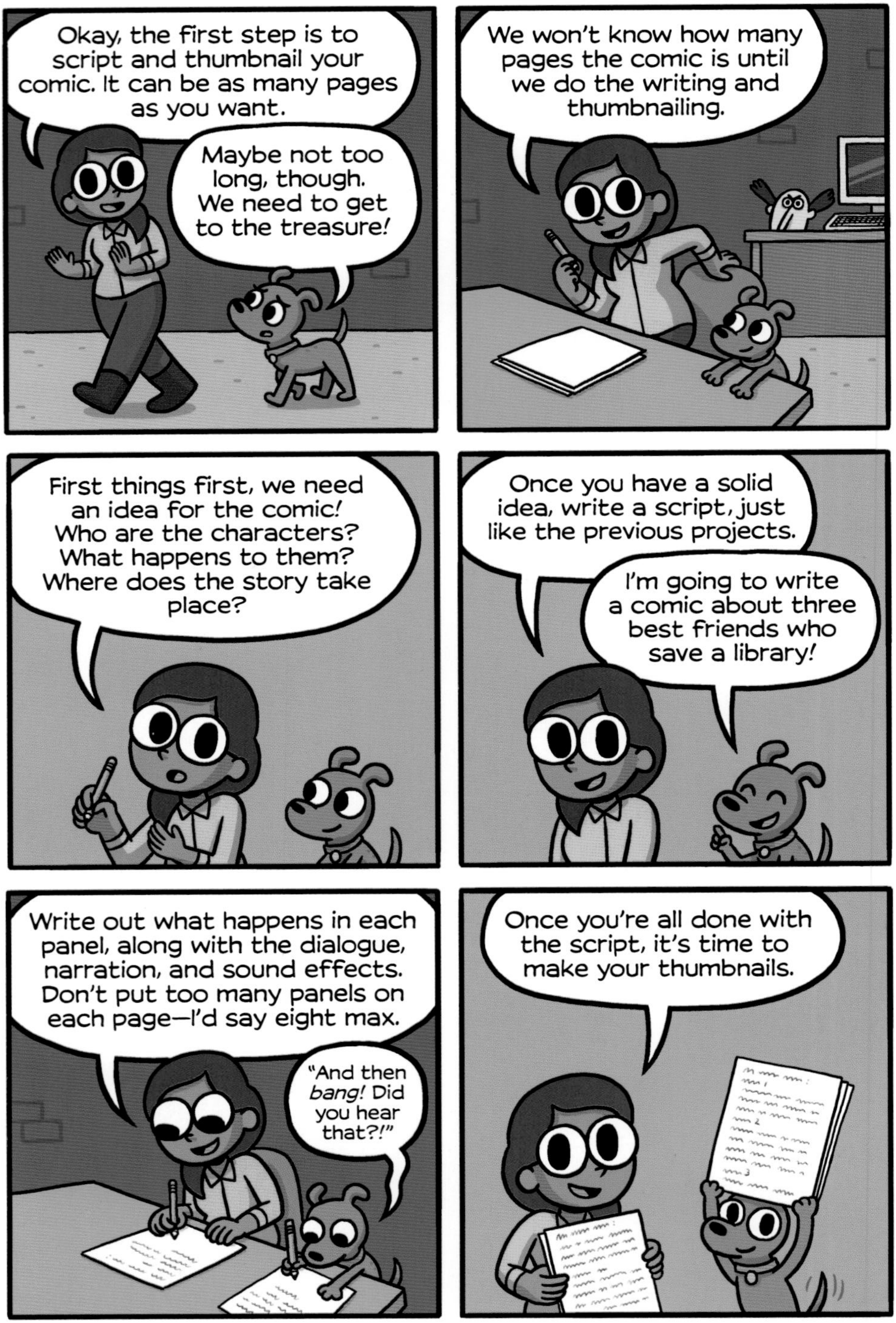
Okay, the first step is to script and thumbnail your comic. It can be as many pages as you want.
Maybe not too long, though. We need to get to the treasure!
We won't know how many pages the comic is until we do the writing and thumbnailing.
First things first, we need an idea for the comic! Who are the characters? What happens to them? Where does the story take place?
Once you have a solid idea, write a script, just like the previous projects.
I'm going to write a comic about three best friends who save a library!
Write out what happens in each panel, along with the dialogue, narration, and sound effects. Don't put too many panels on each page—I'd say eight max.
"And then *bang!* Did you hear that?!"
Once you're all done with the script, it's time to make your thumbnails.

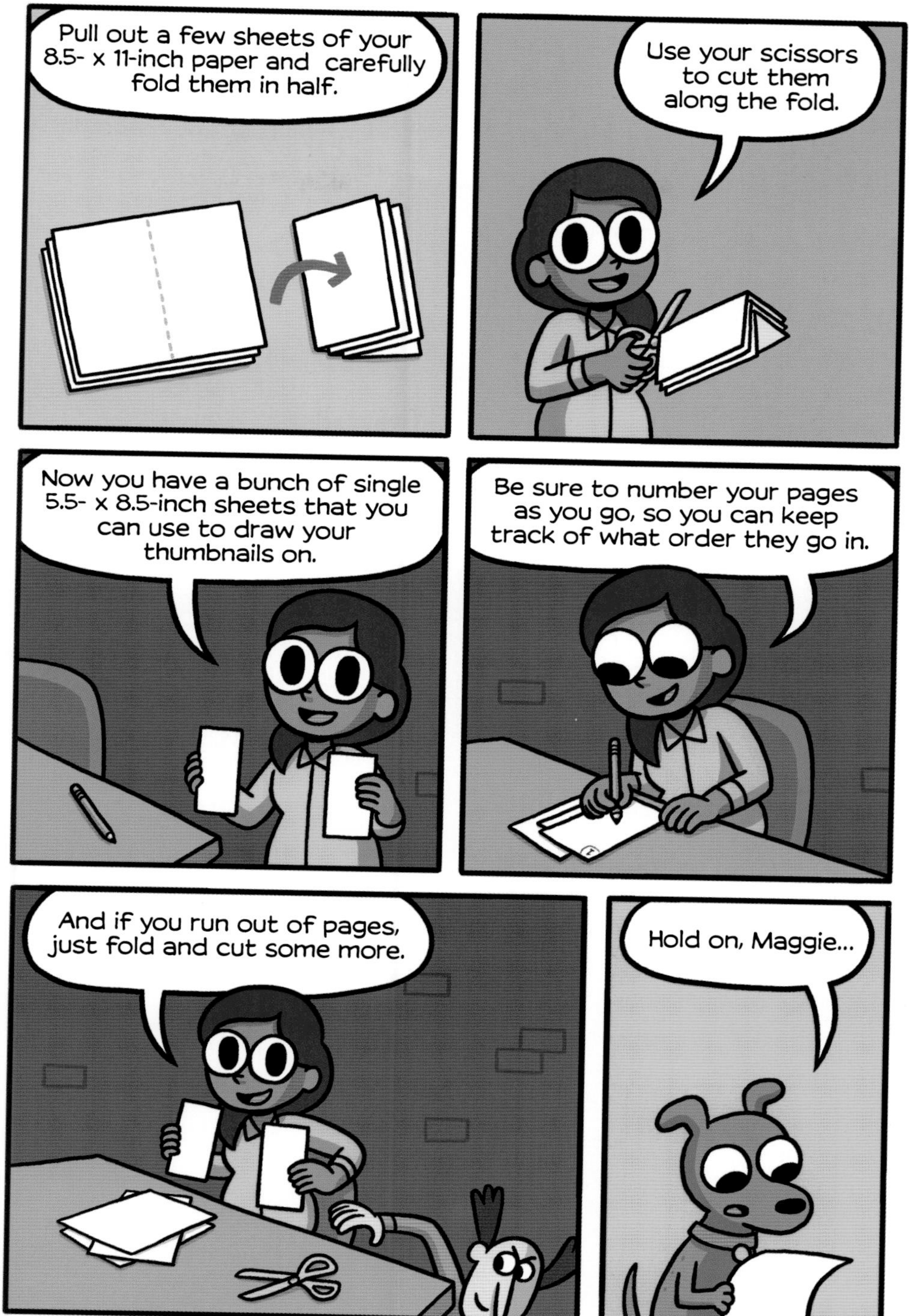
Pull out a few sheets of your 8.5- x 11-inch paper and carefully fold them in half.
Use your scissors to cut them along the fold.
Now you have a bunch of single 5.5- x 8.5-inch sheets that you can use to draw your thumbnails on.
Be sure to number your pages as you go, so you can keep track of what order they go in.
And if you run out of pages, just fold and cut some more.
Hold on, Maggie...

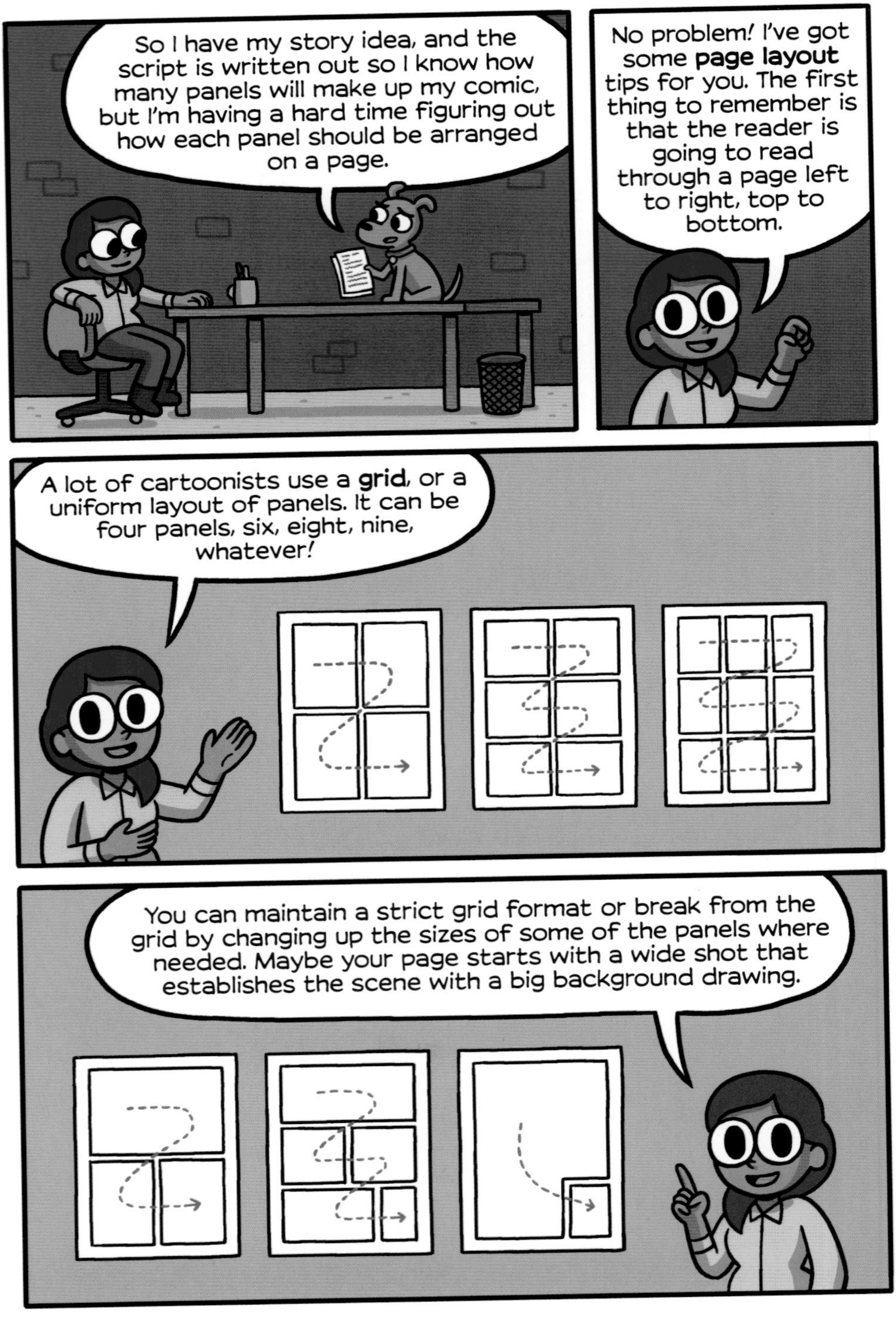
So I have my story idea, and the script is written out so I know how many panels will make up my comic, but I'm having a hard time figuring out how each panel should be arranged on a page.
No problem! I've got some **page layout** tips for you. The first thing to remember is that the reader is going to read through a page left to right, top to bottom.
A lot of cartoonists use a **grid**, or a uniform layout of panels. It can be four panels, six, eight, nine, whatever!
You can maintain a strict grid format or break from the grid by changing up the sizes of some of the panels where needed. Maybe your page starts with a wide shot that establishes the scene with a big background drawing.

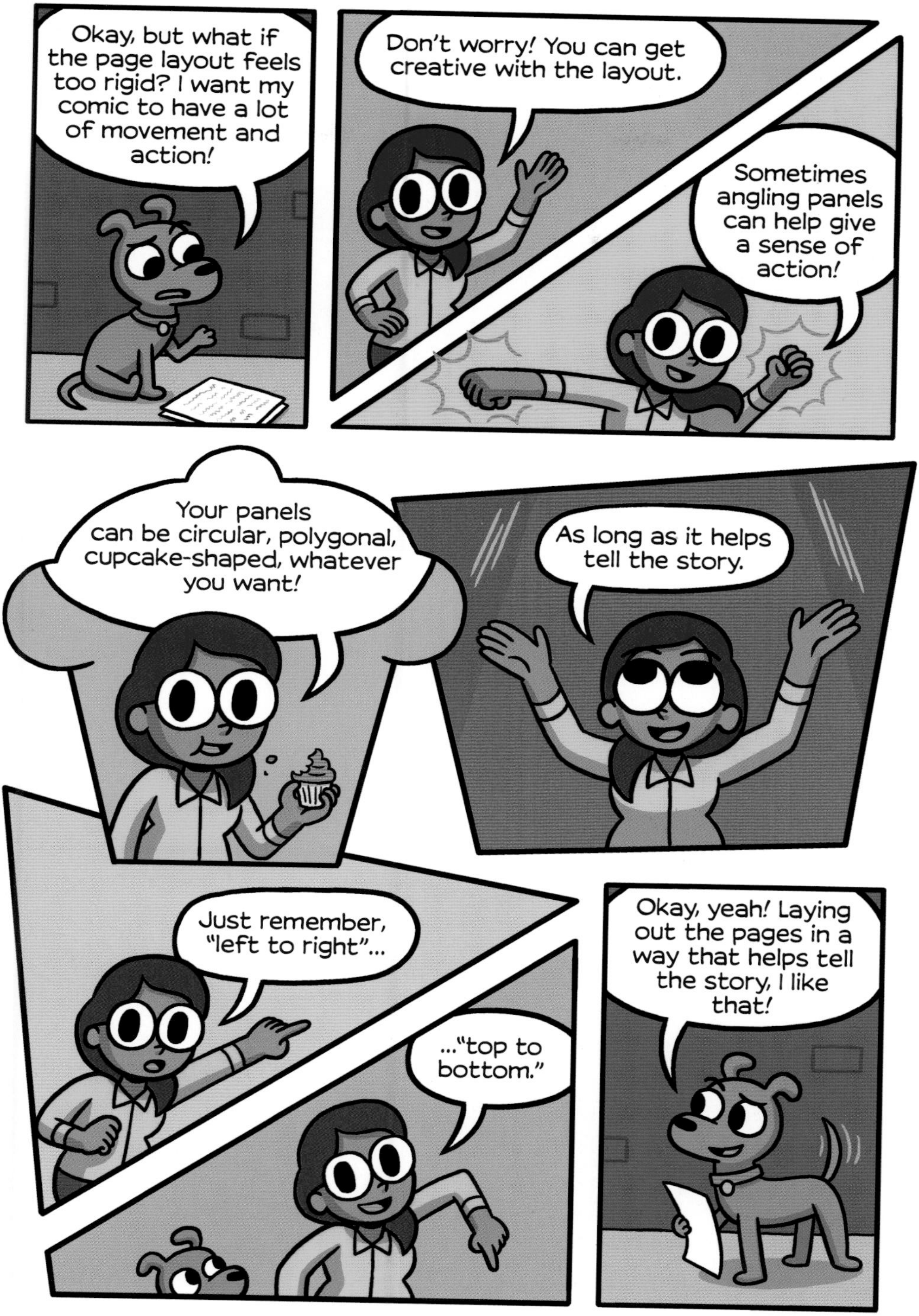
Okay, but what if the page layout feels too rigid? I want my comic to have a lot of movement and action!
Don't worry! You can get creative with the layout.
Sometimes angling panels can help give a sense of action!
Your panels can be circular, polygonal, cupcake-shaped, whatever you want!
As long as it helps tell the story.
Just remember, "left to right"...
..."top to bottom."
Okay, yeah! Laying out the pages in a way that helps tell the story, I like that!

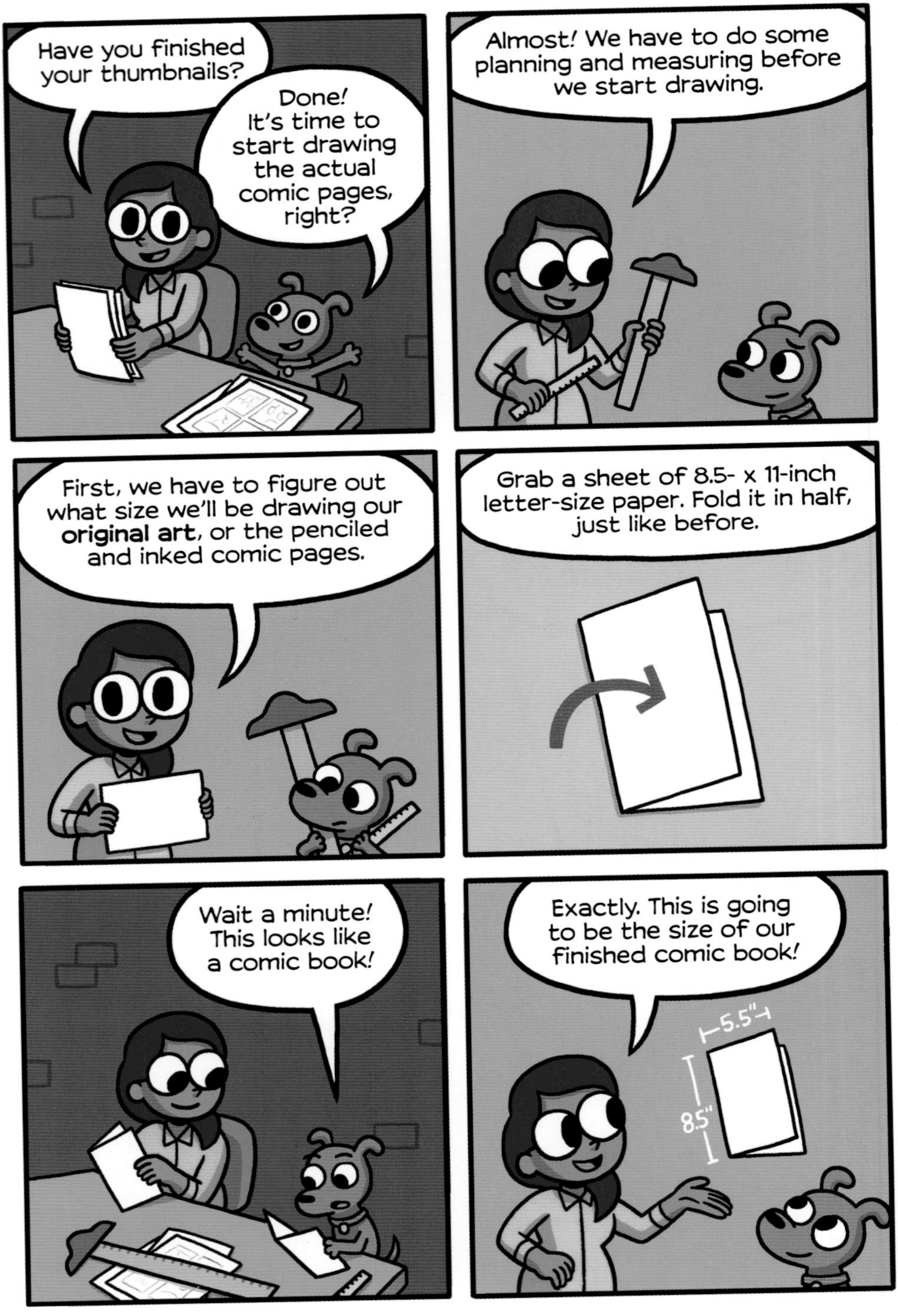
Have you finished your thumbnails?
Done! It's time to start drawing the actual comic pages, right?
Almost! We have to do some planning and measuring before we start drawing.
First, we have to figure out what size we'll be drawing our **original art**, or the penciled and inked comic pages.
Grab a sheet of 8.5- x 11-inch letter-size paper. Fold it in half, just like before.
Wait a minute! This looks like a comic book!
Exactly. This is going to be the size of our finished comic book!
5.5"
8.5"

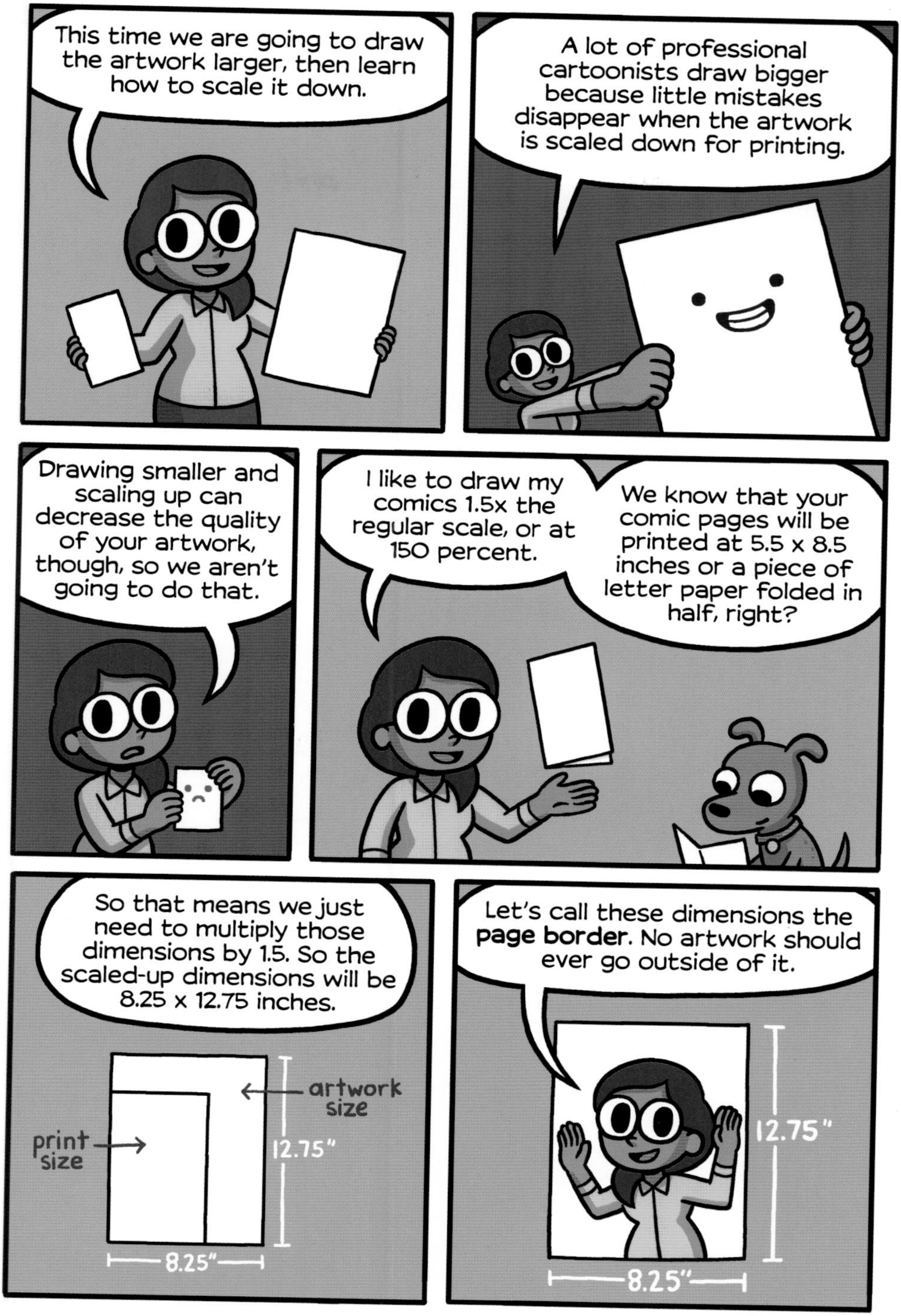
This time we are going to draw the artwork larger, then learn how to scale it down.
A lot of professional cartoonists draw bigger because little mistakes disappear when the artwork is scaled down for printing.
Drawing smaller and scaling up can decrease the quality of your artwork, though, so we aren't going to do that.
I like to draw my comics 1.5x the regular scale, or at 150 percent.
We know that your comic pages will be printed at 5.5 x 8.5 inches or a piece of letter paper folded in half, right?
So that means we just need to multiply those dimensions by 1.5. So the scaled-up dimensions will be 8.25 x 12.75 inches.
artwork size
print size
12.75"
8.25"
Let's call these dimensions the **page border**. No artwork should ever go outside of it.
12.75"
8.25"

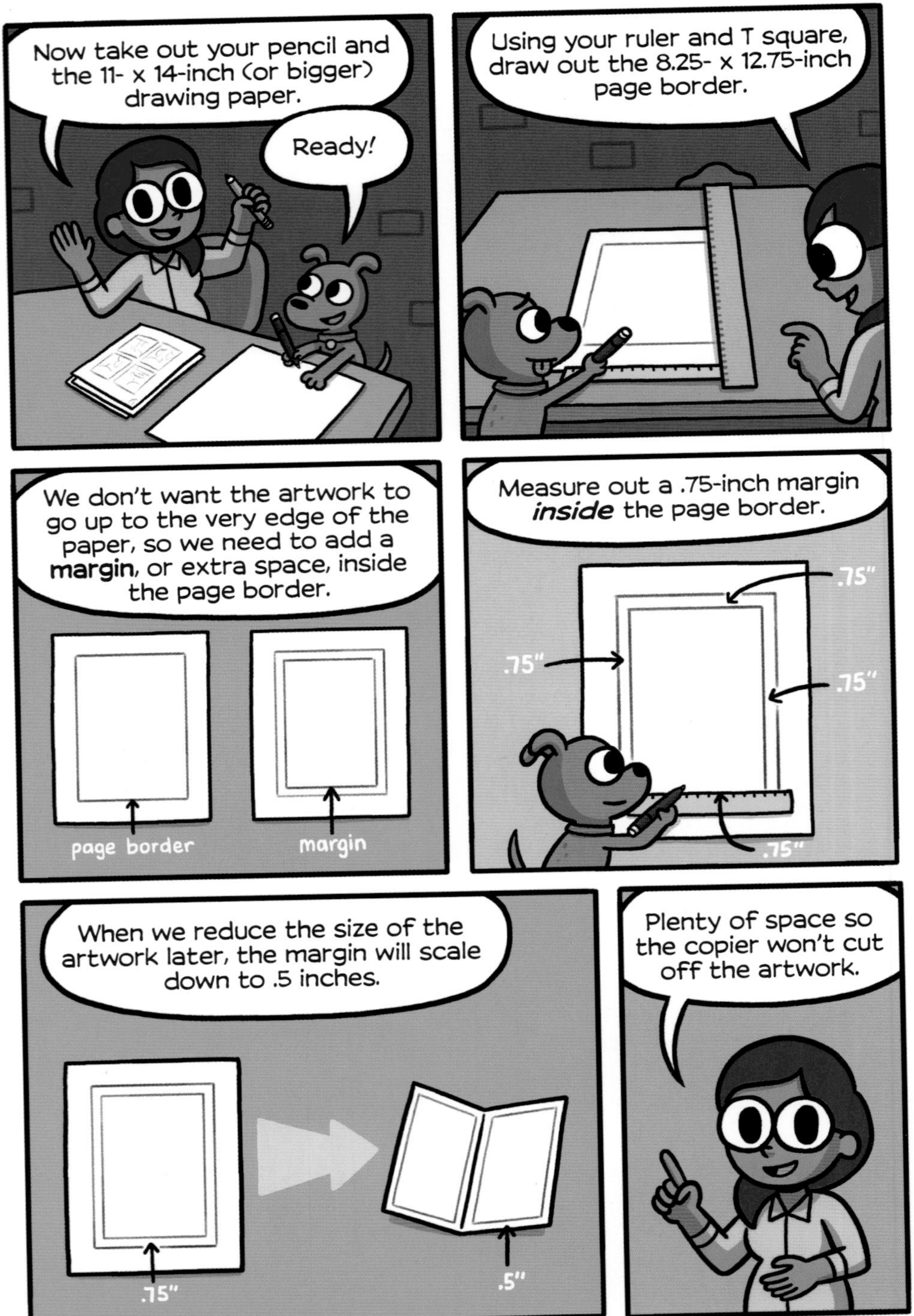
Now take out your pencil and the 11- x 14-inch (or bigger) drawing paper.
Ready!
Using your ruler and T square, draw out the 8.25- x 12.75-inch page border.
We don't want the artwork to go up to the very edge of the paper, so we need to add a **margin**, or extra space, inside the page border.
page border
margin
Measure out a .75-inch margin ***inside*** the page border.
.75"
.75"
.75"
.75"
When we reduce the size of the artwork later, the margin will scale down to .5 inches.
.75"
.5"
Plenty of space so the copier won't cut off the artwork.

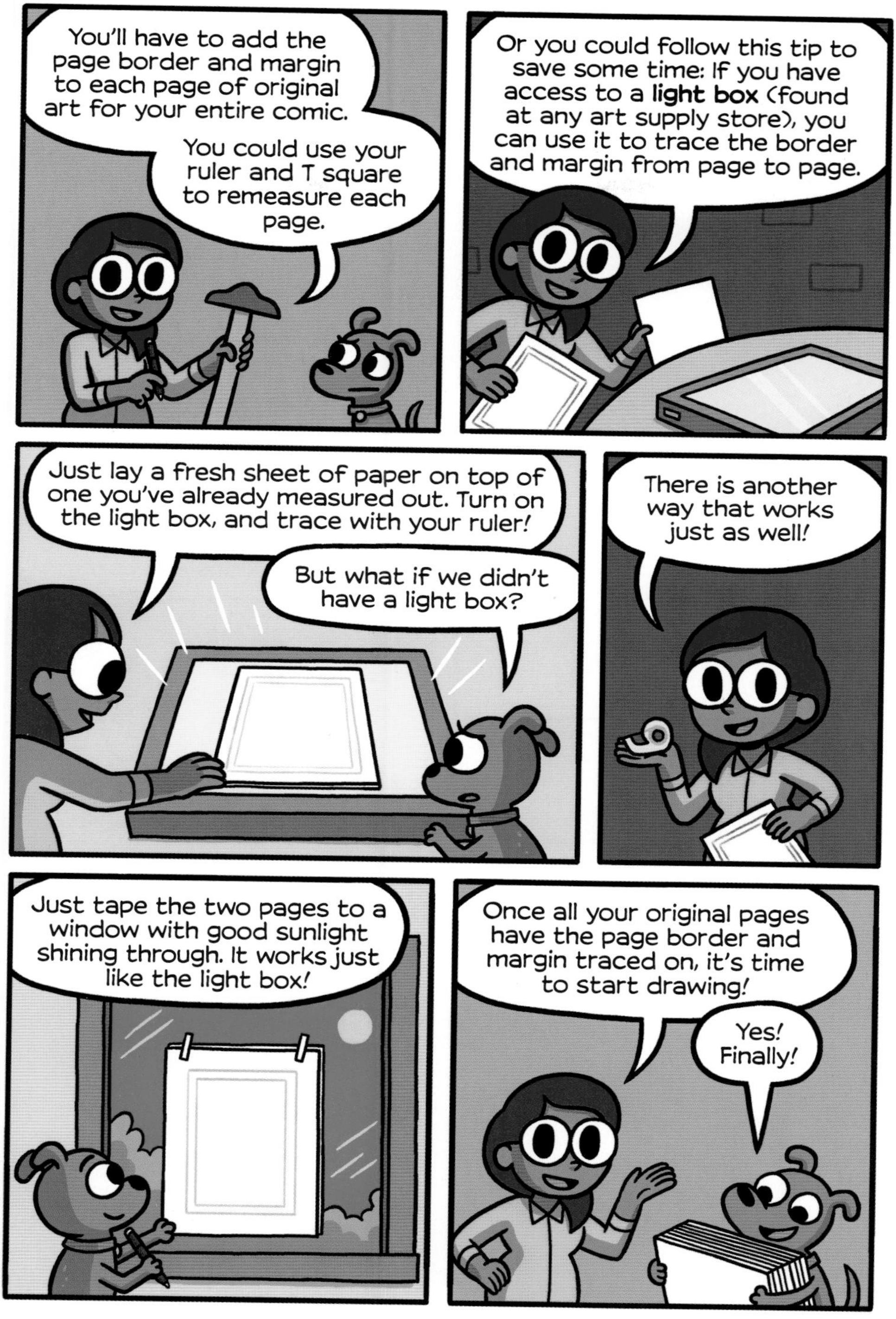
You'll have to add the page border and margin to each page of original art for your entire comic.
You could use your ruler and T square to remeasure each page.
Or you could follow this tip to save some time: If you have access to a **light box** (found at any art supply store), you can use it to trace the border and margin from page to page.
Just lay a fresh sheet of paper on top of one you've already measured out. Turn on the light box, and trace with your ruler!
But what if we didn't have a light box?
There is another way that works just as well!
Just tape the two pages to a window with good sunlight shining through. It works just like the light box!
Once all your original pages have the page border and margin traced on, it's time to start drawing!
Yes! Finally!

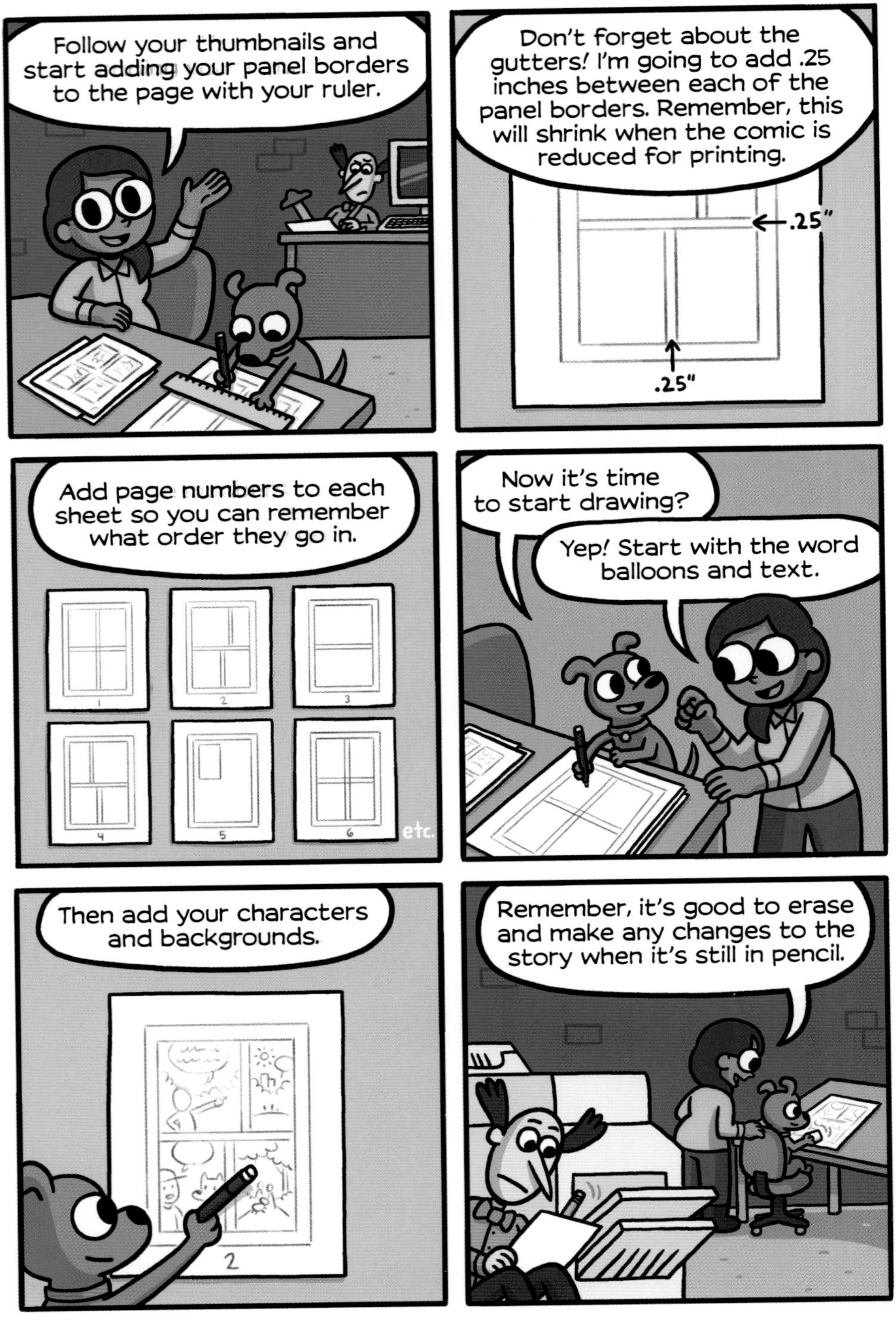
Follow your thumbnails and start adding your panel borders to the page with your ruler.
Don't forget about the gutters! I'm going to add .25 inches between each of the panel borders. Remember, this will shrink when the comic is reduced for printing.
.25"
.25"
Add page numbers to each sheet so you can remember what order they go in.
1
2
3
4
5
6
etc.
Now it's time to start drawing?
Yep! Start with the word balloons and text.
Then add your characters and backgrounds.
2
Remember, it's good to erase and make any changes to the story when it's still in pencil.

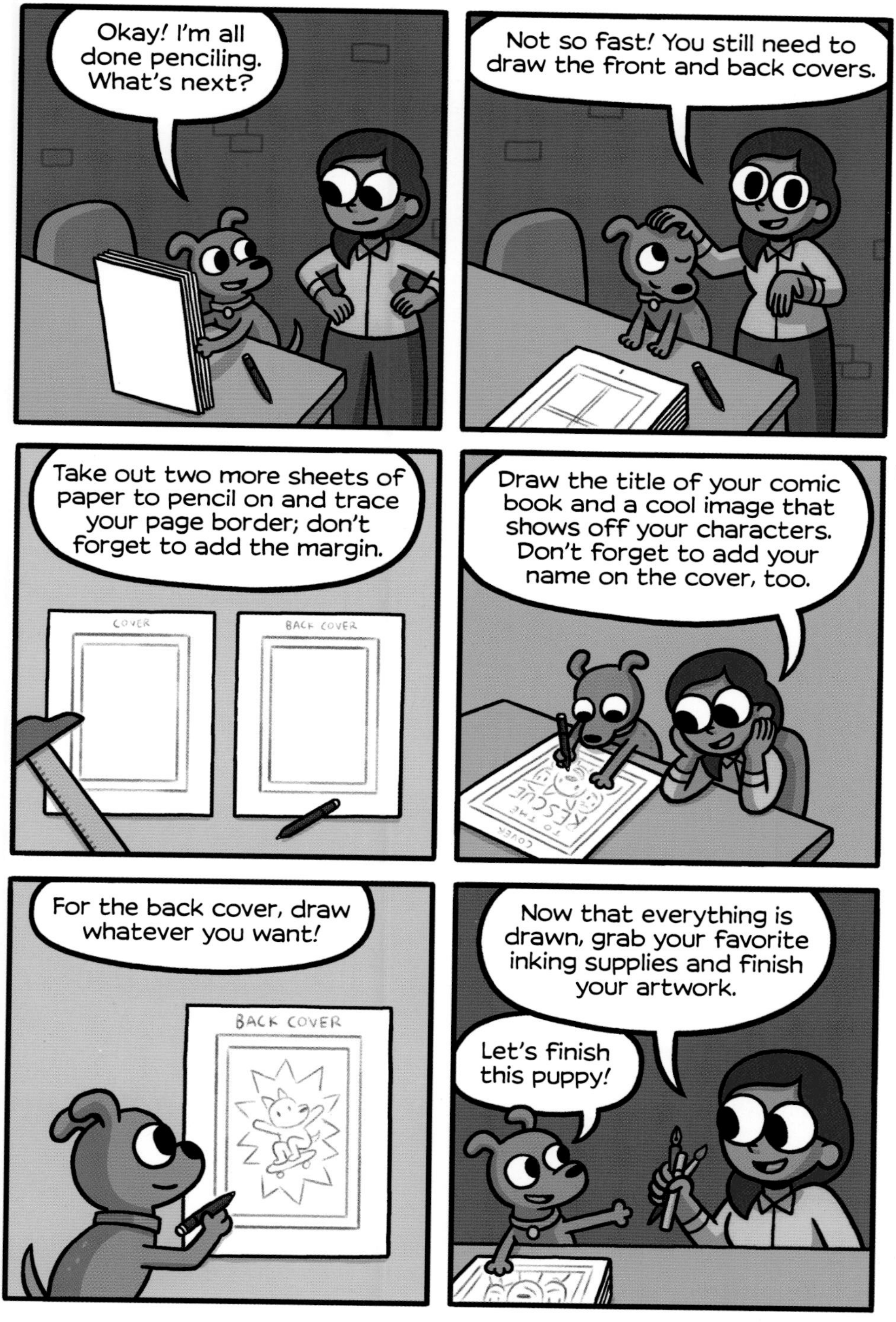
Okay! I'm all done penciling. What's next?
Not so fast! You still need to draw the front and back covers.
Take out two more sheets of paper to pencil on and trace your page border; don't forget to add the margin.
COVER
BACK COVER
Draw the title of your comic book and a cool image that shows off your characters. Don't forget to add your name on the cover, too.
For the back cover, draw whatever you want!
BACK COVER
Now that everything is drawn, grab your favorite inking supplies and finish your artwork.
Let's finish this puppy!

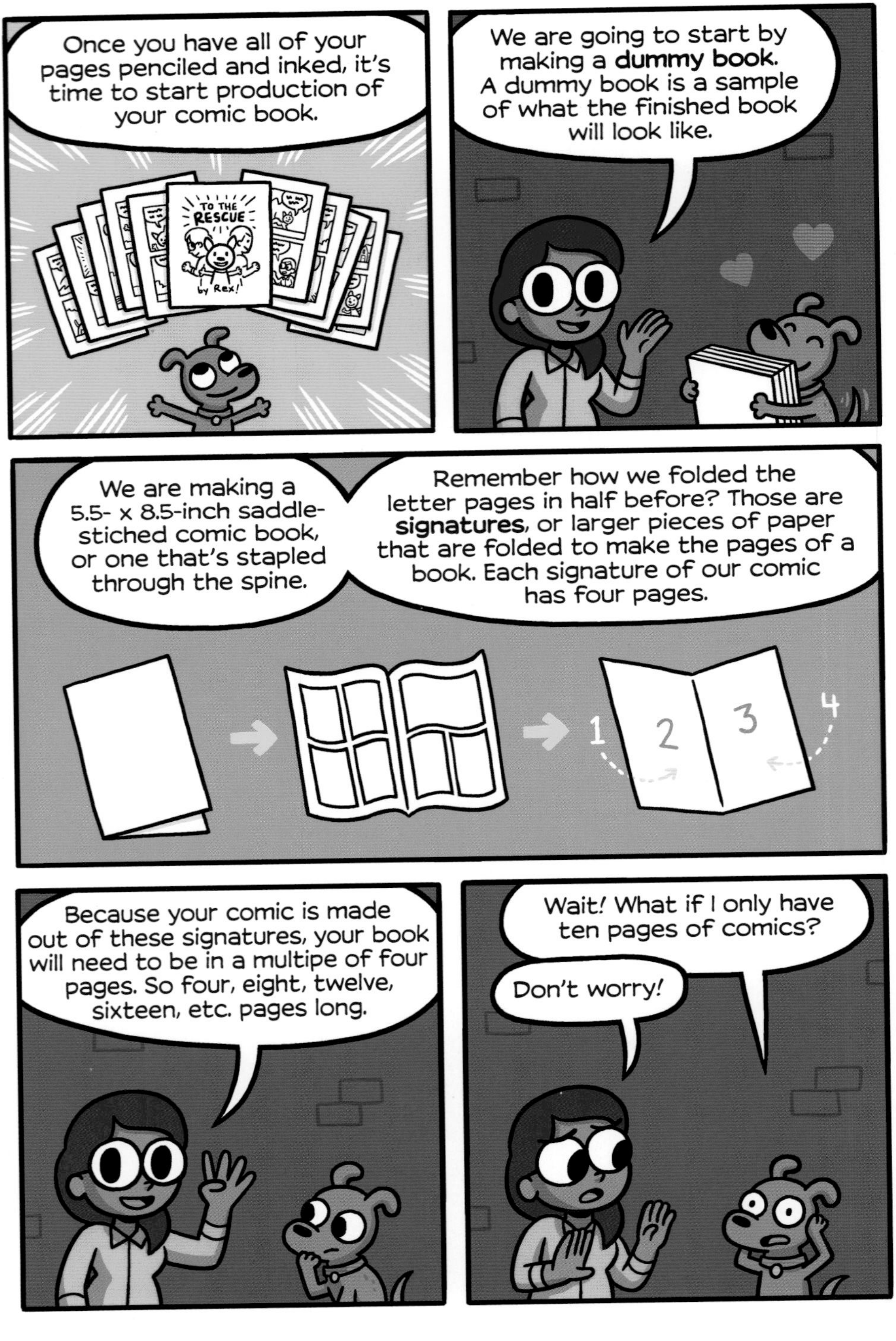
Once you have all of your pages penciled and inked, it's time to start production of your comic book.
TO THE RESCUE
by Rex!
We are going to start by making a **dummy book**. A dummy book is a sample of what the finished book will look like.
We are making a 5.5- x 8.5-inch saddle-stiched comic book, or one that's stapled through the spine.
Remember how we folded the letter pages in half before? Those are **signatures**, or larger pieces of paper that are folded to make the pages of a book. Each signature of our comic has four pages.
1
2
3
4
Because your comic is made out of these signatures, your book will need to be in a multipe of four pages. So four, eight, twelve, sixteen, etc. pages long.
Wait! What if I only have ten pages of comics?
Don't worry!

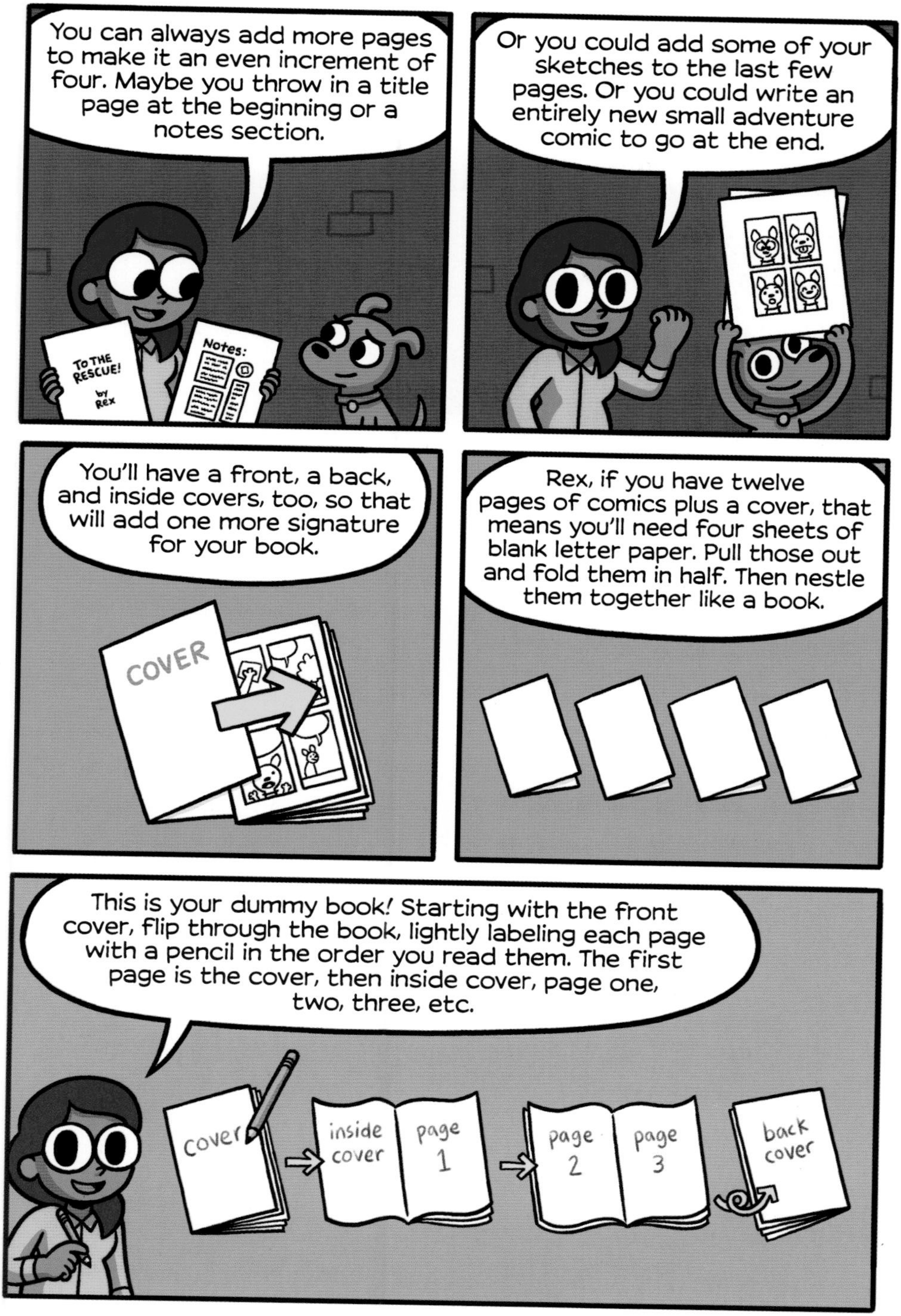

You can always add more pages to make it an even increment of four. Maybe you throw in a title page at the beginning or a notes section.
TO THE RESCUE! by Rex
Notes:
Or you could add some of your sketches to the last few pages. Or you could write an entirely new small adventure comic to go at the end.
You'll have a front, a back, and inside covers, too, so that will add one more signature for your book.
COVER
Rex, if you have twelve pages of comics plus a cover, that means you'll need four sheets of blank letter paper. Pull those out and fold them in half. Then nestle them together like a book.
This is your dummy book! Starting with the front cover, flip through the book, lightly labeling each page with a pencil in the order you read them. The first page is the cover, then inside cover, page one, two, three, etc.
cover
inside cover
page 1
page 2
page 3
back cover

Now that you have a dummy book, you can spread out all the sheets. It should look like this.

back cover | cover

↑ inside back cover | ↑ inside cover

page 12 | page 1

page 11 ⋯ | page 2 ↑

page 10 | page 3

page 9 ↑ | page 4 ↑

page 8 | page 5

page 7 ↑ | page 6 ↑

That's called **pagination**. Using this dummy book as our guide, next we'll lay out the book for printing.

cover

cover

First, we need to make sure your original artwork is properly prepared.

back cover

We'll need to scale down your original artwork so it fits onto the letter-size page folded in half.

cover

It's easy to use a photocopier for this step.

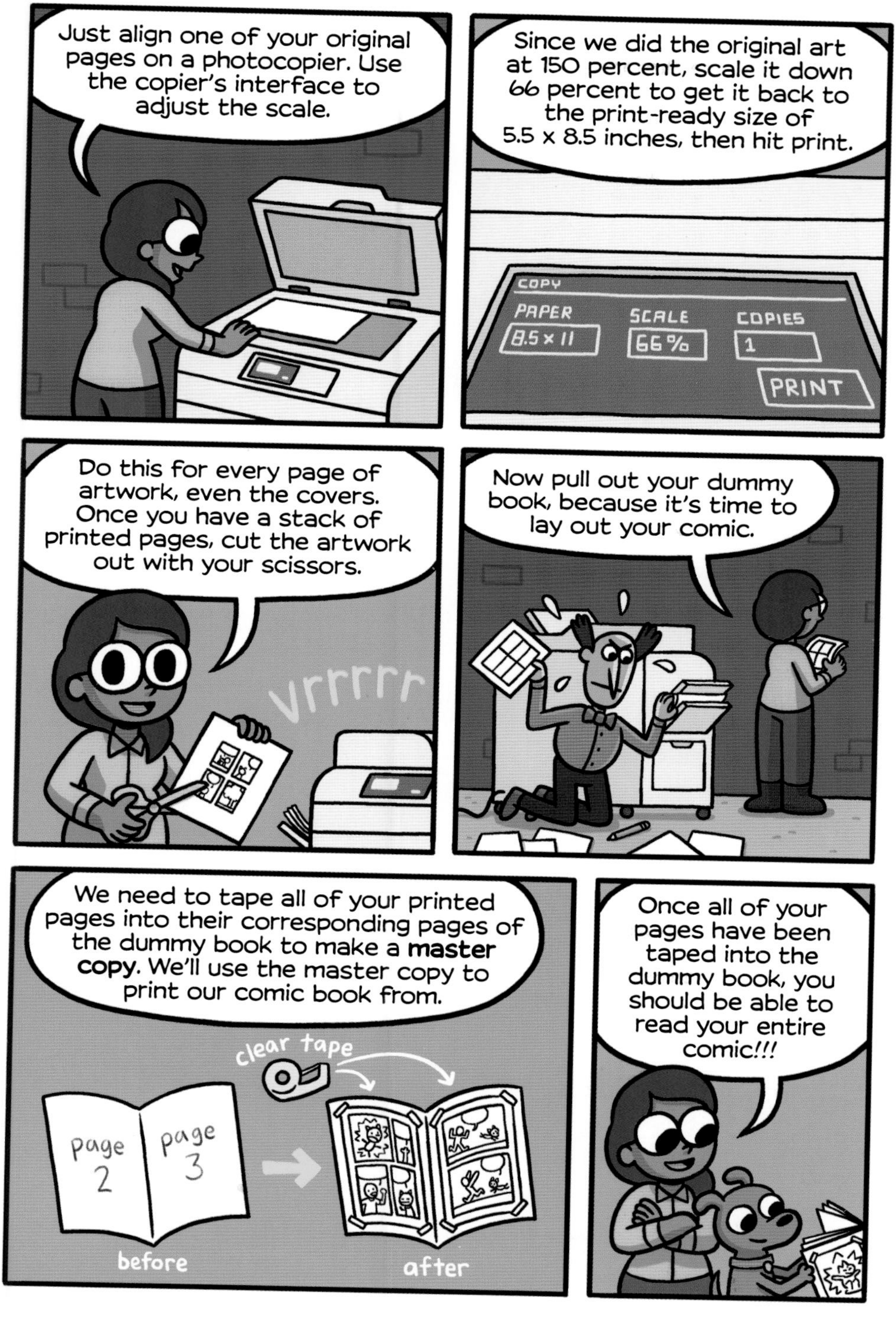
Just align one of your original pages on a photocopier. Use the copier's interface to adjust the scale.
Since we did the original art at 150 percent, scale it down 66 percent to get it back to the print-ready size of 5.5 x 8.5 inches, then hit print.
COPY
PAPER
8.5 x 11
SCALE
66 %
COPIES
1
PRINT
Do this for every page of artwork, even the covers. Once you have a stack of printed pages, cut the artwork out with your scissors.
vrrrrr
Now pull out your dummy book, because it's time to lay out your comic.
We need to tape all of your printed pages into their corresponding pages of the dummy book to make a **master copy**. We'll use the master copy to print our comic book from.
clear tape
page 2
page 3
before
after
Once all of your pages have been taped into the dummy book, you should be able to read your entire comic!!!

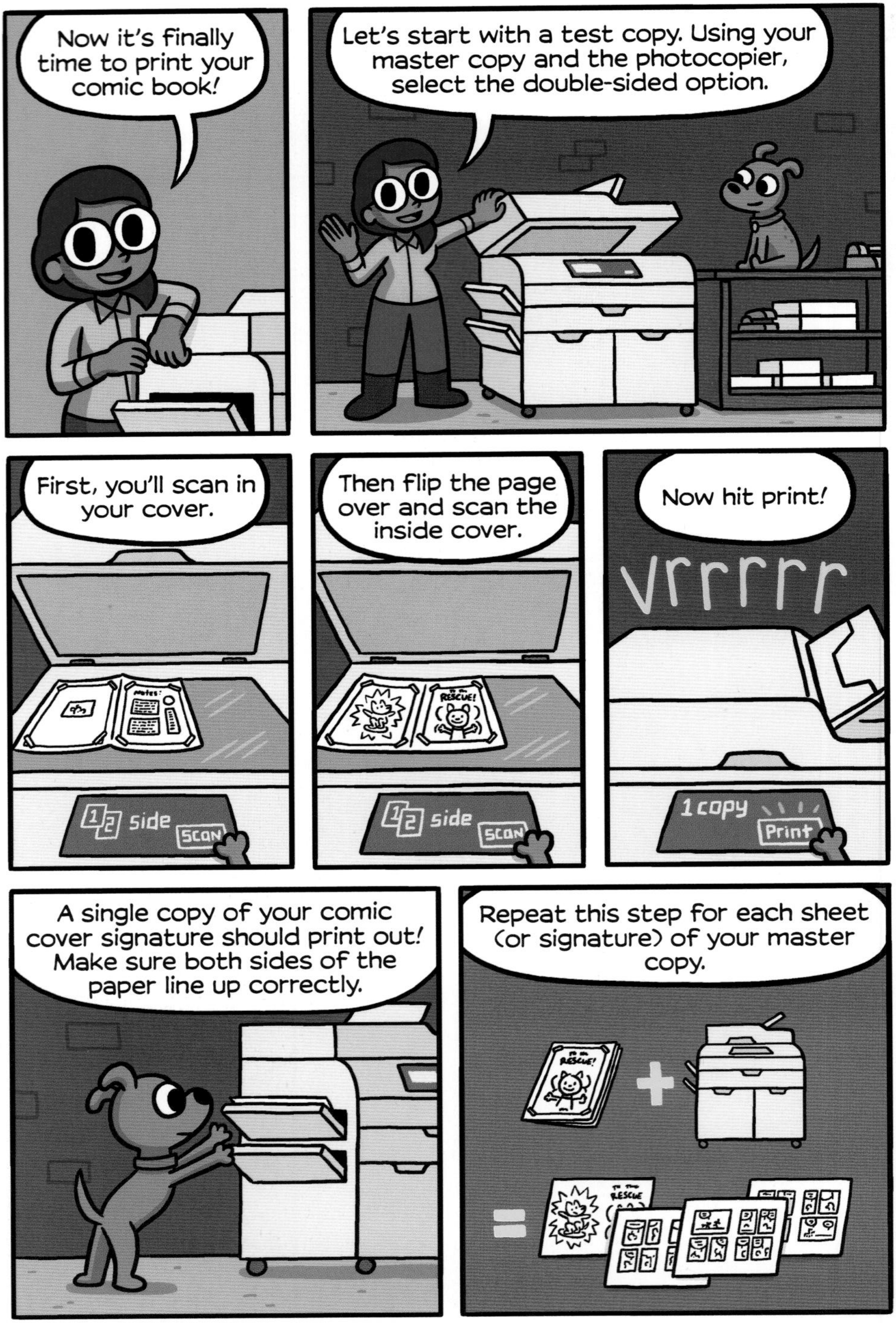

Now it's finally time to print your comic book!
Let's start with a test copy. Using your master copy and the photocopier, select the double-sided option.
First, you'll scan in your cover.
1/2 side
SCAN
Then flip the page over and scan the inside cover.
TO THE RESCUE!
1/2 side
SCAN
Now hit print!
Vrrrrr
1 copy
Print
A single copy of your comic cover signature should print out! Make sure both sides of the paper line up correctly.
Repeat this step for each sheet (or signature) of your master copy.

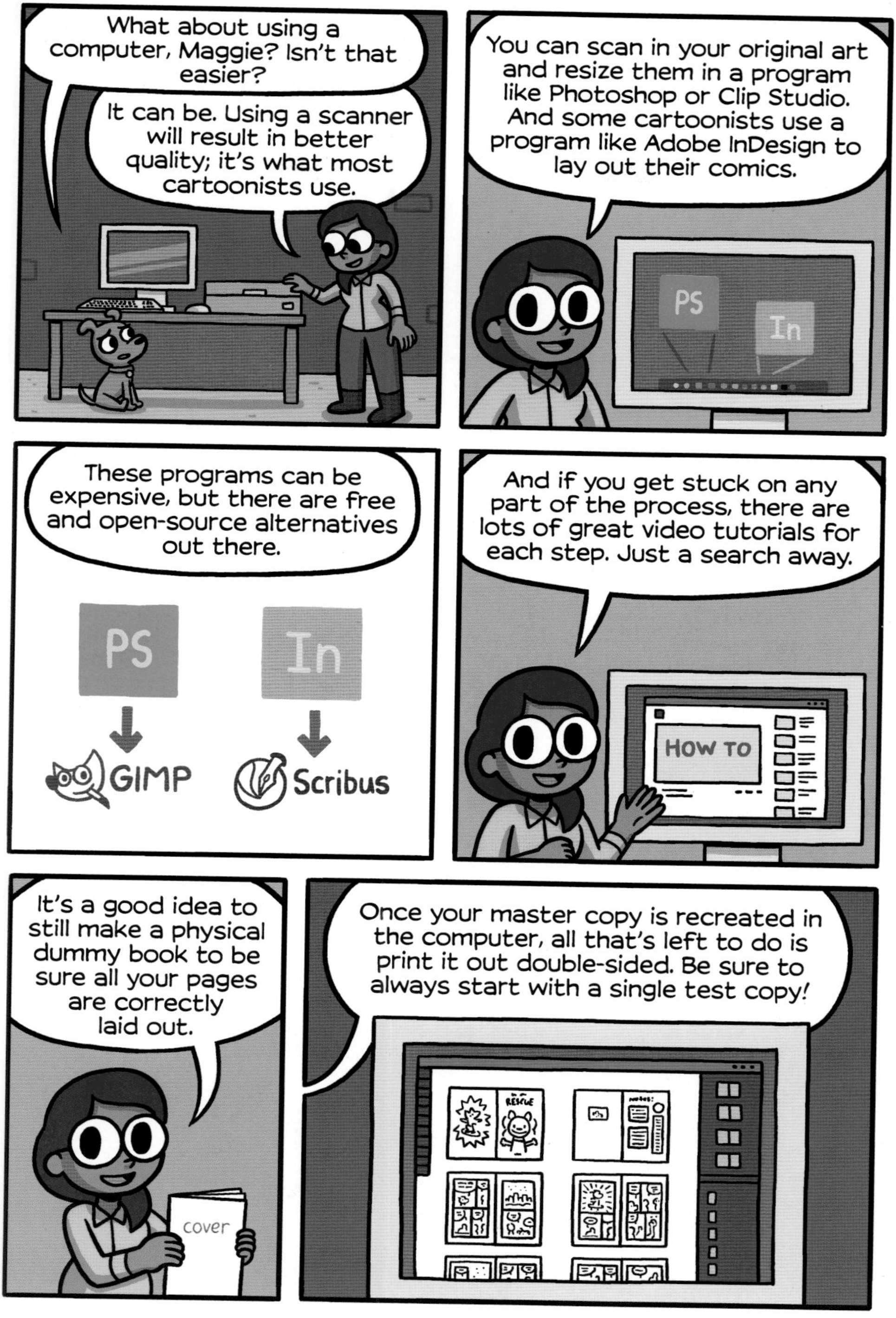
What about using a computer, Maggie? Isn't that easier?
It can be. Using a scanner will result in better quality; it's what most cartoonists use.
You can scan in your original art and resize them in a program like Photoshop or Clip Studio. And some cartoonists use a program like Adobe InDesign to lay out their comics.
PS
In
These programs can be expensive, but there are free and open-source alternatives out there.
PS
In
GIMP
Scribus
And if you get stuck on any part of the process, there are lots of great video tutorials for each step. Just a search away.
HOW TO
It's a good idea to still make a physical dummy book to be sure all your pages are correctly laid out.
cover
Once your master copy is recreated in the computer, all that's left to do is print it out double-sided. Be sure to always start with a single test copy!

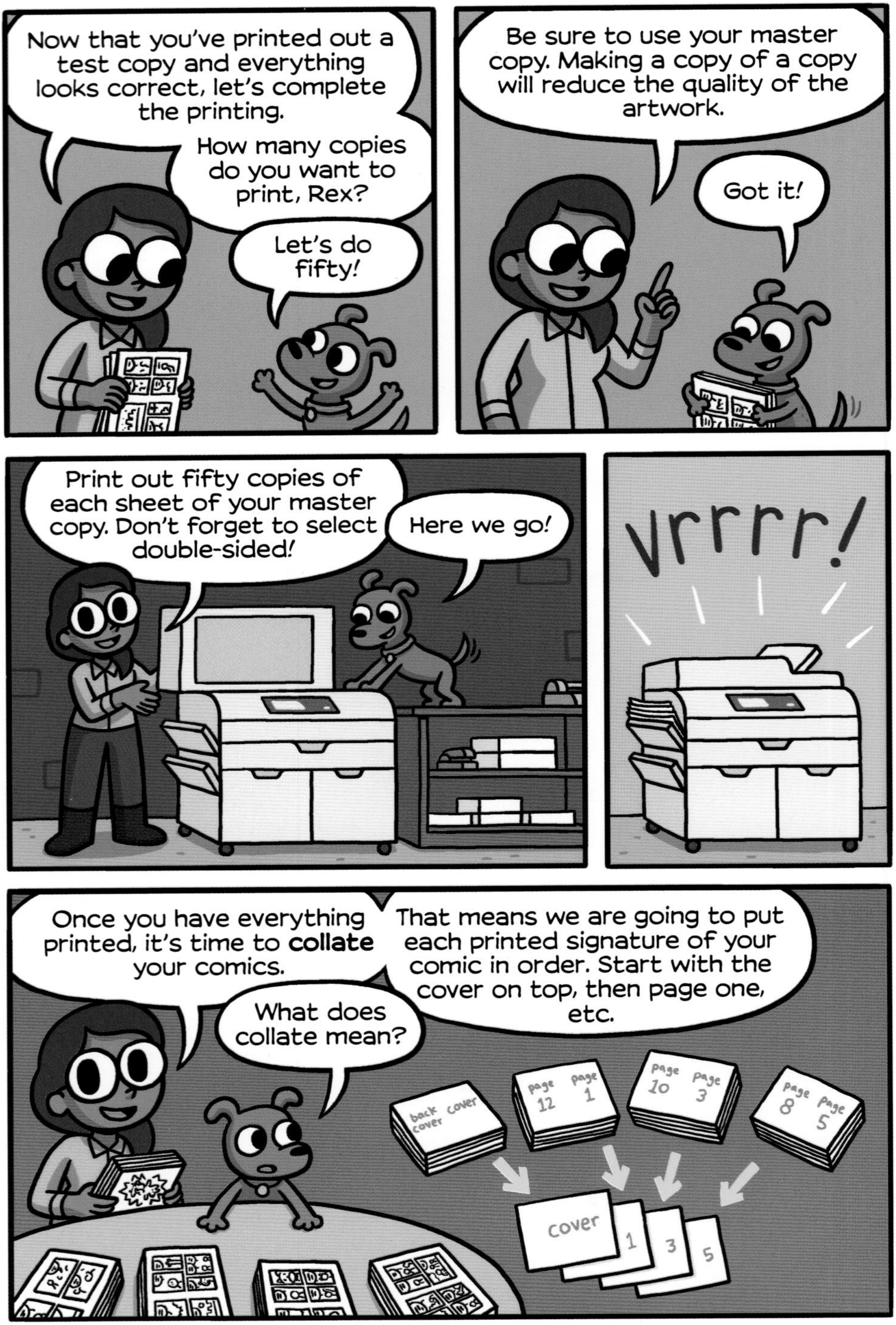

Now that you've printed out a test copy and everything looks correct, let's complete the printing.
How many copies do you want to print, Rex?
Let's do fifty!
Be sure to use your master copy. Making a copy of a copy will reduce the quality of the artwork.
Got it!
Print out fifty copies of each sheet of your master copy. Don't forget to select double-sided!
Here we go!
Vrrrr!
Once you have everything printed, it's time to **collate** your comics.
What does collate mean?
That means we are going to put each printed signature of your comic in order. Start with the cover on top, then page one, etc.
back cover
cover
page 12
page 1
page 10
page 3
page 8
page 5
cover
1
3
5

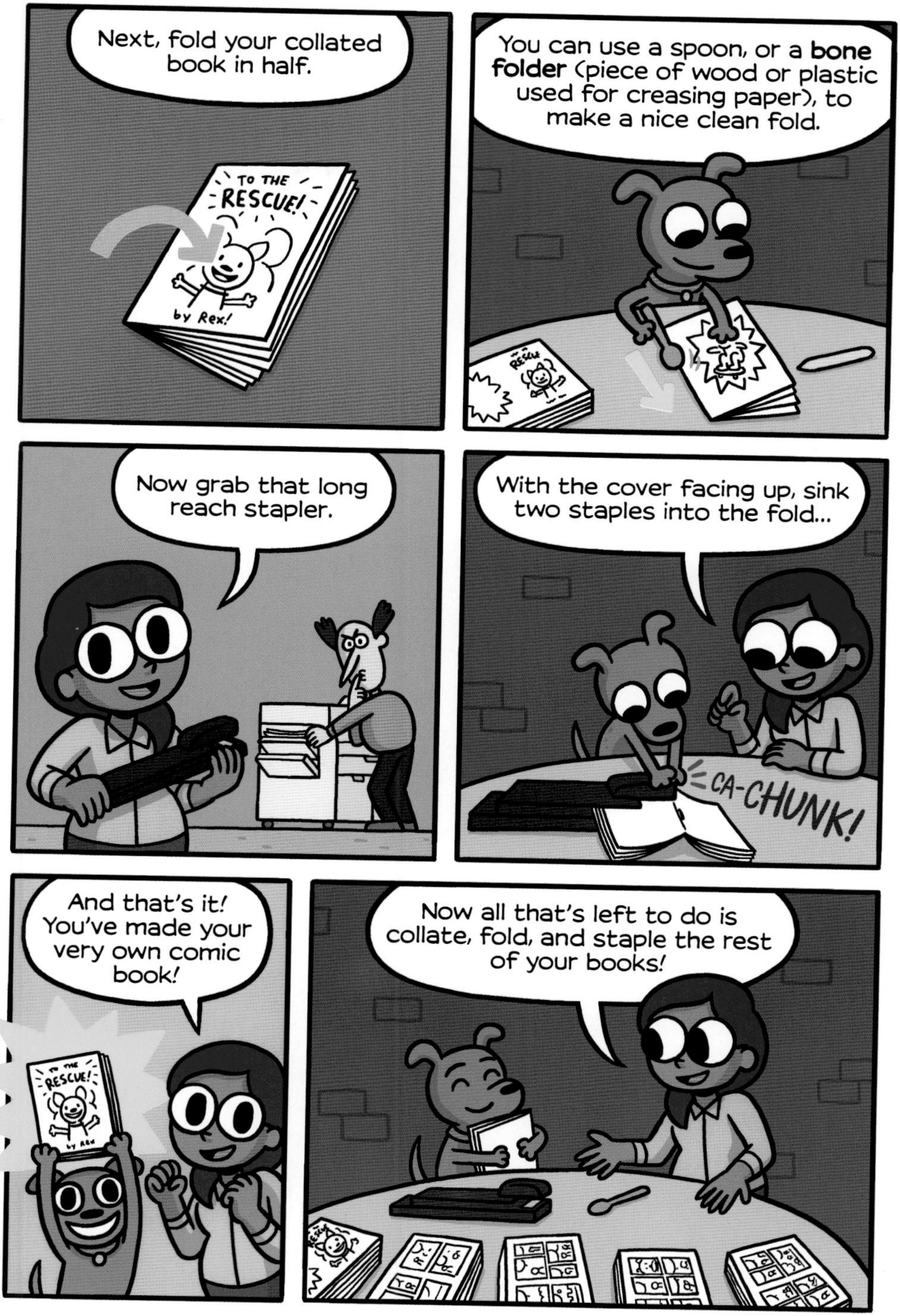

Next, fold your collated book in half.
TO THE RESCUE!
by Rex!
You can use a spoon, or a **bone folder** (piece of wood or plastic used for creasing paper), to make a nice clean fold.
Now grab that long reach stapler.
With the cover facing up, sink two staples into the fold...
CA-CHUNK!
And that's it! You've made your very own comic book!
TO THE RESCUE!
Now all that's left to do is collate, fold, and staple the rest of your books!

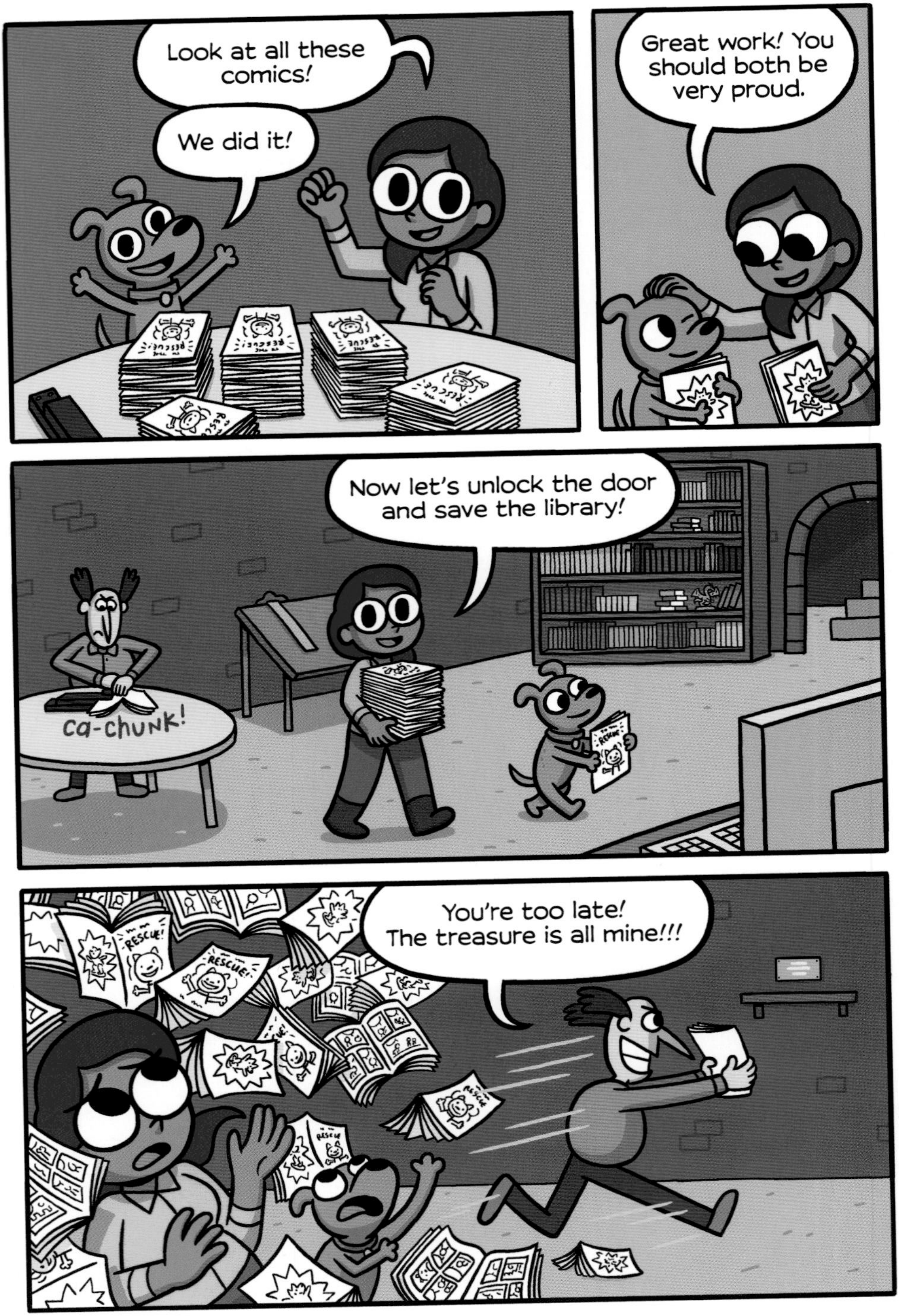
Look at all these comics!
We did it!
Great work! You should both be very proud.
Now let's unlock the door and save the library!
CA-CHUNK!
You're too late! The treasure is all mine!!!

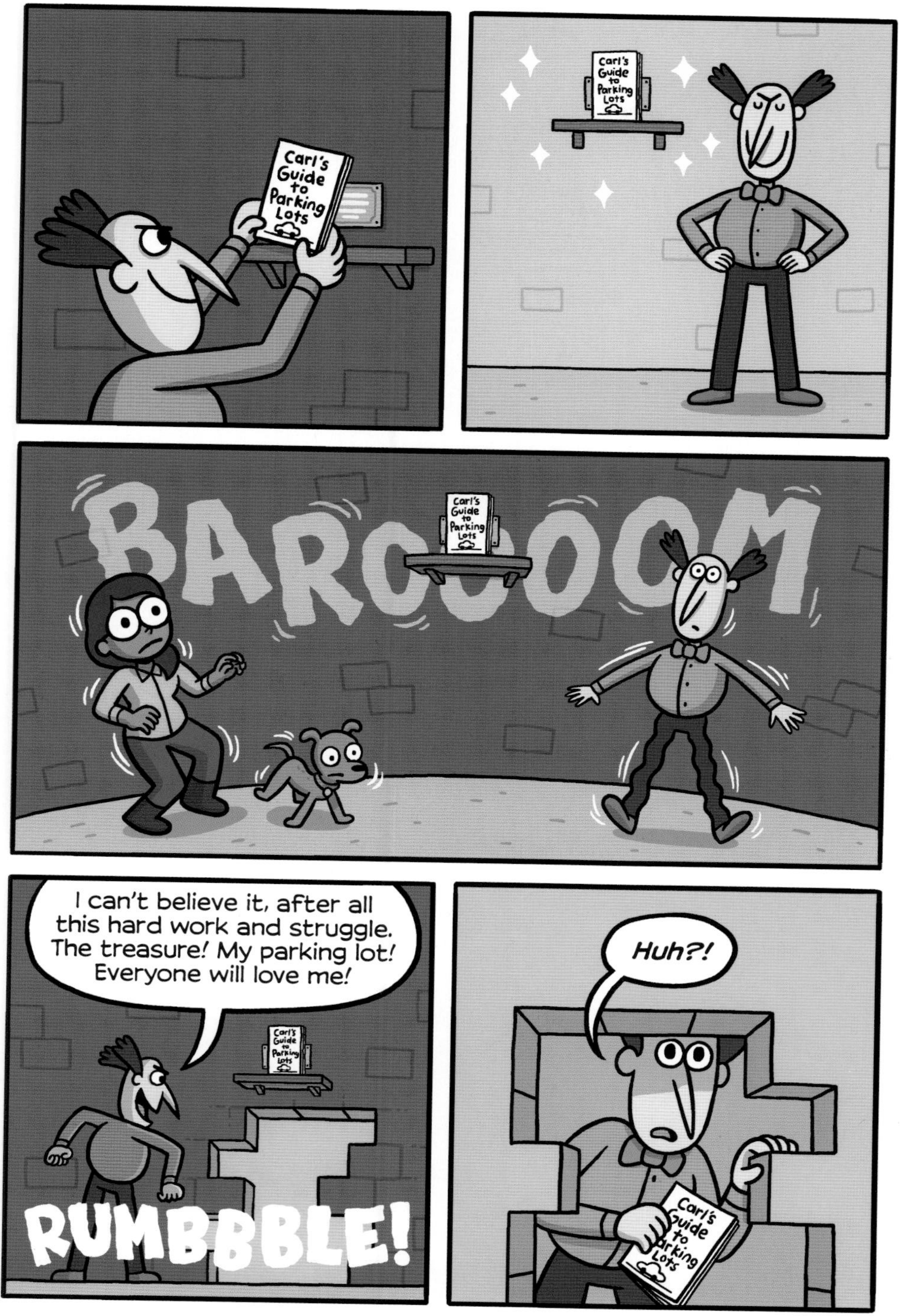
Carl's Guide to Parking Lots
BAROOOOM
I can't believe it, after all this hard work and struggle. The treasure! My parking lot! Everyone will love me!
RUMBBBLE!
Huh?!

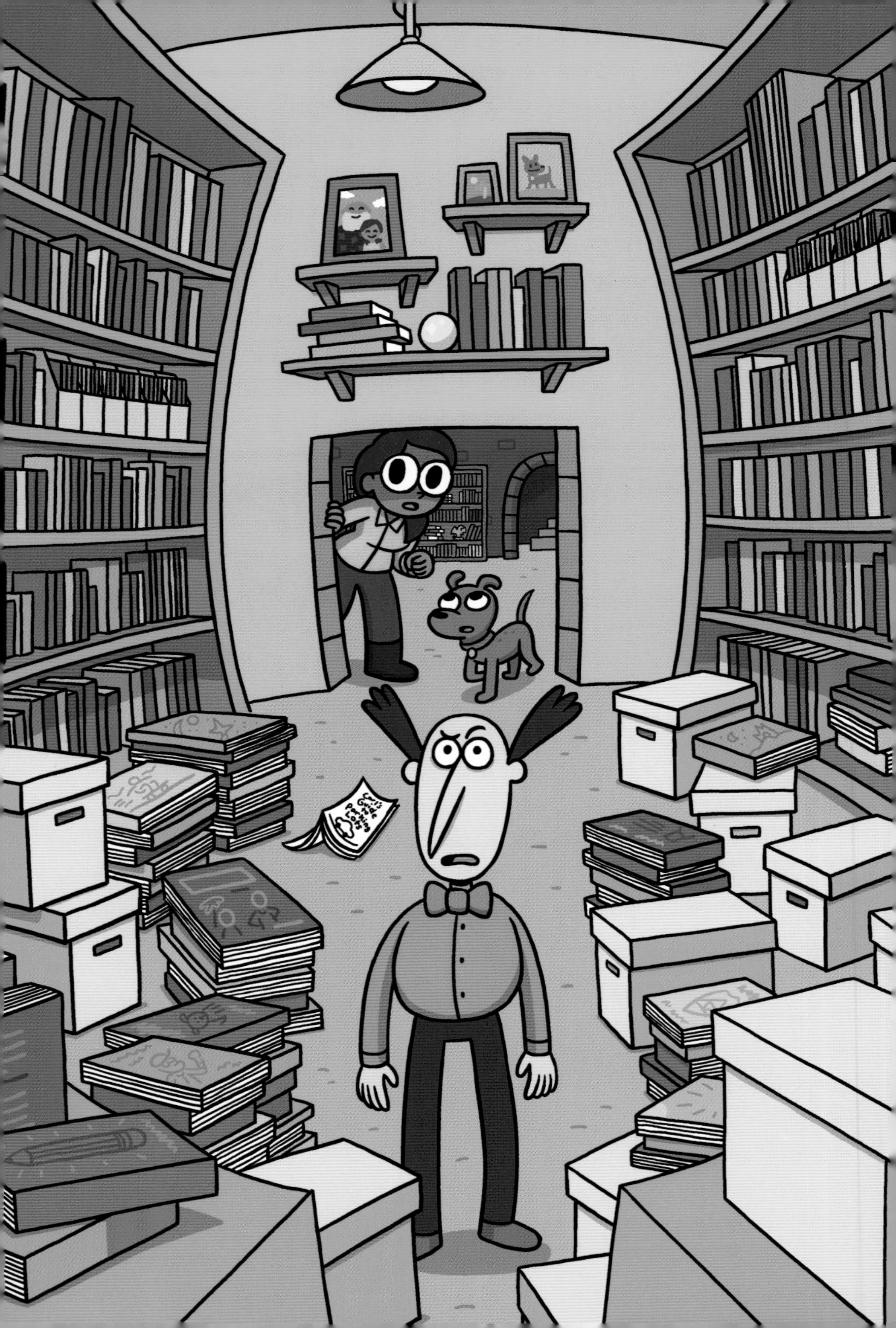
Carl's Guide to Parking Lots

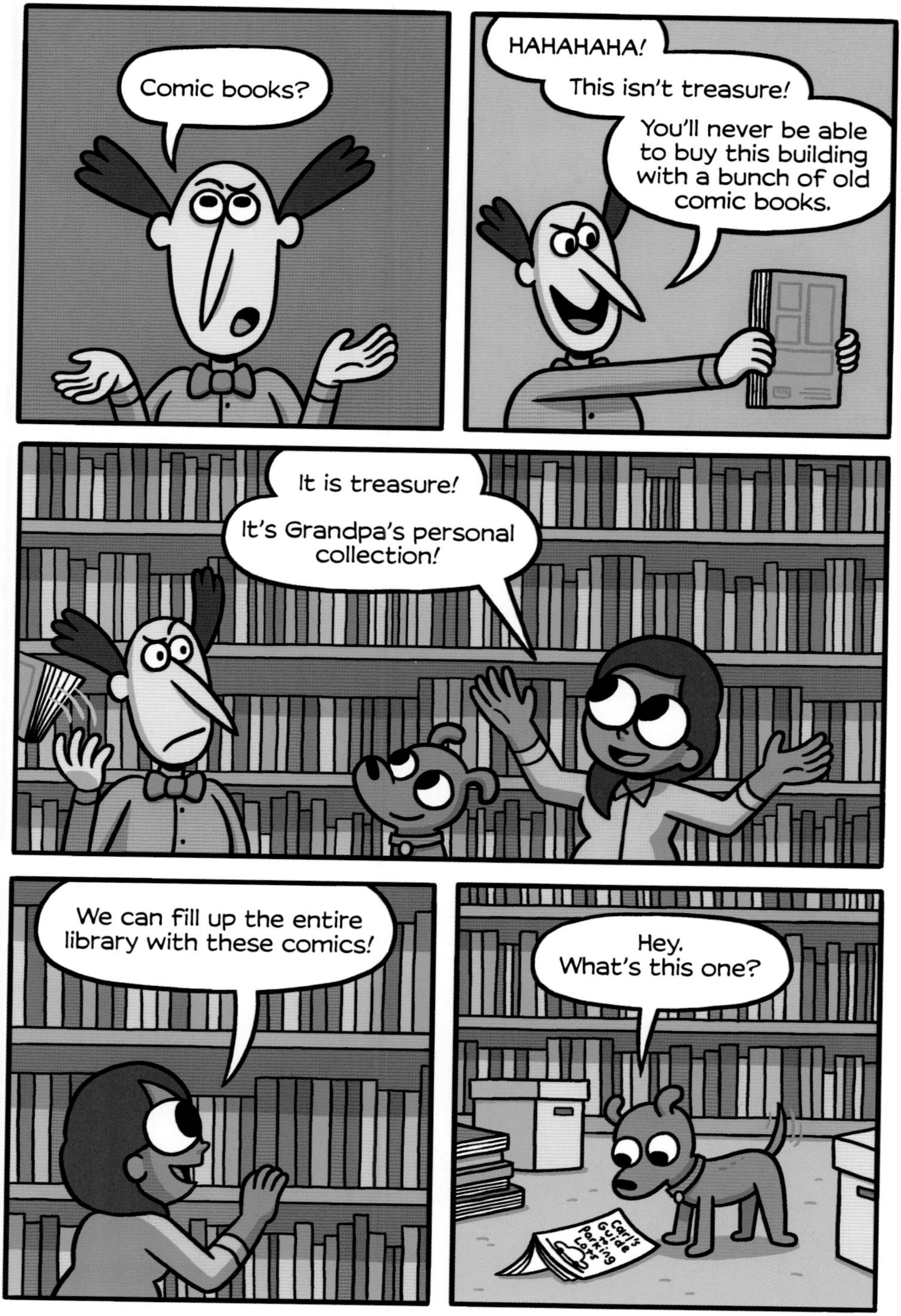
Comic books?
HAHAHAHA!
This isn't treasure!
You'll never be able to buy this building with a bunch of old comic books.
It is treasure!
It's Grandpa's personal collection!
We can fill up the entire library with these comics!
Hey. What's this one?
Carl's Guide Parking Lots

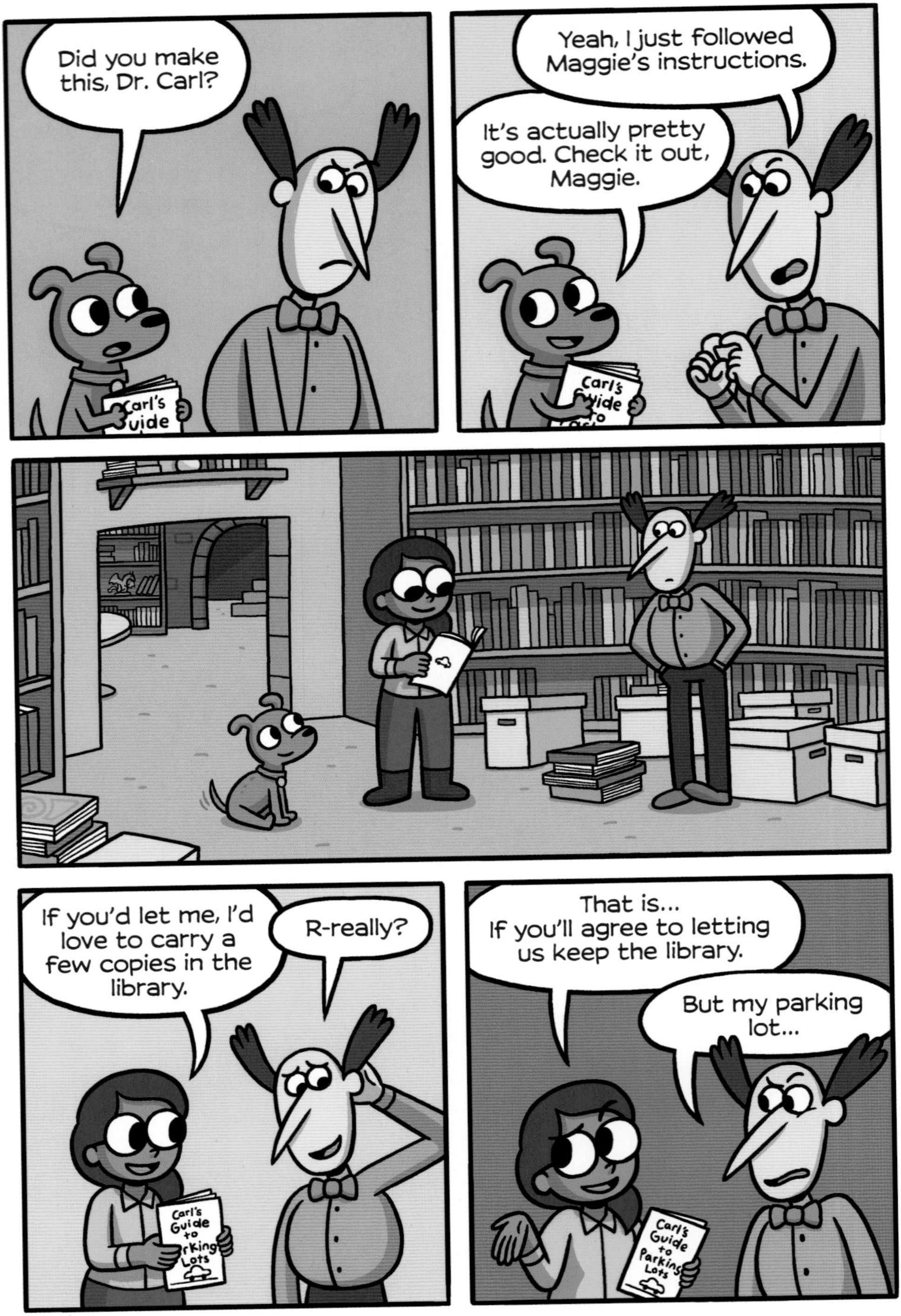
Did you make this, Dr. Carl?
Carl's Guide
Yeah, I just followed Maggie's instructions.
It's actually pretty good. Check it out, Maggie.
If you'd let me, I'd love to carry a few copies in the library.
R-really?
Carl's Guide to Parking Lots
That is... If you'll agree to letting us keep the library.
But my parking lot...
Carl's Guide to Parking Lots

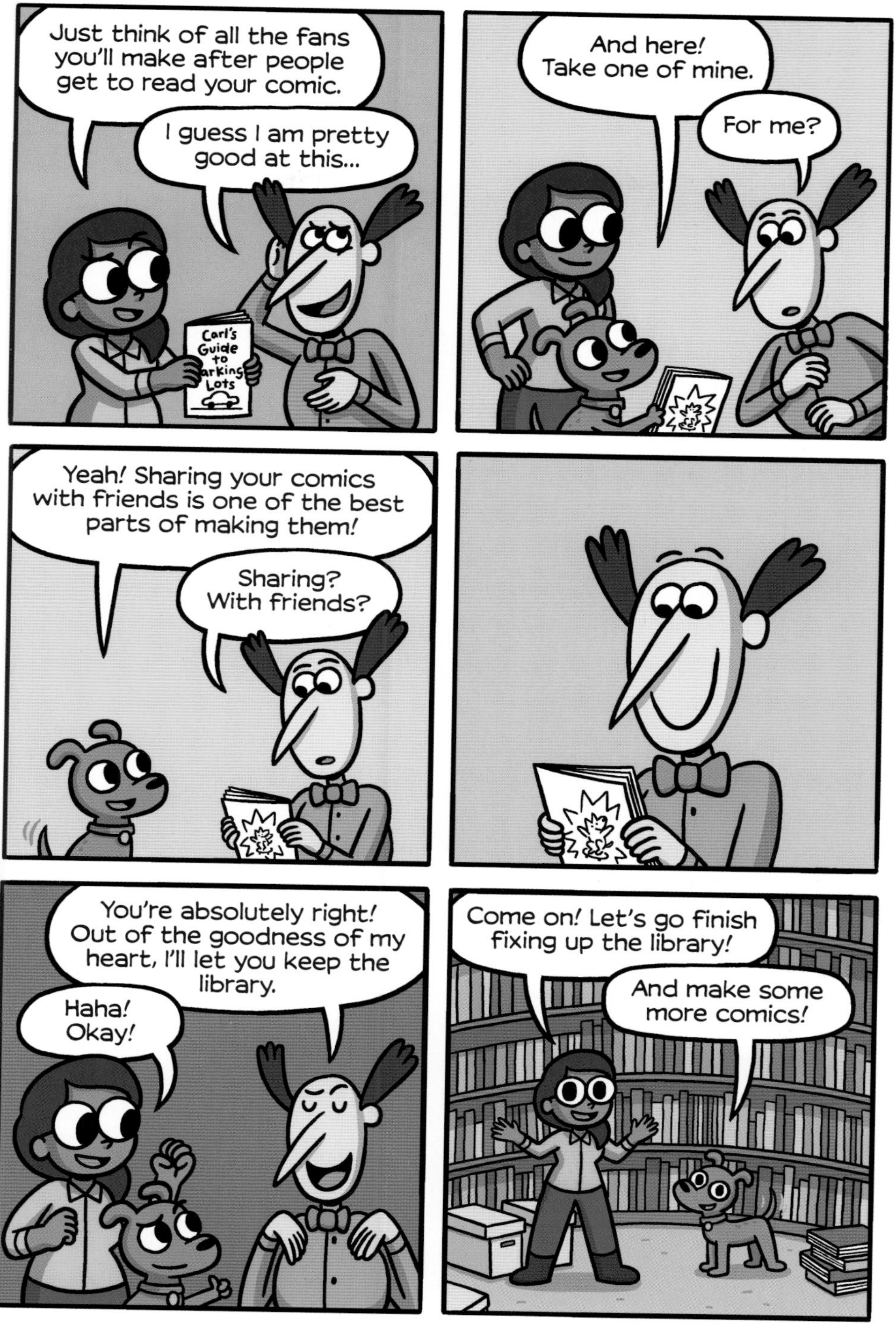
Just think of all the fans you'll make after people get to read your comic.
I guess I am pretty good at this...
Carl's Guide to Parking Lots
And here! Take one of mine.
For me?
Yeah! Sharing your comics with friends is one of the best parts of making them!
Sharing? With friends?
You're absolutely right! Out of the goodness of my heart, I'll let you keep the library.
Haha! Okay!
Come on! Let's go finish fixing up the library!
And make some more comics!

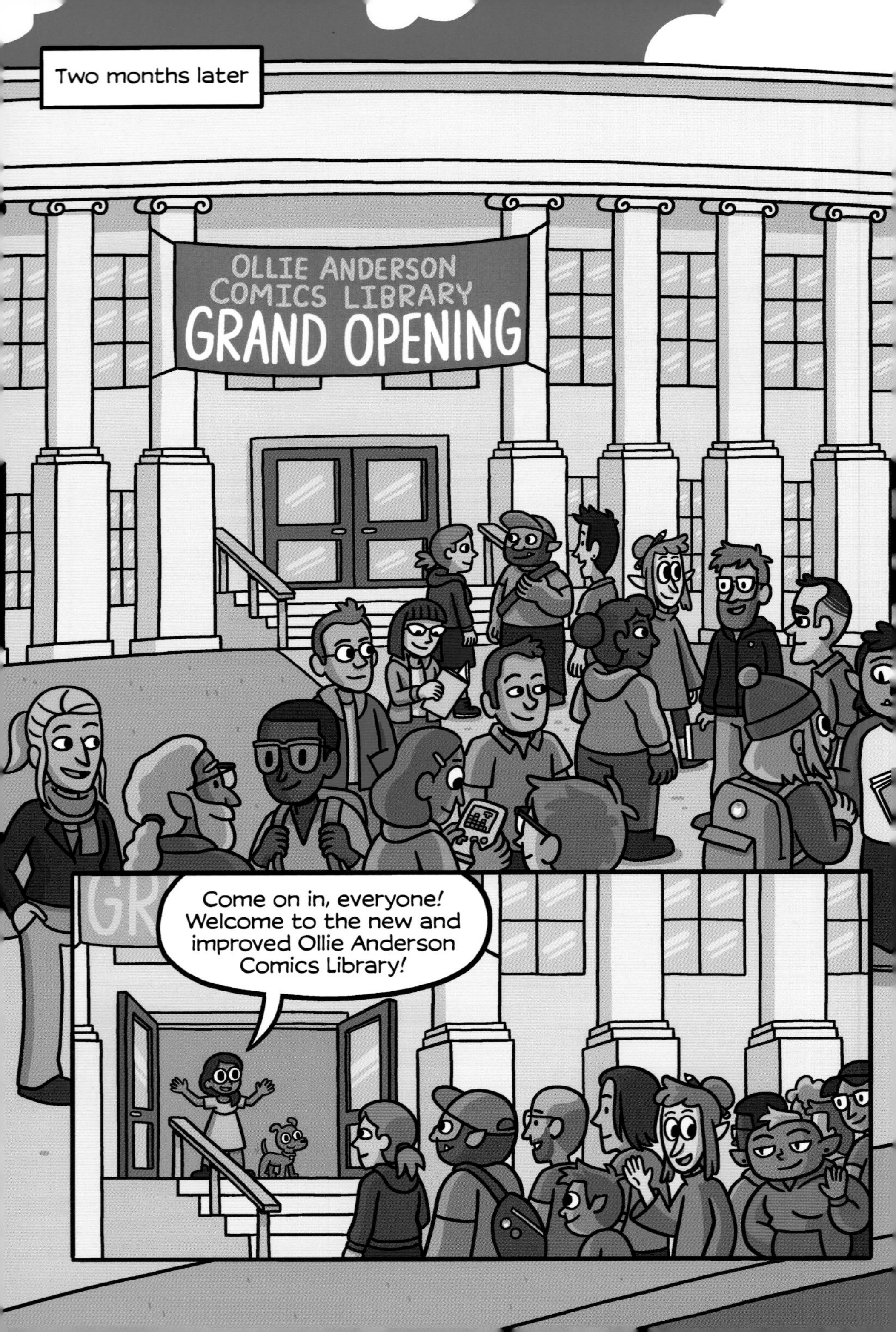
Two months later
OLLIE ANDERSON COMICS LIBRARY GRAND OPENING
Come on in, everyone! Welcome to the new and improved Ollie Anderson Comics Library!

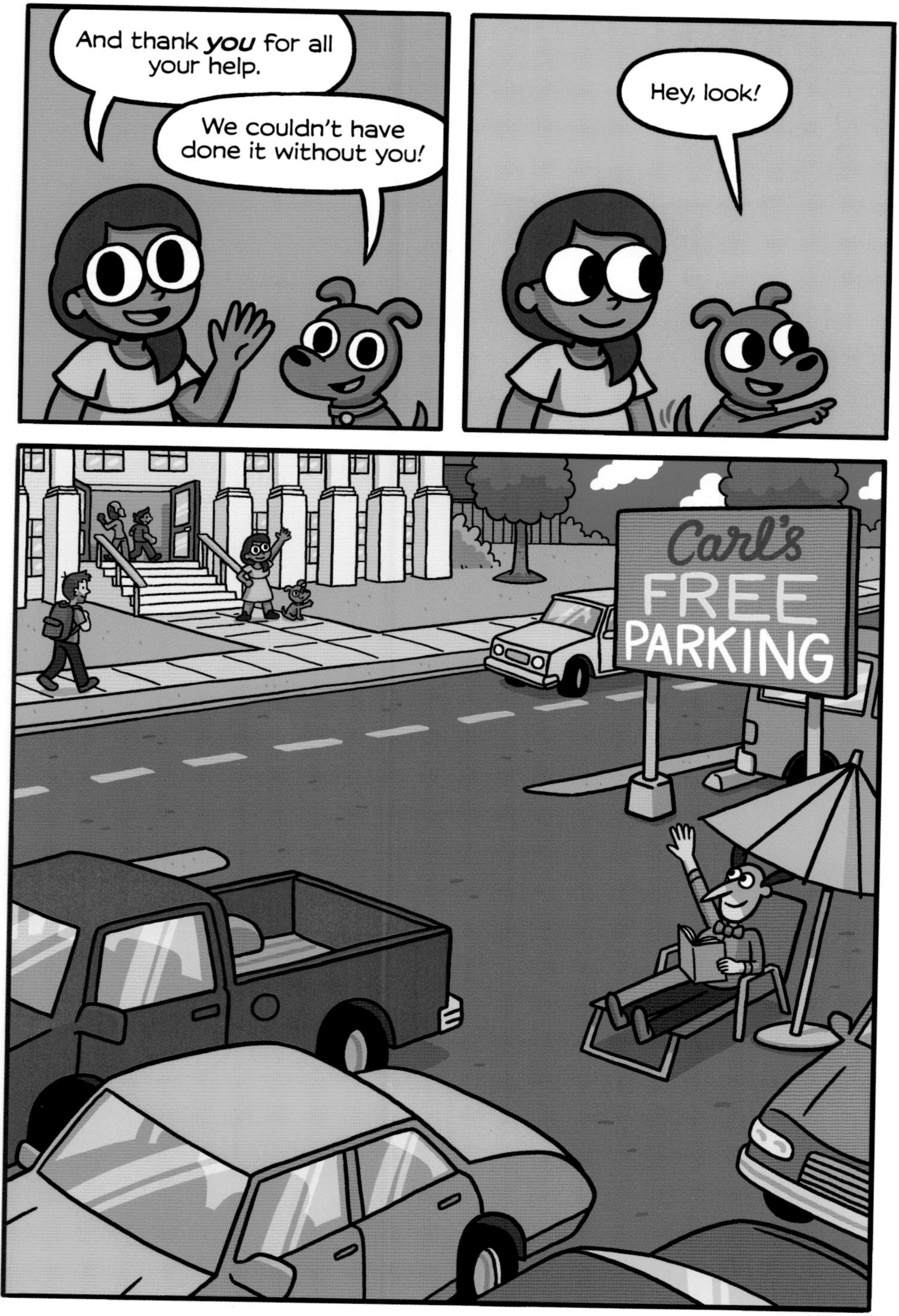
And thank *you* for all your help.
We couldn't have done it without you!
Hey, look!
Carl's FREE PARKING

the end.

NOTES ON MEASUREMENTS

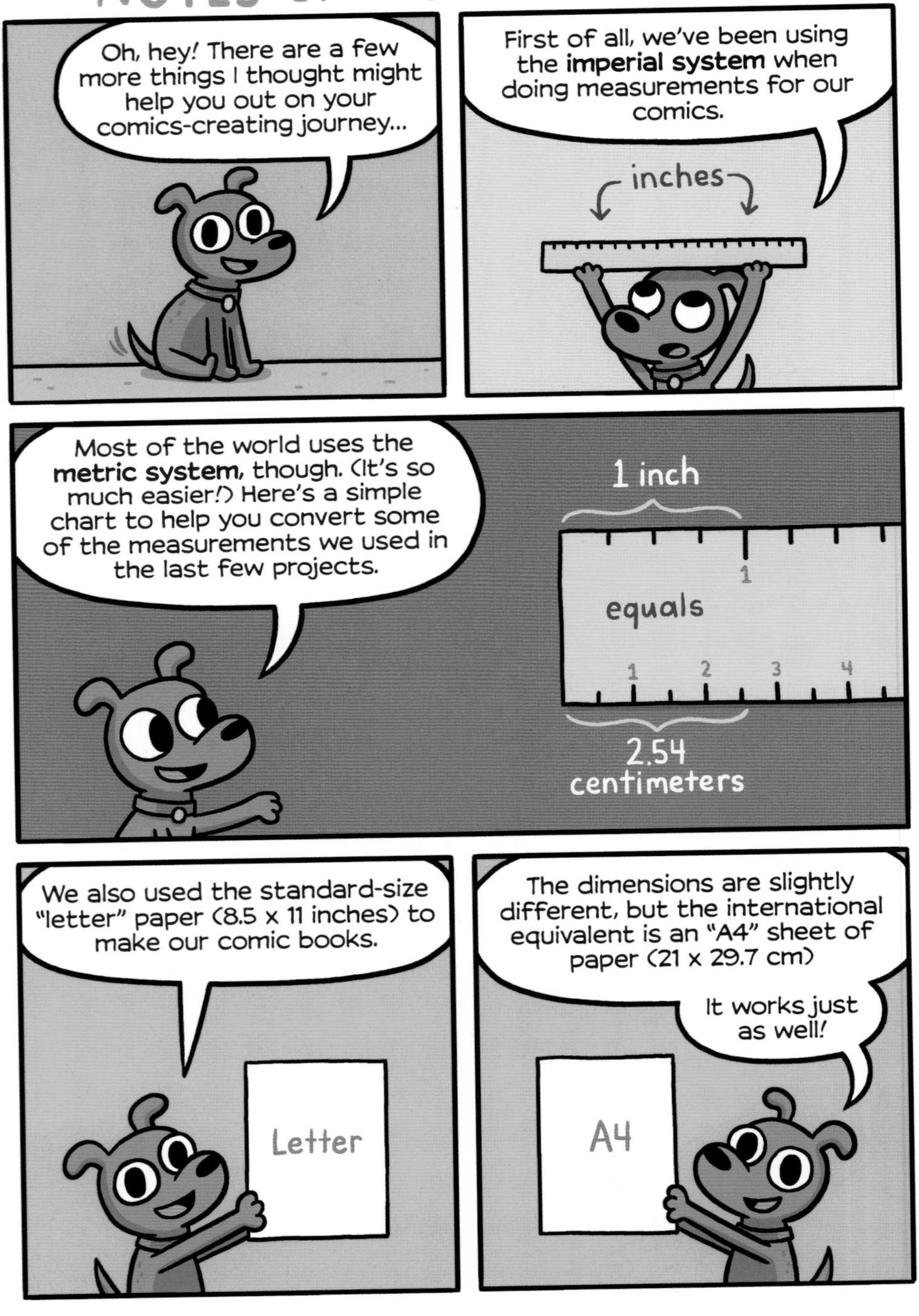

Oh, hey! There are a few more things I thought might help you out on your comics-creating journey...
First of all, we've been using the **imperial system** when doing measurements for our comics.
inches
Most of the world uses the **metric system**, though. (It's so much easier!) Here's a simple chart to help you convert some of the measurements we used in the last few projects.
1 inch
1
equals
1 2 3 4
2.54 centimeters
We also used the standard-size "letter" paper (8.5 x 11 inches) to make our comic books.
Letter
The dimensions are slightly different, but the international equivalent is an "A4" sheet of paper (21 x 29.7 cm)
It works just as well!
A4

TIPS FOR SCANNING

Here's a rundown of how you should scan in artwork, depending on how you drew it.

Black and White or Bitmap

If your ink artwork is only black and white (no shades of gray!), you can scan in this mode. But do it at a really high resolution, like 1200 DPI.

Grayscale

Grayscale mode is for black-and-white artwork that has shades of gray, like pencil or ink wash. Scan in your artwork at 600 DPI in this mode.

Color

If you've made full-color artwork, scan in this mode. 300 DPI is a high enough resolution for color.

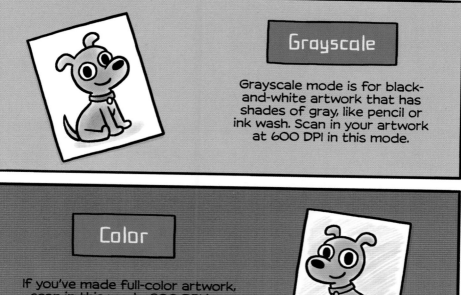

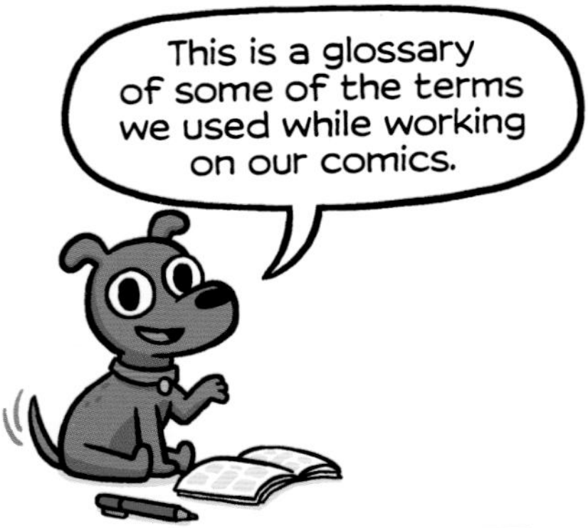
This is a glossary of some of the terms we used while working on our comics.

caption—Boxes with words inside them that provide extra info or give voice to a narrator.

close-up—A framing device used to bring attention to a subject by showing its details.

comic strip—Short comic usually ending in a punch line.

dummy book—Guide used to figure out the pagination of a comic book.

emanata—Symbols used to indicate mood or emotion.

establishing shot—Framing method used to show the subject in an environment.

graphic novel—A bound comic in book form.

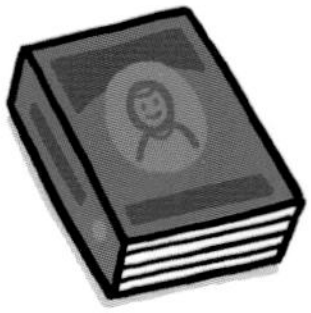

grid—Arranging panels in a uniform way.

gutter—Space between panels.

margin—Space between comic artwork and the edge of a page.

master copy—The finalized, high-quality mock-up of a comic book used for reproduction.

medium shot—Framing method that shows a subject and background elements.

pagination—The order pages are placed into a signature when printing a comic book.

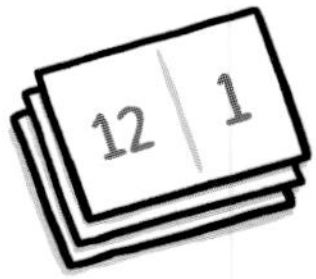
12
1

panel—The boxes with words and pictures that make up a page of a comic.

saddle stitch—Binding method used to create a comic book by folding and stapling signatures.

script—Written plan for a comic.

signature—A single sheet of paper that is folded to create multiple pages of a comic book.

sound effect—Stylized words to indicate sound.

thought balloon—Words in a cloud-like shape that indicate what a character is thinking.

thumbnails—Quick and simple version of a comic used for planning.

traditional comic book—Folded and stapled comic book.

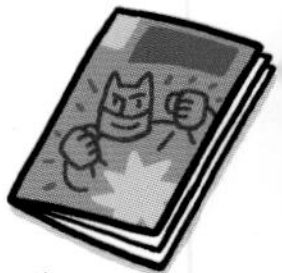

web comic—Comic published on the internet.

word balloon—Words in a circular shape that show a character speaking.

MORE BOOKS TO READ!

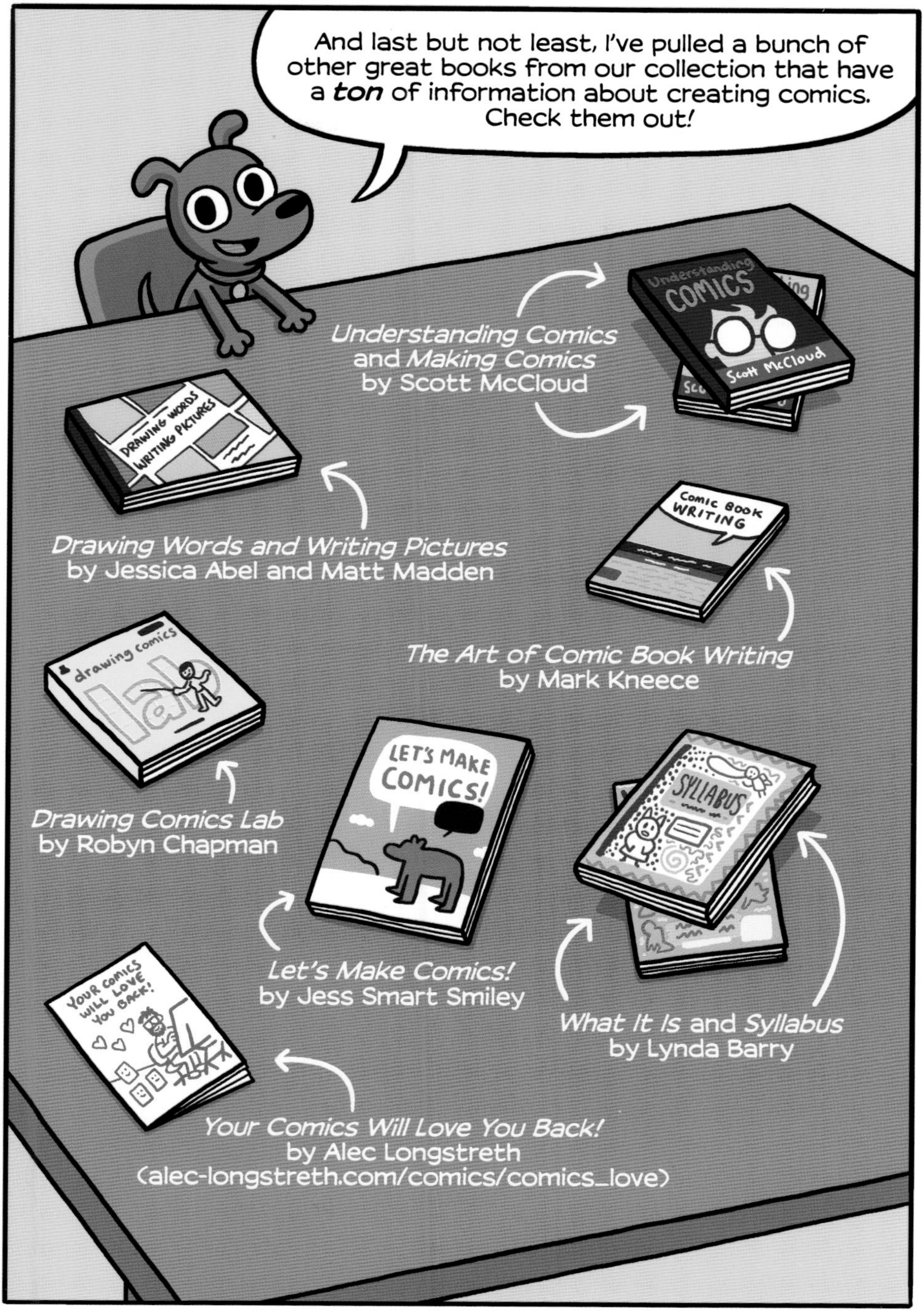

And last but not least, I've pulled a bunch of other great books from our collection that have a *ton* of information about creating comics. Check them out!
Understanding COMICS
Scott McCloud
Understanding Comics and *Making Comics* by Scott McCloud
DRAWING WORDS WRITING PICTURES
Drawing Words and Writing Pictures by Jessica Abel and Matt Madden
COMIC BOOK WRITING
The Art of Comic Book Writing by Mark Kneece
drawing comics lab
Drawing Comics Lab by Robyn Chapman
LET'S MAKE COMICS!
Let's Make Comics! by Jess Smart Smiley
SYLLABUS
What It Is and *Syllabus* by Lynda Barry
YOUR COMICS WILL LOVE YOU BACK!
Your Comics Will Love You Back! by Alec Longstreth (alec-longstreth.com/comics/comics_love)

:01

First Second

All instructions included in this book are provided as a resource for parents and children. While all due care has been taken, we recommend that an adult supervise children at all times when following the instructions in this book. The projects in this book are not recommended for children three years and under due to potential choking hazard. Neither the authors nor the publisher accept any responsibility for any loss, injury, or damages sustained by anyone resulting from the instructions contained in this book.

Published by First Second
First Second is an imprint of Roaring Brook Press,
a division of Holtzbrinck Publishing Holdings Limited Partnership
120 Broadway, New York, NY 10271
All rights reserved

Don't miss your next favorite book from First Second! For the latest updates go to firstsecondnewsletter.com and sign up for our enewsletter.

Library of Congress Control Number: 2018953658

Paperback ISBN: 978-1-250-15212-1
Hardback ISBN: 978-1-250-15211-4

Our books may be purchased in bulk for promotional, educational, or business use. Please contact your local bookseller or the Macmillan Corporate and Premium Sales Department at (800) 221-7945 ext. 5442 or by email at MacmillanSpecialMarkets@macmillan.com.

FIRST
EDITION

First edition, 2019
Edited by Robyn Chapman and Bethany Bryan
Expert consultation by Jon Chad
Cover design by Andrew Arnold and Sammy Savos
Interior book design by Rob Steen
Coloring assistance by Jacie Anderson Coovert

Printed in China by 1010 Printing International Limited, North Point, Hong Kong

Created entirely with a Wacom Cintiq Pro 16 in Adobe Photoshop CC with a variety of brushes.

Paperback: 10 9 8 7 6 5 4 3 2
Hardcover: 10 9 8 7 6 5 4 3 2 1

BY ART
WE LIVE